Central in the formulation of many of the most important Christian theological ideas and doctrines are the analogies of Paul. These word pictures run like a brilliant thread through all of his writings, the metaphorical and comparative shorthand by which he attempts to convey his message. How are they to be interpreted? Diversity in the survey studies Paul- I Thessalonians, Galatians, 1 and II Corinthians, Romans, Philippians, and Philemon. Through this survey Dr. Gale discovers numerous characteristics which persist throughout. He shows how the study of these provides certain controls to help the reader understand the material of the letters more nearly as the apostle himself intended.

By applying the pattern of usage thus derived Dr. Gale shows that three major conclusions can be drawn. These may well provide the missing key Biblical students have long needed for unlocking the approach to Paul's thought.

This book is essential reading for the critical student and scholar, but it is also written for all who are interested in the thinking of that figure whose influence upon the history of Christian thought can hardly be overestimated. In addition to long-needed new knowledge of Paul's meanings, it provides thoughtful Christians with a rewarding familiarity with the mind of the fiery disciple.

THE AUTHOR: Herbert M. Gale ordained Methodist minister. As a bright Scholar he studied at the versity of Berlin and later receive Ph.D. from Boston University. Dr. has served several Methodist pasto He is presently Professor and Chairman of the Department of Biblical History, Literature, and Interpretation at Wellesley College, Massachusetts.

D1154230

THE USE
OF ANALOGY
IN THE LETTERS
OF PAUL

THE USE
OF ANALOGY
IN THE LETTERS
OF PAUL

by
Herbert M. Gale

PHILADELPHIA
The Westminster Press

LIBRARY OF CONGRESS CATALOG CARD No. 64–15581

PUBLISHED BY THE WESTMINSTER PRESS
PHILADELPHIA, PENNSYLVANIA 19107 ®
PRINTED IN THE UNITED STATES OF AMERICA

Contents

Preface

Spoken or written references to the parables of Jesus suggest immediately a more or less familiar body of material to anyone who possesses even a minimal acquaintance with the New Testament and with Christian traditions. It is generally recognized, furthermore, that any serious study of the teachings of Jesus found in the Gospels must take the parables into account. Many books, both scholarly and popular, have dealt with them and with the question of their proper interpretation. It is extremely surprising, on the other hand, that relatively little comparable consideration has been given to the analogies of Paul, to those " pictures " which the apostle presents to his readers as he attempts to illustrate or reinforce the thought which he wishes to convey. The absence of more direct and more comprehensive treatment of the Pauline analogies is particularly remarkable in view of the fact that some of these analogies have played an extremely important role in the formulation and expression of many of the most important Christian theological ideas and doctrines. The Pauline analogies of a sacrifice, of the adoption of a child, and of the human body with its various " members " — to mention only three examples — have had tremendous influence upon theological thinking regarding the significance of the death of Christ, the grace of God, and the church as the " body of Christ."

The present study was undertaken because of the writer's growing conviction that just as a careful analysis of the use of parables in the Gospels has served to provide criteria according to which the parables must be interpreted, so also a careful examination of the use of analogy in the letters of Paul might produce results that could be helpful in determining the extent to which any given analogy can be employed justifiably as a basis for an understanding of the apostle's theological thought. For the writer, at least, the study has been rewarding. There has emerged the fact that in Paul's analogical usage numerous persistent characteristics are to be recognized. Taking these characteristics into account, the interpreter of Paul's writings is provided with certain controls that should help him avoid an improper application of the apostle's analogical material and enable him to understand it more nearly as the apostle himself intended.

It is hoped that the book may be useful not only for the critical student or scholar but also for anyone interested in the thinking of that figure whose writings occupy such an important place in the New Testament and whose influence upon the history of Christian thought can hardly be overestimated. The more general reader will find it possible to follow the main outline of the treatment — without becoming involved in some of the more technical issues — by omitting the paragraphs that are printed in the smaller type face. Greek words appear at many points, but the English translations are indicated consistently so that the sense of a given statement or argument can be recognized even though the reader may be unacquainted with the Greek language. (Practical considerations have necessitated the transliteration of the Greek words as they appeared in the original manuscript.

I should like to express my gratitude particularly to Wellesley College for providing the opportunity for periods of concentrated work in this undertaking, to my students whose questionings and observations have deepened my concern in this area, to my wife for her aid in proofreading.

H. M. G.

Wellesley College, Wellesley, Massachusetts

Introduction

The fact of Pauline influence upon the total history of
Christian thought is well established. It is true that estimates
may vary as to the *extent* of Paul's impact upon the so-called
primitive church. According to Adolf Deissmann this apostle
" not only labored more, but created more " than all the others who built upon the foundation of Jesus Christ; he was the
" Great Power " of the apostolic age.[1] Whether or not this
judgment requires a certain qualification, it must be recognized that very early there was ascribed to Paul an importance that should not be underestimated. More of the documents granted canonical status were written by him than by
any other individual. And the fact that his name came to be
attached to some documents of which he can no longer be
regarded as the author, as well as to some about which his
authorship is at least uncertain, testifies to the significance of
the role that he was believed to have played in the early
Christian community. Evidences of Pauline influence in the
later literature of the New Testament, the Apostolic Fathers,
and the Apologists have been presented in considerable detail by A. E. Barnett.[2] Insofar as Paul's influence in later centuries is concerned, simply to mention such names as Augustine, Luther, and Barth is to point indirectly to the apostle
whose thinking figures so largely in the theology of these
men and of the movements associated with them.

But to say that Pauline influence upon the history of Christian thought has been tremendous is not to say that the results of that influence have been uniform. The diversity of
claims and counterclaims for which the authority of Paul has

9

been asserted is a phenomenon frequently discussed.[3] Although numerous causes may be recognized as contributing to this diversity, particular significance must be attributed to the fact that Paul's media of communication — his language and his forms of expression — are of such a nature that strikingly different meanings have been found in (or read into) that which he wrote. What he wrote ought to tell us what he meant; but since the former has been interpreted at many points in such diverse ways, the result has been a corresponding diversity of opinion with respect to the intended meanings.

The problem is partly one of language. Paul wrote in the language of a culture long since past, and it is always difficult to translate important distinctions in meaning from one culture to another. But the problem of language, in the case of Paul, is vastly more complex than this. The apostle's cultural environment was Hellenistic and his language was Greek, but his religious heritage was Hebraic. And although he used the Greek language in order to express his thoughts, the actual words and phrases that he employed suggest again and again that Hebraic presuppositions and connotations rather than the Greek may be involved. Paul's use of the Greek word *sarx* ("flesh") may serve as an illustration here. Is there present in this usage, for example, the Hellenistic idea of the inherently sinful character of the flesh, or is the more Hebraic notion presupposed? Different answers to this question can lead to marked differences with respect to the understanding of various aspects of Paul's theological position.

It is another kind of problem, however, with which the present study is primarily concerned. As Paul presented his message, whether it be in argument, in rebuke, or in exhortation, he introduced a multiplicity of analogical usages in order to clarify or to reinforce that message. Just as Jesus is represented in the Synoptic Gospels as making extensive use of parables in the course of his teaching, so also Paul resorted to analogies of different kinds. His letters are filled with expressions that present to the reader mental pictures involving

elements analogous to this or that aspect of his thought. In
some cases these pictures are of familiar phenomena, drawn
with a certain measure of detail, as in I Cor., ch. 12, where
Paul compares the community of Christians to the human
body with its various parts or "members." At other points the
pictures are of scenes or events described in familiar literature, as in Gal., ch. 4, where the Old Testament narrative
concerning Abraham and his family is employed. In many
passages the pictures are suggested very briefly indeed: in
I Thess. 2:7 Paul compares himself to a "nurse taking care of
her children"; in I Cor. 9:7 he allows the brief reference to
a picture to speak for itself: "Who tends a flock without get-
ting some of the milk?" Sometimes the picture is offered
suddenly through the metaphorical use of a single word, as
in Phil. 3:2: "Look out for the dogs." Again and again a word
simply *points* to a picture, so to speak, when that word is one
that was frequently associated with a given life situation: in
Gal. 4:5, for example, the verb "redeem" points to the picture of a slave ransomed from bondage; in Rom. 3:24 the
verb "justified" points to a scene in a court of law. These are
only a few of the multitude of analogies that are introduced
either explicitly or indirectly as the apostle attempts to convey his message to his readers.

Although such analogical usages were obviously intended
to clarify and reinforce the Pauline message, some of them
have also tended to produce diversity and confusion. Pictures representing familiar phenomena or life situations may
serve a useful purpose in clarifying and reinforcing certain
Pauline ideas, but since the phenomena or life situations that
they represent usually involve a variety of elements, the interpreter is confronted with the necessity of determining, in
any given usage of a picture, which of the elements within it
are intended by Paul to have significance for the thought that
he wishes to communicate. The problem becomes all the
more complex in the case of pictures used analogically in
earlier literature, for the reader is prone to assume that ideas
emphasized in the previous applications must also be rele-

vant, whether or not they are given explicit expression by the apostle. Diversity in the understanding of Pauline thought is inevitable so long as interpreters are left without clearly defined criteria concerning the extent to which the apostle's analogical material provides a basis for the comprehension of that thought. In Gal. 4:4 f., for example, Paul introduces the picture of ransom as he refers to the saving work of Christ. How many of the elements involved in this picture are intended to be relevant and applicable? In the life situation from which the picture is drawn there is found the idea of deliverance and freedom. There is found the idea of a price being paid. There is found the idea that the slave is set free because someone else paid the price. There is found the idea that the slave's owner released the slave only when he received a satisfactory payment in a strictly businesslike transaction. Are all of these elements to be regarded as having significance with respect to Paul's thought about Christ and man's salvation? If not all of them are intended to have relevance, then which of them are so intended? Reconstructions of the Pauline thought have varied tremendously, depending upon the answers given to such questions as these and depending upon the ways in which interpreters have chosen to apply the elements regarded as applicable.

The situation with respect to the interpretation of Pauline analogies is not unlike that which long prevailed with regard to the interpretation of the parables of Jesus. Very early within the Christian movement there began to appear the allegorical type of interpretation, according to which the various details of a parable were given particular significance. This is not entirely surprising, since the use of allegory was exceedingly common in the Greek world and was adopted by such figures as Philo within Hellenistic Judaism. Accompanying factors may also have been involved, such as " an unconscious desire to discover a deeper meaning in the simple words of Jesus," [4] and the notion that the parables served the purpose of concealing the " secret of the kingdom of God " from those who were " outside " by clothing in the details of the parables certain meanings that would be recognized only by the enlightened (see Mark 4:10-12; Matt. 13:10-15; Luke 8:9 f.). The Synoptic Gospels themselves include examples of such interpretation.[5] During the following centuries the allegorical type of interpretation continued to flourish. A classic illustration of the method, often cited,[6] is found in Augustine's interpretation of the parable of the good Samaritan, according to which almost every noun and verb in the story is claimed to convey a particular metaphorical significance. One of the most extended treatments of the parables involving the allegorical method of interpretation is that of Trench, who draws a distinction, it is true, between parable and allegory in terms of *form*,[7] and recognizes that the "figurative language of Scripture is not so stereotyped that one figure must always stand for one and the same thing," [8] but he accepts, nevertheless, the assumption that "there is import in every single point" of a parable.[9]

It was Adolf Jülicher, at the turn of the last century, whose work established the essential error of the allegorical interpretation of the parables and demonstrated that parables as such are quite unsuited to this kind of interpretation.[10] Although Jülicher's reaction against allegorization may have led him to an oversimplification and to an interpretation of the parables in a much too broad and general way, he did mark the turning point in this area of New Testament studies. Further significant advance in the interpretation of the parables has been made by such scholars as A. T. Cadoux,[11] B. T. D. Smith,[12] and especially C. H. Dodd [13] and J. Jeremias.[14] All of these men moved steadily toward an understanding of the parables *based upon their relationship to the specific and critical situations in the midst of which they were uttered.*

This brief survey of the study of the parables directs attention to the emergence of two related conclusions: (1) the parables uttered by Jesus were not intended to receive the kind of allegorical interpretation that gives to each detail its

own application and significance and (2) each parable must
be interpreted in the light of the particular historical context in which it was used. These conclusions, reached
through the examination of the many parables, thus provide
certain criteria in the light of which any given parable must
be interpreted. This does not mean that all problems of interpretation are therefore solved. Since the gospel traditions
do not offer indications as to the actual historical settings for
every parable, the precise meanings that were intended may
still remain unclear. It does mean, however, that there are
provided controls that at least prevent the kind of fanciful
interpretation that once prevailed, and at the same time
make possible a more trustworthy interpretation within the
limits imposed by the material itself.

All of this can be seen as relevant here when there is formulated the fundamental question that gave rise to the present study: *Has the understanding of Pauline thought been
distorted to any marked degree because interpreters have
taken as clues to that thought more of the ideas suggested by
the various elements or details in Paul's analogies than the
apostle himself intended?*

It is certainly true that from the Pauline analogies have
been drawn some of the ideas and doctrines that, rightly or
wrongly, have been ascribed to Paul. In considerable measure, at least, it is from his use of the picture of ransom and
the picture of sacrifice that there have been constructed
some of the aspects of the allegedly Pauline thought concerning the nature of salvation wrought by Christ, especially through his death. Claims concerning Paul's view of
man's sinful state as due to the " fall " of the first man, Adam,
rest largely on passages in which his references to Adam are
introduced analogically: it is to reinforce the emphasis upon
the saving work of Christ that the picture of Adam is introduced for comparison and contrast (Rom. 5:12-19; I Cor.
15:21 f., 45-49). Since analogies thus play an important role
in such areas as these, there seems to be a need for the kind
of examination of Paul's analogical usages generally which

may determine the persistent characteristics of them and thereby provide some fundamental criteria for the interpretation of any given analogy, just as the study of the parables has provided criteria in that branch of New Testament criticism.

This is not to imply that scholarship has been indifferent to the subject of Pauline analogical usage. Writings in the German language have tended especially to direct attention to the fact of Paul's extensive use of analogy, for in them the reader encounters frequently such terms as *Bild* ("picture," "likeness," etc.) and *bildlich* ("pictorial," "metaphorical"), even more frequently, it seems, than corresponding terms in works composed in English. Bultmann, a half century ago, presented a rather extensive list of Paul's Greek words that have analogical significance, classifying them according to the kinds of phenomena or life situations with which they are (or were) associated.[15] Werner Straub published in 1937 a work devoted wholly to the subject of Paul's analogical usage, *Die Bildersprache des Apostels Paulus*.[16] Here one finds a sixfold classification of the Pauline "picture" usages,[17] some discussion of each usage, and the formulation of certain conclusions. Although the author presents numerous important observations, the treatment of the various analogies is, on the whole, quite sketchy. Commentators, too, often offer observations concerning Pauline analogical usage as they deal with this or that picture which the apostle has employed. It is stated, for example, that "Paul is not careful to maintain the consistency of his illustrations,"[18] or that he "lacks the gift for sustained illustration,"[19] or that "an illustration is not necessarily perfect at every point."[20] Generalizations of this kind may indeed be true, but to express them in connection with the treatment of a single passage only, without the marshaling of evidence provided by an examination of the analogies generally, cannot be wholly convincing. Only as the nature of Paul's usage is analyzed in a large number of cases, and only as the characteristics of that usage are shown indeed to be *persistent*, can the interpreter accept the generalizations as valid and employ them with confidence in the attempt to reconstruct the Pauline thought.[21]

The purpose of the present study is to examine critically a large number of the passages in Paul's letters in which analogical elements are introduced. Only in this way can there be any real hope of determining whether or not there is recognizable a pattern of usage that can serve as a dependable guide to the interpreter as he attempts to grasp the significance of a particular usage, especially in those areas in which the more crucial theological issues are involved. It was the author's original intent to include in this volume a reexamination of these crucial issues in the light of the criteria that might emerge from the analysis of the many analogical usages. It soon became evident, however, that if the preliminary analysis was to be sufficiently comprehensive, this, in itself, should constitute a single volume. The result, therefore, is a study that must be recognized as only the introduction to the total planned undertaking. It is hoped, however, that progress will have been made toward the establishing of certain *means* — the determining of certain criteria — which may be helpful in the subsequent effort to move on to the ultimate *ends*. In view of the plan for the total undertaking some of the analogies that are of particular importance because of their bearing upon central — and controversial — theological issues are treated, at best, only lightly. As already indicated, these are the very analogies that, because of their crucial import, need to be examined with benefit of the recognition of the persistent characteristics in Paul's usage generally. There are omitted here, therefore, extended treatments of the pictures of sacrifice and ransom as media through which there may be apprehended Paul's understanding of the saving work of Christ, especially of his death. There is absent also a detailed consideration of the apostle's analogical references to Adam, references that bear heavily upon the reconstruction of Paul's position in regard to the nature of man's sinful state. Postponed for later treatment likewise is an examination of some of those usages which introduce pictures drawn from legal procedures — the use of the verb " to justify," for example.

There is a further reason also why an examination of the more crucial analogies should be postponed for a later volume. These analogies pertain to theological issues that must be considered, not only in the light of persistent characteristics found in Paul's analogical usages, but also in the light of characteristics seen in other, though related, areas. In reality there is involved the larger question as to how the apostle's mind operated generally as he sought to express his thought. Only as this larger problem is explored can the interpreter move with confidence from the expression to the thought itself. One aspect of this problem involves the question as to whether or not Paul's statements can always be accepted as expressing what he actually means.[22] It is to be noted especially that in the midst of a given discussion Paul sometimes seems to make an assertion which, viewed from a different perspective, he cannot really have meant. His statement, for example, in Rom. 2:6 (" For he will render to every man according to his works ") *seems*, at least, to contradict the emphasis upon justification through faith. His expression of a trichotomous anthropological view in I Thess. 5:23 may not necessarily mean that such a view was firmly held by him.[23] Is it possible, through further analysis of these and similar passages, to recognize additional characteristics of Pauline expression that should be taken into account in the attempt to move from the expression to the underlying thought?

Another especially important aspect of the larger question concerns Paul's use of earlier material, particularly the Old Testament. There have been numerous discussions with regard to the apostle's handling of the Old Testament literature; and in the present study this subject is considered at those points where Paul's analogies are drawn from, or are related to, that source. It would be helpful, however, if it could be shown more clearly whether or not there are to be found *persistent* characteristics in his general use of the Old

Testament which might provide yet additional insight into the relationship between the apostle's expression and his thought. Because considerations of this sort ought to be included in the treatment of the areas in which the more crucial analogies are involved, there is thus some further justification for dealing with those analogies in a later volume.

Since the present study is concerned with the characteristics of the analogical usages on the part of Paul alone, it is necessary to accept as a basis for analysis only those pictures which are found in the "undoubtedly genuine"[24] letters of the apostle. Numerous scholars may accept as Pauline such writings as II Thessalonians and Colossians, and some may accept Ephesians as well. In view of the fact that these are by no means universally regarded as authentically Pauline, however, they can hardly be used with full confidence for the purpose at hand.

The term "analogy" is employed here to refer to any picture of a phenomenon or life situation that is presented to the mind of the reader by the Pauline language in such a way as to suggest that in it is to be found something that corresponds to what is being said. As noted earlier, some of the pictures are drawn with a certain amount of detail, some are introduced very briefly indeed, and some are presented only in flashes, so to speak, as single words may suggest them. Although attempts have sometimes been made to classify the various types of usage under such categories as metaphor, simile, allegory, and the like,[25] such classifications are not offered here, partly because many of the pictures do not fall clearly into one category as over against another, and partly because the very use of such categories in reality prejudges to a certain extent the nature of each analogical usage. The purpose of the present study is not to see how Paul's usages fit into predetermined patterns, but rather to discover his *own* patterns and procedures. (Classifications might be useful if evidence could be found that Paul consistently employed analogies in the different categories in different ways. If judgments are to be made in this respect, however, they must come as a *result* of the kind of study which is now undertaken.)

It has already been explained that some of the analogies that may be regarded as particularly crucial must await later treatment. This does not mean that consideration can be given, even in this study, to every other picture that is suggested by the Pauline language or to every separate allusion to a given picture. Numerous words may suggest pictures of certain phenomena or life situations, but when they become widely used in a figurative sense their appearance need not necessarily indicate that the writer was consciously intending to present pictures *as pictures* to the mind of the reader. Thus, when Paul uses the verb " to bear fruit," he may simply be employing a term that had become a familiar substitute for " to produce results." In some cases the actual picture of an agricultural phenomenon need not be involved at all; in other cases the picture might have been intended to have relevance.[26] In the present study attention is given only to those words which seem to the author to have particular analogical significance. Where a given picture is introduced in more than one context there has been selected for direct analysis that context which throws the greatest light on the nature of its use. If, as is sometimes the case, however, the same picture is used differently in different contexts, more than the one context is examined.

1.

The First Letter of Paul
to the Thessalonians

I THESSALONIANS 2:7

If I Thessalonians is the earliest of the extant letters of Paul, then the first clear Pauline analogical usage that we possess is that found in I Thess. 2:7: "But we were gentle among you, like a nurse taking care of her children." The extent to which analogical usage is involved, however, is a matter of considerable dispute. It is evident that the apostle likens himself and his companions to a "nurse taking care of her children." This is the only analogical element to be found in this verse if there is accepted as authentic the textual reading that includes the form *ēpioi*, translated in the Revised Standard Version as "gentle." A further analogical element appears, however, if, following many early manuscripts, there is accepted as original the form *nēpioi* ("babes," RSV margin). In this case Paul likens himself and his companions to infants before he introduces the metaphor of the nurse.

A large number of interpreters prefer the adjective *ēpioi* ("gentle") as the original form here. It is argued that the metaphor of "babes" is "inappropriate" in a context in which the attitude of a nurse toward her children is also involved.[1] Dibelius believes that "gentle" is the more appropriate as a contrast to the thought expressed in v. 5 and as in harmony with the thought of v. 8.[2] The widespread acceptance of "gentle" is indicated by the fact that it is given as the preferred reading, not only in the Revised Standard Version but also in the King James Version, the American Standard Version, *The New English Bible,* and the translation of Moffatt. It is frequently suggested that *nēpioi* appears in some manuscripts as the result of dittography,[3] the final

21

letter of the previous word being repeated so as to change *ēpioi* into *nēpioi*. It has also been noted that the word for "gentle" appears only once elsewhere in the New Testament (II Tim. 2:24), whereas the word for "babes" is much more common. The proposal has been made that since copyists "are prone to change an unfamiliar into any familiar word resembling it that gives a tolerable sense," and since "babes" is a "favorite expression" of Paul's,[4] the appearance of "babes" in some manuscripts may thus be explained.

On the other hand, *nēpioi* ("babes") is the better-attested reading (XBCDGF, Vulg. . . .). It is used elsewhere nine times by Paul.[5] Frame meets the problem of reconciling the analogy of babes with that of the nurse by offering as the intended punctuation (and meaning), "we became babes in the midst of you, — as a nurse cherishes her own children so we yearned after you, . . ." (vs. 7 f.).[6] In this way "babes" is understood as a contrast to the preceding "apostles" (who "might have made demands," v. 6), and "with its implication of the unripe and undeveloped, far from being meaningless . . . , is a capital antithesis."[7] This understanding of the text is in complete agreement with the fact that throughout the first seven verses of this chapter there appears a series of such contrasts, each introduced by "but" (*alla*). By relating "babes" in this way to that which precedes rather than to that which follows, the problem of reconciling the shift from the one metaphor to that of the nurse is reduced considerably. Neil, although insisting that "gentle" makes "better sense," admits in effect that even a *closer* relationship between the word under consideration and the nurse metaphor would not necessarily exclude the possibility of Paul's use of "babes" here, for he admits that "Paul is quite capable of comparing himself to an infant and a nursing mother in the same sentence — he calls himself a father a few lines farther down (v. 11) and an orphan in the same chapter (v. 17)!"[8] Since, as will be seen more fully in the following pages, Paul frequently moves rapidly from one metaphor to another, there seems to be no real justification for rejecting the reading ("babes") which is the better attested in the manuscripts. And if the form *nēpioi* can be explained as due to the fact that the last letter of the previous word has been repeated and *added* to an original *ēpioi* in some manuscripts (dittography), it is equally possible that in the other manuscripts there has simply occurred the *omission* of one *n* (haplography).[9]

If Paul does indeed liken himself and his companions to babes, the picture is obviously intended to suggest the oppo-

site of " apostles " who " might have made demands " (v. 6).
In this case the relevant element in the picture of babes is
the idea of the absence of an authoritarian attitude, which
may be associated with children as over against their parents
or teachers. The thought is not unlike that which is found
in Mark 10:15 (Matt. 18:3; Luke 18:17), where the idea of
humility on the part of children is at least partly involved.[10]
The analogy may thus be said to suggest a " childlike temper which is untempted to self-advancement . . . a humble,
unassuming disposition," as one writer interprets the reference to children in Matt. 18:3, 5.[11]

While it is this element in the analogy which is applicable
in the passage under consideration, there are other ideas associated with the picture of babes that are not only irrelevant
but also quite inappropriate. In Rom. 2:20, for example, Paul
uses the same word to introduce an entirely different idea.
(The RSV reads, " a teacher of children," but Paul's word for
" children " is the plural of *nēpios*.) There the picture, in
context, is used to suggest " morally and religiously immature persons." [12] Much the same idea is associated with babes
in I Cor. 3:1, where the reference is to those who are so immature (spiritually) that they are still to be fed " with milk,
not solid food " (v. 2); they are still " of the flesh " (v. 3).
The picture of babes as suggesting immaturity is found again
in I Cor. 14:20, where " babes " (though in a verb form,
nēpiazete) and " mature " stand in contrast.

Paul's word for " mature " is *teleios*. In I Cor. 13:10 f. this word
is again contrasted to *nēpios* (" babe "), although in the RSV
the former is translated as " perfect " and the latter as " child."
Here, however, the former may refer primarily to that perfect
state which is to be found " in the risen life " [13] (though the meaning of " mature " still leads Paul to introduce, in contrast, the passing reference to the child).

In Gal. 4:1, 3 still further usages of " babe(s) " (RSV, " child "
and " children ") are found. The total context there shows
that the thought is of those who are not yet sufficiently ma-

ture to be released from the care of "guardians and trustees." That the picture of babes was not uncommonly used to suggest immaturity is shown further by the fact that *teleios* and *nēpios* stand in contrast also in Eph. 4:13 f. and in Heb. 5:13 f.[14]

Altogether it is clearly apparent that the picture of babes was frequently employed, in Paul's time (and later), to suggest the idea of immaturity as well as the idea of a "humble, unassuming disposition" (see above). The important point to be observed here is that in I Thess. 2:7 the idea more generally associated with the picture is precisely the one that can have *no* relevance or applicability. The notion of his own *immaturity* is entirely out of place in a context in which he is defending himself and his conduct. He may deal with others because they are yet immature (I Cor. 3:1 ff.), and earlier he was himself immature (Gal. 4:3), but he speaks or writes as he does because there has been revealed to him and for him a true maturity. There is, certainly, the recognition that there are still limits to his maturity ("Not that I . . . am already perfect [or "mature"]," Phil. 3:12), but within those limits he belongs nevertheless in the category of the mature as over against the immature ("Let those of us who are mature be thus minded," Phil. 3:15). Hence among the "mature" he can "impart wisdom" (I Cor. 2:6).

This examination of the analogy of babes points clearly to the fact that the picture is to be understood and applied to the Pauline thought or argument *only with respect to that idea, associated with it, which is shown to be relevant in the light of its immediate context*. In this case it can be seen that it would be a quite erroneous procedure to attempt to apply to the Pauline thought an element in the analogy which, though frequently involved elsewhere in the use of the analogy, is both irrelevant and inappropriate here.

It may be argued, of course, that the idea in the analogy which *is* relevant (as a contrast to "apostles" who "might have made demands") may also be inappropriate, since at times Paul does not seem to manifest the kind of humility suggested by " babes," especially when he is confronted with those who seriously threaten his interpretation of the gospel (as in Gal., chs. 1; 2, and in II Cor., chs. 10 to 12). His boldness and his demanding disposition there, however, pertain to his concern for his *message* fundamentally, and not to a concern for personal self-seeking. Even if it is true that at other times Paul cannot properly be likened to a babe in this respect, then it becomes all the more clear that the *context alone* must determine the extent to which an element in an analogy may properly be applied or used as a basis for understanding the apostle's thinking.

Admittedly the foregoing discussion must be used with caution in any attempt to describe the persistent characteristics of Paul's use of analogy, for although the position taken here is that " babes " represents the original Pauline text, the fact still remains that many — probably most — scholars reject it in favor of " gentle."

The metaphor of the nurse involves relatively simple usage. As the picture of the nurse is applied it is introduced for the sake of the idea of caring for others. It is quite possible that the nurse in this case is to be understood as also the mother of the children who are being tended, since Paul's word for " her " (children) is the form *heautēs,* which, at least in earlier Greek usage, meant " her own." If this is the thought here, then the analogy may be intended to suggest the idea that Paul and his companions were caring for their *own* children — their own in the sense in which the apostle speaks of himself as having become the " father " of his " child " Onesimus during his imprisonment (Philemon 10).

This point cannot be pressed, however, since it may be argued that in Paul's time the Greek form (*heautēs*) may have lost much of its emphatic force.[15] On the other hand, the similar form *heautōn* (I Thess. 2:8) does seem to carry the emphatic force (" our own ").

In any case the primary emphasis is upon the care that the nurse bestows upon the children.

The application of this idea in the analogy is not spelled out. It is possible, of course, that as Paul writes v. 8, the picture of the (mother) nurse may still be in his mind, since the affection for the Thessalonians which he expresses here can be said to correspond to the kind of tender care that may be associated with a (mother) nurse. Furthermore, it is not impossible that being ready to " share [or " impart "] . . . our own selves " may suggest the feeding of the children from the breast of the (mother) nurse. It seems unlikely, however, that this point of correspondence was intended. Not only does Paul fail to mention such correspondence, but also he shows elsewhere that he was inclined to use his word for " share " or " impart " (*metadounai*) wholly apart from any such picture as that of the (mother) nurse (Rom. 1:11; 12:8; compare Luke 3:11 and Eph. 4:28).

The following facts emerge through this examination of the analogy of the nurse: (1) The picture is introduced for the sake of the idea of tender care, which it suggests. (2) The application of the picture is not developed in any clear or systematic manner. Even if elements in the following verse may be said to correspond to elements in the picture, the absence of any further reference to the picture indicates that the picture occupies, at best, a minor element in his thinking. (3) If, as contended above, the picture of the nurse is preceded by that of babes, the sudden change from the one to the other indicates with particular force that, while a certain association of ideas may be involved (babes may be cared for by a nurse), the *use* of the ideas is determined by the issue to which Paul is addressing himself and not by any careful or systematic application of the analogy itself (Paul could not be babe and nurse at the same time!).

I THESSALONIANS 5:1-11

In this section of I Thessalonians, Paul continues the discussion, begun in ch. 4:13, concerning the expectation of the Parousia, the return of the risen Christ, who, at his second advent, would establish his kingdom. After assuring his readers that those Christians who have already died will not be excluded from the blessings of the new age (in fact, they will " rise first " to " meet the Lord "), the apostle now turns to the question of the " times and the seasons ": when will this " day of the Lord " occur? As he attempts to deal with this question he does so with the use of a rather strange mixture of analogical statements.

The first picture is introduced thus: "(The) day of (the) Lord will come like (a) thief [*kleptēs*] in (the) night " (ch. 5:2).[1] This picture of a thief (or thieves) had already, before Paul's time, become a familiar metaphor or analogy. In the Old Testament it is found in Job 24:14; 30:5; Jer. 2:26; 49:9; Joel 2:9; Obad. 5. The use of it continued throughout the New Testament period. Of particular significance for present purposes is the use of the picture of the coming of a thief as an analogy for the coming of the Lord in Matt. 24:42 f. (compare Luke 12:39).

In comparing Matt. 24:43 with the Pauline language, we note that in the former, Paul's Greek word for " night " is not found. Instead, there appears the word that means " watch " (*phulakē*). Since " watches " were at night, however,[2] the picture is essentially the same (and explains the use of " night" in the RSV).

Other parts of the New Testament also indicate the commonness of the analogy (II Peter 3:10 and Rev. 3:3), though without the mention of night.[3] It has been suggested that " like a thief in the night " would " seem to be a standard use in missionary teaching. The Thessalonians are reminded of it almost as if it were a quotation." [4] Note the preface to the picture: " For you yourselves know well . . ." (I Thess. 5:2). This is generally taken to mean that the Thessalonians " know " this because they are familiar with the tradition reported in Matt. 24:43 and Luke 12:39.[5]

In I Thess. 5:3, Paul indicates the element in the analogy that is intended to have relevance: " When people say, ' There is peace and security,' then sudden destruction will come upon them." The thief comes suddenly at a time that cannot be predicted just as destruction comes suddenly for those who, with a sense of security, are not expecting it. The language certainly suggests that Paul had in mind here the way in which the prophets spoke of the suddenness of God's intervention. Isaiah, ch. 47, stresses the *suddenness* (v. 11) with which the *security* (v. 6) of Babylon will be turned into ruin or destruction. (It is interesting that almost immediately afterward — in ch. 48:3 — there is also a reference to God " suddenly " bringing to pass that which had been determined earlier — a striking parallel to the idea of the Parousia coming suddenly, although the fact of its coming had already been assured.) And Jer., ch. 6, emphasizes the idea that " suddenly " (v. 26) destruction will come precisely at a time when a sense of " peace " (ch. 6:14; compare ch. 8:11) prevails.[6] The probability that Jer., ch. 6, especially, was in Paul's mind here is all the greater as there is observed the combination in this chapter not only of references to peace and a sense of security (v. 14), and suddenness (v. 26) and destruction (vs. 15, 26), but also the picture of a woman in travail (v. 24), all of which are combined by Paul in I Thess. 5:3. In any case, as the apostle adds this sentence immediately after his introduction of the analogy of the thief in the night, it becomes clear that it is the suddenness of the thief's coming that is relevant to the context.[7]

This analogy of the thief is one that indicates with unusual certainty the fact that in Pauline usage the application of an analogy must be limited to that element (or those elements) having relevance in the immediate context. To press this analogy farther can lead to serious difficulties, if not absurdities: (1) To press the point that the day of the Lord is intended to be represented as a thief (*kleptēs,* " one who takes property by stealth ")[8] is meaningless. Or, if the coming of the day of the Lord is simply a kind of circumlocution for the coming of the Lord himself, the representation of the Lord as " one who takes property by stealth " is equally out of place.[9] (2) The coming of a thief is ordinarily not anticipated. The victims are taken by surprise precisely because he is *not* expected. To press this element in the analogy is patently improper, for Paul *was* expecting the Parousia. In view of this, the accompanying analogy of travail coming upon a woman with child (v. 3) agrees more fully with the Pauline expectation, for while the birth pangs come suddenly, at a time that cannot be predicted with exactness, nevertheless there is the obvious expectation that they *will come* in the not distant future (see below, however).[10]

Both of these considerations indicate quite clearly that *the only element* in the analogy of " a thief in the night " that can be intended by Paul to suggest the nature of his thought in regard to the Parousia is that which has relevance to the very immediate point under discussion, namely, its *suddenness*. To draw more from the analogy than that which is relevant to the *immediate* context is to give to it a significance that the apostle never intended.

How limited this significance actually is may be seen further as one moves on to Paul's added words. In vs. 4 ff., Paul turns from the analogy itself, with its idea of suddenness, to an idea that is emphasized even more, the idea that his readers must be ready for the Parousia; they must be " awake." They should be awake as befits those who are " sons of the day " (v. 5) and " belong to the day " (v. 8). As such, they are " not in darkness " (v. 4); they are not " of the night " (v. 5). But if Paul can say this, it is evident that already the analogy of the thief in the night is laid aside, for it breaks down entirely in this new context: if they are " of the day " and are not " in darkness " or " of the night," then the analogy, to be appropriate, would need to be of a " thief in the day," not of a " thief in the night." In other words, one cannot press the details, nor draw from the analogy more than is appropriate for the *most immediate context*. To do this in the case of I Thess. 5:1-11 leads to contradiction and nonsense.

Even if one reduces the analogy to the picture of the thief, disregarding " in the night," a contradiction or conflict still remains if an attempt is made to press the analogy beyond the idea of suddenness. Paul says, in v. 4, " But you are not in darkness, brethren, for that day to surprise you like a thief." [11] If this is the correct reading of the text (see below), Paul is saying that since his readers are not in darkness (" that is, in the realm of wickedness "),[12] the " day " (the Parousia) will *not* surprise them as a thief surprises his victims. That is, the " day " will not surprise them in the sense that it will " overtake " them when they are not prepared or ready for it. But the picture of a thief is normally that of one whose coming involves *both* suddenness *and surprise*. Since Paul in this verse explicitly excludes the element of surprise, he is making it quite clear that this element usually associated with the picture is *not* intended to have significance for his thought regarding the Parousia. Since the Thessalonians are *not* " in darkness," they will not be caught unprepared. Of course the day of the Lord, by implication, *will* involve both suddenness and surprise for those who are " in darkness," but those whom Paul is addressing as " you " in v. 2 are the same persons as those addressed in v. 4. It is to them that the analogy is first directed in v. 2. It is clear that *for them* the picture has applicability only in terms of suddenness; they are *not* to be surprised.

The (RSV) translation of v. 4, given above, is based on the reading of *kleptēs* (" thief ") in the singular (Nestle text) and preserves the same metaphor found in v. 2. A less widely accepted reading, *kleptas* (Westcott and Hort text, " thieves "), would change the metaphor and give the following meaning: " for that day to surprise you as thieves are surprised." If this is the correct reading,[13] then there has occurred an inversion of metaphor: " The figure of the ' thief ' is now transferred from the *cause* of the surprise (v. 2) to its *object*." [14] This reading, which in reality introduces a new picture, does, it is true, allow for a certain correspondence (with respect to surprise) between the metaphor and the Pauline thought, for (presumably) thieves normally prepare themselves against being surprised by the coming of the dawn just as the Thessalonians are said to be prepared (by not being " in darkness "). But even here the (new) metaphor cannot be applied fully. Although it is true that thieves, while working at night, expect the coming of the day, just as the Christians expect the coming of the day of the Lord, there is still an important difference between the picture and the Pauline thinking: the thieves *know* when the dawn will break, but the Christians do *not* know when the Parousia will occur, as the primary emphasis on suddenness makes clear. Altogether, therefore, even with this (new) metaphor the picture has only limited applicability. Furthermore, if Paul has indeed changed the picture, it is all the more evident that instead of developing and applying the original analogy (v. 2) he has allowed the flow of his thought to take precedence over the analogy. The form of the analogy is determined by his thinking with regard to the issue under discussion; the nature of his thinking is not to be understood from an analysis of the analogy itself.

There is found also in this section of I Thessalonians a further analogy: " Then sudden destruction will come upon them as travail comes upon a woman with child " (v. 3). *In context*, as noted above, the picture is obviously introduced to suggest, as with the metaphor of the thief, the idea of suddenness, since the exact moment at which travail comes upon a woman cannot be predicted with exactness. The question needs to be raised, however, as to whether or not further ideas associated with the picture are intended to have significance for the Pauline thought regarding the Parousia.

In earlier writings, " travail " (*ōdin*, " pain of childbirth," " birth pangs ") was frequently mentioned to suggest anguish, sorrow, and pain.[15] It is noteworthy that in the Septuagint an identical phrase, *ōdines hōs tiktousēs* (" pangs as of one bringing forth "), is used in Ps. 47:7 (Ps. 48:6); Jer. 6:24; 8:21; 27:43; Hos. 13:13; and Micah 4:9. This picture of a woman in travail, though not introduced with the same stereotyped phrase, came to be used in connection with references to the coming day of the Lord, as in Isa. 13:6-8. The pain of childbirth as an analogy for the anguish associated with the coming Messianic judgment is actually spelled out in Enoch 62:4:

> " Then shall pain come upon them
> as on a woman in travail, . . .
> When her child enters the mouth of the womb,
> And she has pain in bringing forth." [16]

In Mark 13:8 and in Matt. 24:8 the word translated "sufferings," and used in connection with the events leading up to the inauguration of the new (Messianic) age, in reality introduces the same picture, for it is the plural of the very word that is rendered "travail" in the Pauline passage under consideration and means literally, as already observed, "pains of childbirth." It is true, therefore, as all of this material indicates, that the picture of a woman in travail was commonly employed to suggest the sufferings or woes associated with the coming of the day of the Lord. The question remains, however, as to whether or not the idea of suffering, as well as the idea of suddenness, was intended by Paul to have relevance or significance for his thought in regard to the Parousia. The use of the word "destruction" (*olethros*) and the statement that "there will be no escape" suggest that this signfiicance may have been intended. Upon closer examination, however, it appears that Paul's Greek word, translated "destruction," does not refer to the Messianic woes or sufferings at all. In its context here it seems to mean simply "death." Only four verses earlier (ch. 4:17) it is emphasized that when the Parousia occurs "we shall always be with the Lord." And again, a few verses later (ch. 5:10), the emphasis is also upon the expectation that "we might live with him." Since the natural antithesis to continued life with the Lord is "death," it seems likely that Paul intended this meaning to be understood in his use of *olethros*. The thought is thus very much like that which is found in II Thess. 1:9: "They shall suffer the punishment of eternal destruction and exclusion from the presence of the Lord and from the glory of his might." As death is the antithesis of life (compare II Cor. 2:15 f.), so, apparently, "destruction" is the antithesis of life with Jesus.

In view of the doubtful authorship of II Thessalonians (see the Introduction) this document can hardly be used as a reliable source for a careful analysis of the Pauline thinking. Since in II Thess. 1:9, however, the author's thought, as just observed, is so similar to that which is seen in I Thessalonians, it is at least of interest to consider further the significance of "destruction" in this verse. It was suggested above that "exclusion from the presence of the Lord," parallel with "destruction," might be construed as referring to death. On the other hand, the expression may mean "not the annihilation of the wicked . . . but their separation from Christ." [17] In either case, however, no idea of Messianic sufferings or woes is involved. It is true that "from the presence of the Lord and from the glory of his might" is, in the Greek, an almost exact quotation from the Septuagint version of Isa. 2:10 and 2:21; the wording is identical except for the omission of "of the fear," which, in the Septuagint, follows "presence." It is also true that the passage in Isa., ch. 2, is in a context that concerns the day of the Lord. And since the context includes reference to the haughtiness and pride of man as being brought low on that day, and suggests destruction in various forms, it may be contended that the author of II Thessalonians quoted from the prophecy because it agreed with his own thought of the Messianic woes. On the other hand, *the words actually quoted* center attention, not upon the woes, but upon the fact of separation from the presence of the Lord. Furthermore, the very omission of the word *phobou* ("fear," "dread," "terror"), found in the Septuagint quotation, can mean that the main point involved in the quotation is consciously being separated from the ideas of terror and destruction found in the Isaiah passage from which the quotation is taken. Thus, as the quoted section stands in II Thess. 1:9, (1) it does not necessarily involve the idea of Messianic sufferings or woes, (2) it centers attention upon the idea of separation from the Lord, and (3) it is this separation which is parallel to "destruction." Hence it becomes evident that "destruction" is to be understood in this verse very much as it is to be understood in I Thess. 5:3, at least insofar as there is absent in both usages any suggestion of sufferings as associated with the day of the Lord.

The only other use of this word for "destruction" in unquestioned Pauline material is found in I Cor. 5:5. Here again the expression appears in a context in which the day of the Lord is mentioned. But it is important to observe that the destruction, however interpreted,[18] is mentioned as that which should occur quite apart from the day of the Lord: as a *prior* destruction, due to Satan, it may be efficacious in making possible the saving of the man in question when the Parousia does take place. Once more, therefore, the term is employed in a context where reference is made to the day of the Lord, but it carries no idea of the sufferings or Messianic woes that are associated with this day in non-Pauline literature.

Thus as Paul employed the picture of a woman in travail there is given no convincing evidence whatever that he intended the idea of suffering, naturally associated with it, to be applied to his thought concerning the day of the Lord, even though such an application was frequently made.[19]

Finally, the analogy of travail is one that might suggest the *inevitability* of the Parousia, since a " woman with child is certain to be faced with travail." [20] The words at the end of v. 3 (" there will be no escape ") might be interpreted as the application of this element in the picture. But since the following sentence (v. 4) includes the verb " surprise " (or " overtake "), there is indication that the essential thought has not shifted from that of suddenness to that of inevitability. And the discussion that then continues (vs. 5 ff.), with its admonition concerning preparedness (being " awake " and " sober "), has relevance with respect to suddenness but not to inevitability. It is probable, therefore, that the clause that *might* suggest the inevitability of the Parousia (" there will be no escape ") arises " not from the comparison but from *olethros* [" destruction "]," [21] which, as previously seen, is probably introduced because of the influence of the prophetic idea that destruction will fall suddenly in the midst of a sense of peace and security.

Reference has already been made to Paul's use of the word " day " in vs. 4-8. Actually a wordplay is involved here, for " day " refers both to the day of the Lord and to daytime or daylight. In a sense there is also a wordplay on " night," which can perhaps be understood as referring to the Last Judgment [22] and also to nighttime. Insofar as the day of the Lord is compared to daylight and the judgment is compared to nighttime there is introduced still another analogy. The relevant idea involved in this picture seems to be that just as men are awake and sober in the daytime, while others are asleep and drunk at night, the Thessalonian Christians should be prepared for the day of the Lord even though its coming will be sudden, and they should not be unprepared as those who are asleep or drunk. In saying that " those who sleep sleep at night, and those who get drunk are drunk at night " (v. 7), Paul is probably extending the analogy rather than applying it. In vs. 5 f. the use of the first and second person ("we," "you ") provides unmistakable evidence of application. Here, however, attention seems to be directed back to the picture. But even so the picture is not being drawn with complete accuracy. While men may usually sleep at night and may often be drunk at night, the latter, especially, is by no means invariably the case. Isaiah 5:11 associates drinking with daytime as well as with night. Paul is apparently adapting his picture to his thought rather than developing it in any careful or systematic manner. The analogy is extended farther through the references to "light " and "darkness." As men live in the light of day, as over against the darkness of night, so the Christians are living " in the full enlightenment of the Christian faith." [23] At least this seems to be the essential meaning, although Paul is content to convey these points of comparison without careful explanation or development. It is still the idea of the suddenness of the coming of the Parousia that provides the reason for the new analogical material: men who are awake and sober and enlightened will be ready for the *sudden* coming of the day of the Lord, as the merging of this analogy with that of the thief in the night (v. 4) indicates. It has already been noted, however, that there emerges a fundamental contradiction if one attempts to apply the details of these two pictures: if the Thessalonians "belong to the day " (v. 8), then the coming of the day of the Lord cannot properly be compared to the coming of a thief " in the night."

Of particular interest is the use of the picture of those who sleep, which, as already seen, is a part of the larger picture involving day and night. In v. 7 " to sleep " is to be understood literally. In v. 6, however, a metaphorical usage is in-

volved: men are not to sleep in the sense that they are not
to be indifferent to, or oblivious to, the impending day of the
Lord; they are not to be unready or unprepared at the sudden arrival of the Parousia. But only four verses later (v. 10)
the same picture of those who sleep is introduced in order to
convey quite a different idea. In this verse, " sleep " is clearly
intended to refer to death, just as in I Thess. 4:13-18, where
those who have " fallen asleep " are those who have died.

A different Greek verb is used in I Thess. 4:13-18. Paul uses
both verbs, however, to refer to death. At three points the RSV
gives a form of the verb " to die " where Paul's Greek verb means
literally " to fall asleep." See I Cor. 7:39; 11:30; 15:18. Death is
obviously meant in I Cor. 15:6, 20, 51.

This means that the picture of those who sleep is employed
by the apostle to convey quite different meanings in different contexts, even when such contexts stand in close proximity. It is evident that the significance of the picture must
therefore be determined by the setting in which it is placed;
the picture itself does not provide a reliable clue as to the
apostle's thought. In the passage under consideration the
picture is so flexible that Paul can use it to communicate two
entirely distinct ideas within the same paragraph.

Much the same may be said with regard to the parallel, or
contrasting, picture of those who are " awake." In v. 6 to be
" awake " means to be alert, ready, prepared (for the sudden
coming of the day of the Lord). In v. 10, however, the same
Greek verb is used to convey the idea of being alive (as opposed to being dead). While the former metaphorical usage
is found frequently in the New Testament — sometimes expressed by means of the English verb " to watch " (Matt.
24:42 f.; 25:13; 26:38, 40, 41; etc.) — the latter usage appears
only here. Paul undoubtedly introduces it in v. 10 as a contrast to " asleep " (meaning " dead "). It is worthy of note
that in doing so he deviates from common practice, for
whereas " asleep " often denoted death (Matt. 27:52; Acts
7:60; 13:36; II Peter 3:4), " awake," as already observed, is

not found elsewhere in the New Testament to mean " alive."
Thus two facts emerge: (1) As in the case of the picture of
those who sleep, the parallel picture of those who are awake
is employed for the sake of two quite different ideas in statements that stand very close together; it is the immediate
context, and not the picture itself, that is determinative for
the meaning. (2) The " occasional " nature of Paul's usage is
particularly apparent here, since in shifting from the thought
of preparedness to that of aliveness he gives to the picture
of those who are awake a metaphorical meaning that has
been suggested by the context, even though it is a meaning
not commonly associated with the picture.

It is true that according to the RSV to be awake is contrasted
to being dead in Eph. 5:14 (" Awake, O sleeper, and arise from
the dead"). Here, however, the Greek verb is *egeirō*, not *grē-*
goreō, and suggests the idea of arousing much more than that of
being awake. The fact remains that Paul's word for being
" awake " in I Thess. 5:10 is nowhere else used to suggest aliveness as opposed to death.

In v. 8 still another picture is introduced, that of the armed
soldier: " Let us . . . put on the breastplate of faith and
love, and for a helmet the hope of salvation." [24] The Pauline
language here may have been determined, partly at least, by
that of Isa. 59:17, where, in the Septuagint version, the same
Greek words are used for " put on," " breastplate," " helmet,"
and " salvation." Particularly significant is the fact that the
only two pieces of equipment mentioned by Paul are the
very same ones designated explicitly in Isa. 59:17. In both
passages " helmet " is associated with " salvation." With Paul,
however, " breastplate " is made to represent " faith and
love " instead of " righteousness." Since in his use of this
picture the apostle seems to be borrowing largely from an
Old Testament pattern, there is provided only limited evidence as to the nature of his own independent use of analogy. One fact that emerges, however, is that by changing
the application of " breastplate " he shows an inclination to-

ward the adapting of his analogical material to his own thinking.

This picture of the armed soldier, like all the other pictures found in this section of I Thessalonians, is made to contribute to the idea of the sudden coming of the day of the Lord. The essential thought is that men should be prepared for that day no matter how sudden its coming may be, just as the soldier is equipped and ready. This meaning is reinforced through the mingling of the picture with that of day (and night): as men are " awake " in the daytime — and hence prepared for a sudden occurrence — so also they must be prepared like an armed soldier. The correctness of this interpretation is suggested by the fact that in Rom. 13:11-14 the same kind of thinking is expressed through the use of the same kind of analogical material. When Paul writes that " salvation is nearer to us now than when we first believed " (v. 11), his thought here also pertains undoubtedly to the idea of the Parousia.[25] And although the suddenness of its coming is not indicated explicitly, it is nevertheless implied in the statement that " it is full time now for you to wake from sleep." Furthermore, these words, together with the claim that " the night is far gone, the day is at hand " and with the references to being awake, to " darkness " and to " light," involve the same kind of mingled analogies found in I Thess. 5:1-11. Of particular interest is the admonition that there should be " put on the armor of light." Thus the metaphor of the armed soldier is clearly related to several of the other pictures combined similarly in I Thessalonians, and all are related to the thought that the day of the Lord may come suddenly.

It is also of interest to note that in the immediately preceding verses in Romans (ch. 13:8-10), Paul has emphasized the centrality of love with regard to human relations. In I Thess. 5:8, it is precisely " love " (along with " faith ") that he introduces as the " breastplate " instead of " righteousness," as in Isa. 59:17.

In v. 11 a final picture is suggested briefly, that of the construction of a building: " Build one another up." " Since both

a Christian church and individual Christians are likened to
a building or temple in which God or the Holy Spirit dwells
(I Cor. 3:9, 16 f.; II Cor. 6:16; Eph. 2:21), the erection of
which temple will not be completely finished till the return of Christ from heaven, those who, by action, instruction, exhortation, comfort, promote the Christian wisdom of
others and help them to live a correspondent life are regarded as taking part in the erection of that building, and
hence are said *oikodomein* [" to construct a building "]." [26]
Since this picture is only lightly touched upon here, and
since Paul's use of it will be discussed much more fully in
connection with a study of I Cor. 3:5-17, it will suffice at
this point simply to note that the inclusion of the picture
here shows the apostle's tendency to combine analogical materials of various sorts and to move rapidly from one picture
to another, often without development or any attempt at
careful application.

In this section of I Thessalonians are thus to be observed
several characteristics of Pauline analogical usage. Particularly conspicuous is the fact that numerous pictures are here
combined: a thief in the night, a woman in travail, day and
night, sleeping and being awake, drunkenness and sobriety,
an armed soldier, and the construction of a building. None
of these pictures is developed carefully or applied systematically. All of them revolve around the central idea of the sudden coming of the day of the Lord for which men must be
prepared and ready if they are to survive. Each picture has
significance for the Pauline thought only with respect to
that element in it which has relevance in its immediate context; other elements associated with a picture have no importance, and an idea associated with one picture may even
stand in conflict with an idea associated with another picture (the day of the Lord will come like a thief " in the
night," yet the Christians are " not of the night "). Altogether
we see here the way in which Paul's mind is at work as he
employs a multiplicity of analogical materials. One central
thought predominates, and yet through association of ideas,
suggested in part by earlier literary usages, the apostle

reaches out in various directions to seize upon numerous pictures that may reinforce his emphasis. It is still his own thinking, however, which is determinative for his analogical usage. The pictures themselves are of such secondary importance that not only are they left undeveloped but they can even be adapted to suit the immediate flow of thought (as in the case of the picture that suggests that men are drunk only at night).

2.

The Letter of Paul
to the Galatians

GALATIANS 3:15-18

In Gal. 3:15-18, Paul introduces the analogy of the "human " will or covenant. The Greek word, *diathēkēn*, appearing both in v. 15 and in v. 17, is ambiguous, since it was sometimes used, on the one hand, with reference to a man's " will " or " testament," and, on the other hand, with reference to a " covenant " or " agreement." In v. 17 the allusion is apparently to Gen., ch. 17, so that *diathēkēn* must be understood as " covenant." The meaning intended in v. 15 is less certain and has been debated extensively.[1] For purposes involved in the present study it is, for the most part, unnecessary to carry the debate farther, since, interestingly enough, similar characteristics of the Pauline use of the analogy can be recognized whichever meaning is given to the word.

If the meaning in v. 15 (as well as in v. 17) is " covenant," [2] Paul's thought is this: just as an agreement between human beings, once ratified, is not to be annulled or altered by additions (v. 15), so it is that the covenant ratified by God, involving promises " made to Abraham and to his offspring " (v. 16), is not annulled by the law, which came later (v. 17). The element in the analogy which has relevance for Paul's purpose, and because of which the analogy is employed, is the fact that in an agreement or covenant between two human beings neither party, acting alone, can nullify or modify the contract.[3] The picture is introduced for the sake of this point and this point alone. It is apparent, in fact, that

41

other elements involved in the analogy itself not only are irrelevant but if applied to Paul's thought regarding God's
covenant with Abraham and his descendants, would distort
what is otherwise known to be his thought. For example, in
human relationships there exists the possibility that " even
the most solemn compact may be set aside or altered by mutual consent." [4] Paul, of course, ignores this possibility. In
fact, for him to use the analogy at all it was necessary for him
to omit all reference to such a possibility, since the analogy
is introduced precisely to reinforce the claim that the covenant with Abraham and his descendants could *not* be annulled.

There is also a second element involved in the analogy of a
human covenant which is not applicable to the thought of
Paul regarding the covenant made between God and his people. There is a very real sense in which the latter is to be
distinguished from the former. Burton, in his commentary
on Galatians, shows that the Old Testament term for covenant was " commonly used not for a compact between two
parties of substantially the same rank, but for a relationship
between God and man graciously created by God, and only
accepted by man." [5] Burton recognizes that the term was often used with reference to a " mutual agreement between
men," but it " is still more commonly employed of a covenant
between God and men." It is true that in the latter usage
there is sometimes emphasized the " mutuality of the relation," but the usage " in general carried the suggestion both
of divine initiative and of mutuality." [6] He notes further that
the Septuagint renders the Hebrew term as *diathēkē*, as over
against the " ordinary " Greek word for a compact, *sunthēkē*,
in order, probably, to preserve this distinction.[7] " It is not
that God and man strike, as it were, a bargain, but rather that
God makes a gracious offer to man [8] upon certain conditions
of obedience, and that man accepts the offer on these conditions; in other words, it is an agreement made not so much
between God and man as by God with man." [9] It becomes
clear, therefore, that in at least two respects the analogy of

human " covenant " does not apply.

It is important to observe a further point here. Earlier it was seen that it is impossible to apply to the Pauline thought of God's covenant (in Gal. 3:15-18) the fact that a " human " covenant *may* be annulled or modified by mutual consent, since Paul has introduced the analogy to support his claim *here* that God's covenant could *not* be annulled or changed. It is worthy of note that *even the one point in the analogy which is relevant in this context is not relevant in a different context.* In I Cor. 11:25, in his reference to the Last Supper, Paul represents Jesus as having said, " This cup is the new covenant in my blood." [10] Whatever may have been Paul's immediate source of information regarding the words ascribed to Jesus himself, the apostle here seems clearly to be speaking of a covenant that is " new " as over against that which is " old." In fact, elsewhere Paul speaks of the " old covenant " (II Cor. 3:14). The contrast intended is between the covenant now based on faith and that earlier covenant based on law, which was ratified at Mt. Sinai (Ex., ch. 24).

The expression " new covenant " is probably derived ultimately from Jeremiah's use of it in Jer. 31:31.

That Paul was thinking of the Sinai covenant is indicated by the fact that he adds (in I Cor. 11:25) " in my blood," suggesting a consciously intended parallel between the sacrificed blood of Christ [11] and the blood of the animals that were sacrificed at Mt. Sinai (see especially Ex. 24:8).[12]

In this contrast between the new and the old covenants there is clearly an idea of the one displacing or superseding the other.[13] Even in Galatians, in the very letter in which Paul uses our analogy to press the point that a covenant, once ratified, cannot be annulled, he can speak of faith as that which replaces law (chs. 3:23 to 4:7) in such a way as to suggest that *now* a new relationship *is* established between man and God which is vastly superior to the old.[14]

The point that needs to be made in the present study is the fact that in the context of I Cor. 11:25, or II Cor. 3:7-15, or

even in Gal. 3:23 to 4:7, the very element in the analogy
which Paul finds useful in Gal. 3:15-18 is certainly not applicable, for in *these* contexts there *is* a sense in which a covenant has been annulled or changed.

This does not mean that Paul has actually contradicted
himself insofar as his total thought is concerned. It would be
a mistake to say that at one point he flatly states that God
did " not annul a covenant previously ratified " (Gal. 3:17),
while at other points he insists that the opposite is true.
What he is stating in Gal. 3:15-18 is essentially that the covenant made with Abraham and his descendants is not annulled by the *law*. In this context, " law " is not to be confused with " covenant." It was introduced, not to replace the
covenant of promise made with Abraham and his descendants; rather, it was given " with the express purpose of making them realize how far short they were falling of the glory
of God " [15] by bringing to light man's transgressions.[16]

" The statement [17] is not in contradiction with verses 15 ff.,
because the law in the apostle's thought forms no part of the
covenant, is a thing distinct from it, in no way modifying its provisions." [18]

It is true that in the contrast made between the " new covenant " and the " old covenant," as mentioned above, the latter expression does seem to refer to the giving of the law at
Mt. Sinai as involving the establishing of a covenant. The
same is true in the case of the allegory of the two mothers
(Gal. 4:21-31).[19] In these cases, however, Paul seems to be
assuming — for the moment, as it were — the Jewish position
and categories, saying, in effect, that *even if* the giving of
the law involved the establishing of a covenant, that covenant has now been superseded. His *own* position is that
what, from one point of view, may be looked upon as the establishing of a new covenant, is actually not this at all, but is,
rather, the reestablishing of that same covenant of promise
made with Abraham and his descendants.

The fact remains, in spite of all of this, that in the contexts where Paul does speak of a new covenant as over against an old covenant (however secondary this may be to his primary emphasis), even the one point in his analogy of the human covenant which is applicable in Gal. 3:15-18 is not applicable at all in the other contexts, for in *them* a covenant (that made at Mt. Sinai) *is* spoken of as being annulled and superseded by a superior covenant.

What has been made clear, then, in his use of analogy — in this instance — are two facts: (1) The only element in the analogy which is intended to have significance is that which has a bearing upon the central point that is being made: a covenant, once made, cannot be annulled or modified. (2) Even the element in the analogy which has significance in one context does not necessarily have a similar significance in other contexts. In other words, *apart from its immediate context, the analogy cannot be taken as providing any clues whatever as to the nature of Paul's actual thought.*

In the discussion up to this point it has been assumed that *diathēkē*, in Gal. 3:15, was used by Paul in the sense of " covenant." If the Greek word is understood as having the meaning of " will " or " testament," [20] the nature of Paul's use of the analogy, interestingly, remains essentially the same. That is, only a single aspect of the analogy (and even then in a limited way) can be intended to have significance, namely, the fact that, once a will is made, *no one else* can annul it or add to it. (Although the Greek word *oudeis* means simply " no one," the " else " must be presupposed to give any real sense to the application, for it must be recognized that the maker of the will could himself subsequently annul or modify it.) [21]

The fact that the maker of the will *could* annul or modify it during his lifetime is completely ignored, not only because it is irrelevant to the argument with which Paul is engaged, but also because, if applied, it would *refute* Paul's contention that God's covenant with Abraham and his descendants could *not* be annulled or changed.

There is also a further element involved in the analogy

which clearly is without significance in the Pauline usage. One characteristic of a will is the fact that it takes effect only upon the death of its maker. Since, in v. 17, it is explicitly stated that the *diathēkē* was ratified *by God,* to apply this fact from the analogy would require the idea of the death of God, an idea that deserves no comment.[22]

It becomes evident, therefore, that in his usage of this analogy (whether *diathēkē* in v. 15 is taken as "covenant" or as "will"), Paul employs it for the sake of only one element involved in it. Other elements not only are irrelevant but in some cases, if applied, would suggest ideas that stand in obvious contradiction to Paul's thought as seen elsewhere. In other words, the thought of the immediate context provides the clue to the significance of the analogy. The analogy cannot be taken as the clue to his thought.

GALATIANS 3:23 TO 4:7

In this section of the letter to the Galatians, Paul has introduced once more a multiplicity of pictures, including that of the "custodian," that of a minor heir of an estate, that of slavery, that of ransom, and that of adoption. The material needs to be examined carefully, not only to discover the nature of the Pauline usage of each picture but also to determine the relation of each picture to the others.

The first analogy is offered thus: " Now before faith came, we were confined under the law, kept under restraint until faith should be revealed. So that the law was our custodian until Christ came, that we might be justified by faith. But now that faith has come, we are no longer under a custodian." The Greek word for "custodian," *paidagōgos,* has also been translated as "schoolmaster" (KJV), "tutor" (ASV), and "attendant" (Goodspeed). Among both Greeks and Romans it was used with respect to a family slave assigned to the task of supervising the conduct of the boys of the family and attending them wherever they went.[1]

The picture of the custodian as an analogy for the law is not drawn in any detail, but it is of such a nature that nu-

merous ideas are suggested by it: (1) the temporary character of the supervision, since it continued only until the boys
of the family attained a certain maturity; (2) the subjection
of the ward or wards under the custodian; (3) the disciplinary function of the custodian; (4) the teaching function of
the custodian; and (5) the protective function of the custodian. Part of the problem here is to determine how many of
these ideas were intended by Paul to have relevance or significance for his thought concerning the law.

The context indicates the relevance of: (1) the temporary
nature of the custodian's supervision. Verse 25 ("But now
that faith has come, we are no longer under a custodian")
shows clearly that the thought involves "the historic succession of one period of revelation upon another and the dis-
placement of the law by Christ." [2] The same thought is conveyed by the first words of v. 23 ("Now before faith
came").

It must be recognized that in the Greek text the reference (both
in v. 23 and v. 25) is to "the faith" (with the definite article),
not simply "faith." In the Pauline thought, "faith" may be said
to have come long before the law was given (Gal. 3:6-9, 15-18;
Rom., ch. 4). "*The* faith," however — "faith in Jesus Christ" [3]
(v. 22) — came after the law. Hence Paul can speak in terms of
this sequence.

If the Greek expression (*eis Christon*) in v. 24 is correctly
translated "until Christ came," this would provide still further evidence that the idea of temporariness is intended to
be conveyed by the analogy (but see below).

The context suggests, further, the relevance of the idea of:
(2) the subjection of the ward to his custodian: "We were
confined under the law, kept under restraint" (v. 23). The
prepositional phrase here, "under the law," is undoubtedly
parallel to the similar phrase, "under a custodian," in v. 25.
In other words, under the law man is held in subjection,
"kept under restraint," just as the ward is restricted by his
custodian. That the idea was prominent in the Pauline

thought at this point is suggested by the fact that the apostle
turns again to it a few verses later (ch. 4:1-7), characteriz-
ing this restraint as virtual slavery. (Compare also Gal.
4:21-31; 5:1.)

It is possible also that Paul intends the idea of: (3) the
disciplinary function of the custodian to have significance.
The Moffatt translation of ch. 3:24 even centers attention
upon this point: " the Law thus held us as wards in discipline, till such time as Christ came." Again the Pauline context supports this conclusion, for the latter part of the verse
(" that we might be justified by faith ") suggests the disciplinary function of the law. The meaning seems to be that
the law, like a custodian, created in us a recognition of pow-
erlessness " and left us with no alternative but to cast ourselves in faith on Him who came to emancipate us." [4] (See
Rom. 3:9-20; 7:7-25.) This appears to be the Pauline thought,
especially in view of Gal. 3:22 with its idea that the law
" consigned all things to sin," confronting man with the fact
that he could not find justification on the basis of his own
merit [5] and showing him that only the way of faith led to
salvation.[6]

The Greek text of v. 24a may possibly bring out this element
in the analogy in a still further way: " So that the law was our
custodian [*eis Christon*]." If this phrase should be intended, not
in the temporal, but in the so-called pregnant sense (compare this
use of *eis* in Rom. 8:18, 21), the meaning becomes: " So that the
law was our custodian *to bring us to Christ.*" [7] In other words, the
law, as above, serves the disciplinary purpose of turning us to
Christ and to the justification that is to be found only through
faith in him by making manifest the inefficacy of man's own efforts
at self-justification.

One may, of course, question the validity of Paul's use of this
element in the analogy of the custodian. The slave assigned
to the task of supervising the boys of a family was "not always the best" [8] and might be "no very high character." [9]
In fact, in I Cor. 4:15 *paidagōgos*, in the plural (KJV: "in-
structors"; RSV: "guides"), is employed by Paul in a some-

what derogatory way. It may seem somewhat inappropriate, therefore, for Paul, in Gal. 3:24-25, to use the figure of the *paidagōgos* to suggest a meaningful and effective disciplinary function. However, since Paul does use the term negatively in one context, and positively in another context, a characteristic of the Pauline use of analogy is thus made manifest: *the significance of the picture is determined by the context of thought in which it is to be found; the thought is not to be determined by all the implications that the picture may provide.*

As noted at the beginning of the discussion of this analogy, the King James Version renders *paidagōgos* as " schoolmaster." This, like " tutor " (ASV), suggests: (4) the idea of *teaching*, which may have been included among the duties of the Roman *paidagōgos* if not of the Greek.[10] Even if Paul should have had in mind a practice of the Roman environment rather than of the Greek, the notion of teaching or of education appears to have no relevance in Paul's use of the analogy here. There is nothing in the context that gives any hint that Paul at this point was thinking of the law as providing a body of positive information. Of course it is true that in a *different* context the idea of the law as providing teaching or instruction might be said to correspond to this function of the custodian. When Paul states, for example, in Rom. 3:20, that the law provides " knowledge of sin " (compare Rom. 7:7 ff.), the idea of teaching is involved. In the Galatians passage now under consideration, however, there is nothing whatever that points to this idea. Man's *experience* with the law may teach him, as it disciplines him (see above), that salvation is not to be realized through the law, but this is quite different from the idea that the law itself offers such knowledge in the form of teaching or instruction. Rather, the emphasis here is upon the temporary and restraining aspects of the law.

It has been suggested that: (5) the protective function of the custodian is intended to have relevance in Paul's use of the analogy.[11] It appears from the total context, however, that it is the restrictive (see above) rather than the protective function that Paul has in mind. While it may be said that "God in fencing off His chosen nation from their Gentile neighbors by ordinances which might seem a grievous limitation of their freedom, was in this very way protecting and preserving them," [12] this idea is entirely out of place here. Verse 25 ("But now that faith has come, we are no longer under a custodian") as well as the earlier (v. 23) and the still later statements (ch. 4:1-7) make very clear that the *paidagōgos* is introduced for the sake of the negative rather than positive ideas (such as the protective) which are associated with the picture.

It is true that the Greek word *ephrouroumetha*, rendered "confined" (RSV) in ch. 3:23, is used by Paul in Phil. 4:7 to mean "guard" ("keep," KJV and RSV) in a protective sense. (Compare II Cor. 11:32.) That this is not true in Gal. 3:23, however, is shown by the fact that the word is immediately followed by another, *sunkleiomenoi* ("shut up"), which is found in the New Testament only in the restrictive sense.

The foregoing discussion has shown that the Pauline analogy of the custodian is used in a manner somewhat different from the way in which previously considered analogies have been employed, for here it appears that *several* ideas associated with the picture are intended to have significance for the thought that is being conveyed. This does not mean, however, that the picture can be applied in all respects. There are still other ideas suggested by it that cannot be regarded as having significance, chiefly because they involve aspects of the custodian's activity which are not at all relevant to the context and which, if applied, would suggest a much more favorable judgment upon the law than that which appears to be made.

As Paul continues his argument that man, who was previously confined under the law, is now confronted with the possibility of freedom through faith, he adds a new analogy to that of the custodian — the picture of the minor heir of

an estate (Gal. 4:1-3). It must be recognized that in dealing
with this particular analogy, one cannot arrive at entirely
fixed conclusions regarding the nature of the apostle's analogical usage. The difficulty arises out of the fact that it is
impossible to know exactly what picture it is that Paul held
before his mind's eye as he wrote. And if there is uncertainty
as to the picture that is being introduced, there cannot, of
course, be certainty as to the manner in which it is employed.
Perhaps the best procedure is to consider the more important possibilities as to the life situation that Paul has in
mind and see what conclusions of a tentative nature may
emerge.

If Paul is thinking of a minor orphan under Roman law, it
becomes apparent that one relevant element in the analogy
is the fact that such a child might be placed under a person
like those whom the apostle calls " guardians and trustees."
At least Roman law somewhat later than the time of Paul
provided for a " tutor " until the age of fourteen and then for
a " curator " until the age of twenty-five.[13] As applied by
Paul this would mean that just as the child is subject to the
persons over him, so also man under the law is subject to
the law and is in reality " no better than a slave." Of course
it is true that in v. 3 Paul speaks, not of slaves to the law,
but of " slaves to the elemental spirits of the universe " (literally, " the elements of the world ").[14] His expression, however, may actually involve an indirect reference to the
law.

The meaning of Paul's Greek phrase has been the subject of
dispute from very early times. If the reference is to what might be
called " the rudimentary religious teachings possessed by the
race," [15] Paul could have included the law in this expression. If,
on the other hand, the reference is to the angelic or demonic
powers that were often thought to be active in the world (as the
RSV suggests), it is conceivable that even in this case the law
was in Paul's mind. In the previous chapter he seems to have associated angels with the giving of the law (ch. 3:19); hence " he
could urge that, in accepting Jewish ritual as a necessary part
of their religion, the Galatians, so far from advancing in their new

faith, were actually *turning back to serve the Elemental spirits* from which Christ had delivered them." [16]

In any case Paul shows in the following verse (v. 4) that it is still the law that is chiefly under consideration.

It is true that in the Greek the definite article is absent before both usages of the word for "law" in v. 4. Literally the phrase *hupo nomon* should be rendered "under law," not "under the law"; it can therefore be taken as a reference to law generally. The context indicates, however, that it is the Mosaic law that is central in the Pauline thinking [17] — in Gal. 3:23 as well as here — although it has also been held that the apostle "extends the application to all those subject to any system of positive ordinances." [18]

It appears that a second element in the analogy, closely related to the first, is also intended to have relevance. The words "as long as he is a child" (ch. 4:1), taken together with the later clause, "when the time had fully come" (v. 4 — literally, "when the fullness of time came"), suggest the temporary nature of the child's subordinate position. Therefore, just as the child will one day be free from the domination of "guardians and trustees," so also man may now be freed from the law (compare ch. 3:23-25).

It is obvious, however, that other elements in the analogy cannot be relevant. In presenting the picture, Paul speaks of the heir, for example, as "owner of all the estate" (literally, "lord of all"). It is impossible to believe that this aspect of the picture is intended to have significance for the thought that Paul is attempting to convey. By application it would mean that even though man was under the domination of the law, virtually as a slave, nevertheless he was lord of all the inheritance: it was rightfully his! For Paul, of course, man has no claim upon sonship to God and to the privileges of sonship. Man is freed from slavery under the law and becomes son of God only through God's gracious act: "God sent forth his Son . . . to redeem" (vs. 4 f.). Man's new status becomes a reality, not because by his very nature he is "lord of all," but because of God's gift (Rom. 3:24).

There is a second element in the analogy which cannot be taken as applicable. The picture of the heir under guardians and trustees involves the idea that the father of the child is no longer alive,[19] an idea that obviously can have no real place in Paul's thought, since God, the father of all men, has not died.

There is perhaps a sense in which Paul *might* have said that God was dead. Just as he could express the thought of sin as not holding sway over man with the words "sin lies dead" (Rom. 7:8), so it is conceivable that he might have represented man under law — and hence not under God directly as son — with the picture of God as dead to that man. There is no indication anywhere, however, that Paul employed the picture in this way.

There is yet another element in the analogy which is inapplicable to the Pauline thought. In general practice the minor heir was freed from the control of his "guardians and trustees" and attained his freedom as "owner" *automatically*, as it were, as soon as the specified point of age or of time had been reached. It is clear that for Paul the realization of man's new status is in no way automatic. The status is realized "through faith" (Gal. 3:26) and as a result of God's gracious act (ch. 4:4). God acted, not in such a way as to produce results from which man automatically profited, but rather, "so that we *might* receive adoption as sons" (v. 5). The construction in the subjunctive here indicates the purpose of God's action but does not indicate that the realization of the purpose is inevitably assured. It is as man responds in faith, not (as in the analogy) when a certain moment in time has been reached, that man is transferred by God's grace from the position of virtual slave to that of son.

If it should be held that Paul's view of predestination included the idea that sonship for a given individual is predetermined, then, of course, there is a sense in which it could be said that the realization of that sonship is automatic; it occurs simply accord-

ing to plan. Even so, however, some provision for the response of
faith must be made. In the case of the minor heir no factor corresponding to such a response is involved.

Finally, it is inappropriate to apply here the picture of the
minor heir insofar as the child under guardians and trustees
would benefit from the *protective* function of such persons.
It has already been shown, in connection with the analysis
of the picture of the custodian, that this idea is quite foreign
to Paul's purpose in the present context.

What has been said thus far would also hold true if the
basis for Paul's analogy is to be found in Syrian-Greek law
rather than in the Roman. If Paul was drawing upon Syrian-
Greek practice, however, an additional, though not necessarily intended, point of partial correspondence between picture and thought might be claimed in connection with the
reference to " the date set by the father " (v. 2). As over
against Roman custom, according to which the terminal
dates for the control of tutors and curators were apparently
determined by the child's age (see above), in Syrian-Greek
procedure a testator was allowed to determine the age at
which a son was to receive control of an estate.[20] This element in the picture, suggested by the words " the date set
by the father," could be said to be applied in Paul's reference to the time that " had fully come." Just as the father
determined when his child should be given control of the estate, so also God had provided in " the divine plan of the
ages " [21] for the time of the sending forth of " his Son." The
correspondence is not entirely accurate, however. In the picture the " date " refers to the moment when the child receives fully the inheritance; in the suggested application the
" time " refers, not to the moment when men are given their
new status under God, which would be the proper parallel,
but rather, to the time when God provided the means by
which this might be realized. Again, association of ideas may
have influenced Paul in choosing his form of expression, but
careful application of this element in the picture is not to
be found.

There remains yet to be considered the possibility that the basis for Paul's analogy here is to be discovered neither in common Roman nor in common Syrian-Greek practice, but rather, in some special case that was known to him. Attention is sometimes directed to the case reported in I Macc. 3:31 ff.[22] According to this document, Antiochus Epiphanes " determined to go to Persia. . . . He left Lysias, a distinguished man of royal lineage, in charge of the king's affairs from the river Euphrates to the borders of Egypt. Lysias was also to take care of Antiochus his son until he returned." If there were any reason to believe that Paul did have this account in mind, then there could be eliminated one of the above-mentioned points of conflict between picture and thought, for in this case the father (Antiochus Epiphanes) of the child left under a guardian would be alive during the period of guardianship. But there would then be the problem of accounting for Paul's use of the plural " guardians and trustees," since in I Maccabees, Lysias alone seems to have been responsible for the child. Altogether it is quite impossible to believe that Paul was thinking of this report. If, for the sake of the fullest possible application, he was drawing upon such a special case rather than upon more common practice, it would be necessary for him to have made this fact clear, for otherwise his readers would naturally assume that he was referring to the more usual kind of situation regarding a minor heir.

To the picture of the minor heir of an estate is joined that of a slave in bondage. In a sense the reader is confronted with an analogy within an analogy, for the picture of the slave seems at first to be introduced in order to emphasize the idea of subjection in connection with the minor heir: " The heir . . . is no better than a slave " (v. 1). At the same time the picture of slavery is one that has its own independent significance for the Pauline thought: " So with us; . . . we were slaves " (v. 3). That the two pictures are in reality merged, however, is seen in the comment that we were slaves " when we were children."

Although the picture of the slave is not introduced explicitly until ch. 4:1,[23] the idea of being in a state of subjection runs throughout this part of the letter, as observed above. With the explicit introduction of the picture the idea of servitude is now given full force: [24] as a slave is held in bondage, so also men have been subject to the law and to the "elemental spirits of the universe" (see above) until freedom from that bondage was made possible by the sending of Jesus Christ.

It is particularly important to observe that not all ideas associated with slavery can be applied in the present context. Whereas elsewhere (see especially the analysis of Rom. 6:15-23) Paul employs the picture of slavery for the purpose of reinforcing the idea of submission and obedience, the notion of a slave's *obedience* is quite irrelevant in the passage now under consideration. Here slavery is pictured wholly negatively; it is a state of bondage from which man desires to be free, not a condition in which the obedience or submission of the man in servitude carries the positive thought of the Christian's proper response to God (Rom. 6:22) or to "righteousness" (v. 18). Here the oppressive and restrictive aspect of the picture is wholly dominant. This is quite different from the image of the slave who can be said to correspond to the Christian, the *doulos* ("slave") of Jesus Christ (Rom. 1:1; compare I Cor. 7:22; Gal. 1:10; Phil. 1:1).[25] Thus there is provided a conspicuous case where the same picture is employed in different contexts for entirely different purposes. The picture can be applied to the Pauline thought only as the immediate context allows.

The picture of ransom, which is also found in these verses, is very closely akin to that of the slave in bondage. There is a sense, in fact, in which it is a part of the picture of the slave — a slave who is ransomed, set free from his bondage. The picture is not explicitly drawn, however; it is only presupposed as it is applied: "God sent forth his Son . . . to redeem those who were under the law. . . . So through God you are no longer a slave" (vs. 4 f., 7).

Although the word for " ransom " (*lutron*) found in Matt.
20:28 and Mark 10:45 does not appear here (or elsewhere
in the Pauline letters), the apostle's verb, *exagorasēi* ("redeem "), can mean not only " to buy up," but also " to deliver at cost of some sort to the deliverer," [26] — " to ransom,"
" especially from slavery." [27] In Moffatt's translation the verb
" to ransom " is actually used. At other points, also, Paul's
language suggests the picture of the ransomed slave: " You
were bought with a price " (I Cor. 6:20; 7:23).

As indicated in the Introduction, the analogy of ransom
will be treated in detail in a subsequent volume. Since it may
be regarded as one of the more crucial analogies, loaded
with possible theological implications with respect to the
saving work of Christ, it should be considered only after
there have been determined the persistent characteristics of
the Pauline use of analogy generally. It may be noted that
in the immediate context here, however, the only elements
in the picture of the ransomed slave which seem to have relevance are: (1) the idea of *deliverance:* as a slave is delivered from bondage, so also man may be freed from his servitude under the law and under the elemental spirits of the
universe and may experience that freedom for which " Christ
has set us free " (Gal. 5:1); and (2) the thought that man's
freedom through faith is not his own attainment but rather
the consequence of God's action: as a slave is ransomed by
the act of another, so also " God sent forth his Son . . . to
redeem " (ch. 4:4 f.; compare ch. 5:1). There is no hint
whatever that Paul's thinking, in connection with the immediate context, included reflection upon the precise nature of
the ransom paid, or the recipient of the payment.

The final picture that is woven into this complex of analogies is that of adoption. Paul's word here is *huiothesia*,
" adoption as sons " (ch. 4:5).

This Greek word appears neither in the Septuagint nor in clas-
sical Greek usage,[28] though it was common in Hellenistic times.[29]
Paul employs it upon four occasions (Rom. 8:15, 23; 9:4; and
here; it is found also in Eph. 1:5). It is to be observed that al-

though the Greek practice of adoption was not found in Judaism,[30] Paul nevertheless employs the picture with respect to Israel in Rom. 9:4, as he refers to God's establishing of Israel's sonship to himself (see Ex. 4:22; Deut. 14:1; Jer. 31:9; Hos. 11:1; and especially Jubilees 1:21).

Special attention should be called to the fact that in Rom. 8:15 and 9:4 Paul's word is the same as is translated " adoption as sons " in Rom. 8:23 and Gal. 4:5, even though the RSV renders it simply as " sonship " in the former passages.

It is evident that the picture is introduced in order to heighten the contrast between the condition of man under the law and the condition of the Christian, who through faith may now, as son, stand freely in the most intimate relationship with God. Whereas formerly man was a slave, now he is son and heir (v. 7; compare ch. 3:26). The picture is clearly intended to suggest what Lietzmann calls the *Sohnesqualität* (" the quality of sonship "), which is granted the Christian [31] and which stands in contrast to " slave."

In order to grasp the relevance and full force of this picture it is necessary to recognize something of the nature of the practice of adoption which Paul must have had in mind, a practice found in the Roman and Greek world, though not in the Hebraic.[32] Those who were adopted included not only orphans but also many who for a variety of reasons were transferred from one family to another while one or both of their natural parents still lived. Particularly significant for the present study is the fact that in Roman practice the procedure in adoption was in some respects strikingly similar to that which was involved when a slave was sold or ransomed. " The same term (*mancipatio*) was applied to a process of this kind, whether a man parted with his son, or his slave, or his goods." [33] And since the term (*mancipatio*) meant a " making over " or a " transfer," it was also used in the sense of " purchase," even though the transaction in the case of adoption might be called a " fictitious sale." [34] Thus it can be seen that as Paul introduces the picture of adoption he is not moving as far from that of slavery and of ransom as at first may appear.

Since the references to "the covenants" and to "the giving of the law" in Rom. 9:4 point to the report of the event at Mt. Sinai that marked the establishing of a new relationship between Israel and God, and since in the Old Testament that event is closely connected with the release of the Israelites from Egyptian bondage, it is conceivable that as Paul inserted *huiothesia* in that verse he may have had in mind this connection between the act of adoption and the action whereby there occurred a ransoming from slavery. The immediate context provides no evidence, however, that this connection was in Paul's thought at the moment of writing.

In view of the above considerations, it appears that the picture of adoption is sufficiently related to that of a ransomed slave to justify the contrast that is expressed in the application in Gal. 4:7: "You are no longer a slave but a son."

A further point appears also to be involved in Paul's use of the picture of adoption. Not only is the condition of the Christian contrasted in this way to the condition of men under the law; as the picture is introduced it seems to be intended to emphasize, as does the picture of ransom, the fact that the quality of the new relationship between man and God has depended upon God's own gracious act. As it is the decision and act of the adopter that elevates one to the status of son, so also it is God who has taken the initiative in lifting man to a status that man himself could not achieve. Men receive "adoption as sons" because *God* has "sent forth his Son." Thus there is suggested in this picture (as well as in that of ransom) the Pauline insistence upon the idea that man has no claim upon God for his new status; he enters into the new relationship, as son of God, because he has been "justified" by God's grace "as a gift" (Rom. 3:24). Man is *made* a son even though he has no claim upon sonship. Furthermore, the word *huiothesia* ("adoption as sons") seems to stand as an intended contrast to "his Son." The picture of adopted sons suggests, therefore, not only that men become sons only by God's action but also that their sonship must be distinguished from that of "the Son," Jesus Christ. "We are sons by grace; he is so by nature."[35] While all of these applications are not stated explicitly, the nature of the language in the immediate context carries the implications.

But although the picture of adoption is applicable in certain respects, it is also evident that not all ideas associated with it can be applied to the Pauline thought. When a man adopts a child as his son, that child is one who, normally at least,[36] was in no sense the child of the man previously — the offspring of the man. In the thought of Paul, on the other hand, God is the Creator (as in Rom. 1:25); in this sense he is father of all men. Hence when men receive the status of "sons of God" they are entering into a relationship with him who, in one sense, was already their "father."[37] The fact that a child is normally not adopted by his original father thus does not lend itself to consistent application.

Paul's thought here, about God and man, has been compared with that which is presented in the parable of the prodigal son (Luke 15:11-32): "We have cut ourselves off from the Father, and have no longer the right to be called His sons. The Father, however, has never disowned us, and now in Christ He has taken steps to bring us home and to get us installed again in the family."[38] The fact that this comparison is possible serves to point up the limited applicability of Paul's picture. The father in the parable installs as son one whose father he already was. When a child is adopted, on the other hand, no such prior relationship is normally involved, as has just been emphasized. In other words, the parable of Jesus is better suited for possible application to some aspects of the Pauline thought than is the picture of adoption.

It is possible now to consider the analogical usage in this section of the letter to the Galatians with respect to the relationship of each picture to the others, although at a few points certain connections have already been discussed.

It is immediately apparent that the first three pictures include a common element that receives application. In the case of the custodian, the minor heir of an estate, and the slave there is involved the negative idea of *subjection* — a subjection that is made to correspond to man's subjection under the law. (In the first two there is suggested also the notion of the temporary character of such a condition. If the picture of the slave is combined with that of the ransom of a slave, the same thought may again be suggested.) The last two pictures likewise possess a common element. In the case of ransom and of adoption there is presented the idea of deliverance from an inferior condition to one that involves freedom and privilege, corresponding to man's new state which may be received through faith. Insofar as Paul's fundamental argument is concerned, therefore, the various pictures present a consistent unity.

As soon as the pictures are examined more closely, however, it can readily be seen that many details in them are quite inapplicable to the thought of Paul. In every case such inapplicable elements have been discovered. Furthermore, the apostle's indifference to the relevance of secondary elements in the pictures is seen in the fact that in numerous instances the detail in one is inconsistent with that in another. A few of these may be noted. (1) Although, as already observed, the picture of the slave is employed at first in connection with that of the minor heir (Gal. 4:1), the further independent use of the former (v. 3) nevertheless introduces in reality a conflict insofar as detail is concerned. Man's condition under the law may be likened both to that of the minor heir and also to that of the slave, but in the life situations from which the pictures are drawn the status of the one is actually vastly different from that of the other. Paul himself suggests this real difference when he speaks of the heir as "no better than a slave." Lietzmann is entirely correct when he asserts that in this respect the picture of slavery is essentially foreign to that of the minor heir.[39] It is obvious, therefore, that in moving from the one picture to the other Paul is wholly indifferent to the kind of details in the two pictures that are thus in conflict. There is clearly no intent to develop the analogy of the minor heir systematically and in detail. (2) Much the same may be said regarding the shift to the picture of ransom. A slave may be ransomed, certainly, but a minor heir is hardly one in connection with whom ransom would properly be considered (though such an heir might be involved in the somewhat legally parallel act of adoption). (3) Again, a slave may be ransomed, but not the child or children under a custodian. In fact, in the life situation it is likely that the *custodian* was actually a slave for whom the hope of ransom might exist! (4) A careful development of the picture of the minor heir, in view of the element in it which is applied by Paul, would require as a proper contrast to the child's inferior condition (its minority), not adoption, as Paul gives it, but *Mündigkeits-erklärung* ("declaration of majority").[40] (5) The absence of concern for systematic and careful analogical development and application becomes particularly conspicuous as one compares the use of "heir" in ch. 4:7 with that in v. 1. In v. 7, as Deissmann observes, there is suggested the practice "in which the testator adopts some one as his son and makes him the heir."[41] In this case the verse continues the application of the picture of adoption, the picture of one who was neither son nor heir *becoming* son and heir. In v. 1, on the other hand, the heir is pictured quite differently. As vs. 1 and 2 show very clearly, he is *already* an heir, although he is not yet allowed the privileges that are provided for him. Since such inconsistencies appear as one compares the various details in the separate pictures, it follows that details of this kind are simply not intended by Paul to be applicable in all respects and that the apostle was quite indifferent to a systematic development of his analogical material.

Certain facts thus emerge from all of this. It is apparent that in this section of Paul's letter to the Galatians his analogical usages are determined primarily by his thinking concerning man as he is under the law and man as he enters into a new condition through faith. Paul reaches out in various directions for pictures that can reinforce this or that aspect of his argument. A particular word or a particular aspect of one picture may suggest another picture through a simple association of ideas, but there is certainly no general consistency between the details of one picture and those of the others. In each picture there are elements also that are inapplicable to the Pauline theological thought. Instead of systematic development and application of analogical material there is found a use of pictures only for the sake of those elements in them which are useful and meaningful in the immediate context.

It should not go unnoticed that the four pictures that are woven together in Gal. 4:1-7 are combined again by Paul in ch. 8 of his later letter to the church at Rome, where once more he is concerned with the new life of those who are no longer under the law. Here again are the pictures of the child as heir (v. 17), slavery (v. 15), ransom (v. 23), and adoption (vs. 15 and 23). There is also, of course, the further striking parallel in the use of " Abba! Father! " (Rom. 8:15; Gal. 4:6).

Both in Gal. 4:1, 7 and in Rom. 8:17 Paul's word for " heir " is *klēronomos*, although in Rom. 8:16, 17, 21 he uses forms of *teknon* for " child " instead of *nēpios*, the term found in Gal. 4:1, 3. In Rom. 8:23 the noun for " redemption " is *apolutrōsis*, while in Gal. 4:5 the verb for " redeem " is *exagorazō*, but both suggest ransom. The word for " adoption as sons " (*huiothesia*) appears in Rom. 8:15 and 8:23 as it does in Gal. 4:5, although, as noted earlier, the RSV renders it simply " sonship " in Rom. 8:15. It is true that in Rom. 8:23 " adoption as sons " is pictured as lying in the future, as something for which we " wait," whereas in Gal. 4:5 ff. it is referred to as something already present.[42] The variations that are found do not, however, negate the fact that the same pictures appear in the two passages.

GALATIANS 4:19

In Gal. 4:19, Paul offers once more the picture of a woman in travail: " My little children, with whom I am again in travail until Christ be formed in you! " Here the picture is introduced for the purpose of suggesting pain or distress. Like a woman suffering the pains of childbirth, Paul is suffering, he tells the Galatians, " until Christ be formed in you." In this context the apostle is using the picture in a manner that was not at all uncommon, for, as has been shown elsewhere, it was frequently employed to describe suffering and distress. (See the consideration of I Thess. 5:1-11.) What is noteworthy, however, is the fact that in the present context there is no thought whatever of the idea of *suddenness,* for the sake of which the same picture was used in I Thess. 5:3.

Nor can other aspects of the analogy be applied here. The wording shows, for example, that, in the very same sentence in which Paul inserts the analogy, he is deviating from any strict and thorough application. In addressing the Galatians as his (spiritual) children with whom he is " again " in travail, he is actually contradicting the obvious fact that a mother is in travail for the same children only once. That the analogy is not intended to be applied in detail may be suggested also by the last clause of the sentence: " until Christ be formed in you." Although these words may have no relationship to the picture of a woman bearing a child [1] — in which case Paul's sudden turning from the picture indicates no interest in further use of it — it is at least possible that the same picture *is* involved in reverse, as it were, " those who were just spoken of as babes in the womb, now being pictured as pregnant mothers, awaiting the full development of the child begotten in them " (compare Gal. 2:20).[2] A possible reversal of the same sort may be found in I Thess. 2:7 (compare also Rom. 7:4). In this case the picture of the woman in travail has suggested to Paul, by association of ideas, the child, or the children, being born. But this means that the analogy itself is used with extreme looseness and must not be applied in any thorough way. Just as the picture has significance only for the point (suddenness) that is relevant to the context in I Thess. 5:3, so also it has significance here only with respect to the *different* point (suffering or distress) that is relevant to the present context.

GALATIANS 4:21-31

In this section of his letter to the Galatians, Paul uses as an " allegory " (v. 24) the Old Testament account of Abraham and his two sons, Ishmael and Isaac. He employs the picture that this story presents in order to reinforce certain emphases already made and to lend Scriptural authority to his claims.

The first clause in v. 24 ("Now this is an allegory") raises numerous problems of interpretation. Paul's Greek words might more literally be rendered, "Which things are allegorical utterances,"[1] or, perhaps, "Which things are spoken allegorically." The former translation allows the interpretation that the story as it stands in the Old Testament may now be seen to have allegorical significance even though this significance was not intended originally. The latter translation may suggest an allegorical purpose on the part of the original writer (or writers). Since the present study is not directly concerned with Paul's understanding and interpretation of the Old Testament, the various issues, linguistic and otherwise, which are involved here cannot be considered.[2] For immediate purposes it is enough to recognize that Paul himself uses the Old Testament account allegorically in order to reinforce his argument.

Since the major issue discussed in this letter pertains to faith versus law as efficacious for salvation, and since this analogical section stands in the midst of an emphasis upon law as confining and enslaving, whereas through faith there is release and freedom (Gal. 3:23 to 4:7; 5:1, 13), it appears that the picture is intended primarily to support the claim that the way of the law is indeed the way of enslavement and the way of faith is indeed the way of freedom. Both the opening and the closing words of the section serve to indicate that this is the essential thought: "Tell me, you who desire to be under law, do you not hear the law? For it is written that Abraham had two sons, one by a slave and one by a free woman. . . . So, brethren, we are not children of the slave but of the free woman" (ch. 4:21-22, 31).[3]

It has been suggested that this section of the letter is introduced "apparently as an after-thought."[4] Ramsey, on the other hand, believes it likely that the treatment here was "forced on Paul from the outside": it was a necessary reply to the argument, originating in Galatia, that the Jews are the true descendants of

Abraham, through Sarah, and that Gentile Christians must remain in an inferior position unless they conform to the law as do the true descendants.[5] Whatever the motives may have been, however, Paul nevertheless begins and ends the section with the contrast between the "slave" and the "free woman."

Various elements drawn from the account in Genesis are introduced to suggest the contrast between those who follow the way of law and those who follow the way of faith: Just as the one son of Abraham (Ishmael) was the son of a slave mother, and hence, by inference, was likewise a slave, so also the Jews (the children of "the present Jerusalem") are in slavery (ch. 4:25). Just as the other son (Isaac) was the son of a free mother, and hence was likewise free, so also the Christians (the children of "the Jerusalem above") are free; at least this is the clear implication in v. 26 and v. 31.

Paul also uses the account, however, to reinforce another emphasis previously made — the emphasis on the fact that the covenant (of faith) was made with Abraham by "promise" (compare v. 23 with ch. 3:16-18), whereas the covenant established in the giving of the law involved no such promise.

It is true, of course, that in ch. 3:16-18 Paul avoids the use of the term "covenant" in connection with the giving of the law. The very nature of the argument there compelled him to speak of one covenant only. On the other hand, as shown earlier, Paul indicates elsewhere that he *did* think of a covenant as having been involved in the giving of the law (see the discussion of Gal. 3:15-18).

The Genesis account serves a purpose here. Just as the son of the free mother was born "through promise" (ch. 4:23), so also the Christians are "children of promise" (v. 28) and "heirs" of promise (if v. 30b is related to ch. 3:29). Similarly, although the other side of the contrast is not stated explicitly, the idea is implied that just as the son of the slave mother was not born through promise, but only "according to the flesh " (ch. 4:23), so also the Jews are not " children of promise "; hence they stand in a position inferior to that of the true children of Abraham, who may be called " men of faith " (ch. 3:7), and, like the son of the slave, they " shall not inherit " with those who are like the son of the free woman (ch. 4:30).

Although Paul does not say explicitly that the son of the slave was not born " through promise," the antithesis that he does offer (" according to the flesh " as over against " through promise ") seems to require this meaning. Actually both Ishmael and Isaac were born " according to the flesh " (that is, naturally, or " in the ordinary course of nature ").[6] The contrast is to be found, therefore, in the fact that Ishmael was born *only* " according to the flesh," whereas Isaac was born, besides this, " through promise." (See Gen. 15:4 and 17:19.)

There is a sense, of course, in which a promise was involved in the case of Ishmael also (Gen. 16:10 f.). The situation was not quite the same with him as with Isaac, however, since his mother was *already* " with child " when the promise was given. Paul gives no attention to this point. As Lightfoot has observed, " In his choice of words here, St. Paul regards not only the original history, but the typical application, the Jews being the children of Abraham after the flesh, the Christians his children by the promise." [7] Here again, it may be noted, is a case where the Pauline thought determines the use made of the analogy; it is not the analogy that in itself provides the clue to his thought.

Thus the Old Testament account, allegorically interpreted, becomes an analogy for the reinforcement of the Pauline claims. Insofar as major emphases are concerned, the application of the story is fairly clear. For a consideration of the distinctive characteristics of Paul's usage of analogy, however, more careful and more detailed analysis is necessary.

Perhaps the chief characteristic of the use of the story of Hagar and Sarah and of their sons is what might be called the fragmentariness of his treatment. That is, the apostle does not proceed from the story itself, showing how the various elements within it correspond to certain facts in the contemporary situation as he understands it. He moves,

rather, from one idea to another as these ideas arise out of
the contemporary situation and then grasps momentarily at
this or that element in the story which might be said to
offer some kind of correspondence. The absence of systematic development arising from the story itself is seen in
two ways especially: (1) in the way in which a single figure
in the story is used at one moment to represent one thing or
one idea and at the next moment to represent something
quite different and (2) in the way in which even single
points of correspondence are not developed or carried
through to their full conclusions.

(1) The references to the two mothers, Hagar and Sarah,
demonstrate with particular clarity the sudden shifts in representation. The former, Hagar, stands in v. 24 for " one " of
the " two covenants," obviously the covenant involved in the
giving of the law at Mt. Sinai, the covenant suggested by the
language in II Cor. 3:14. In v. 25, however, she represents,
or " corresponds to," the Jews (" the present Jerusalem ")
and also perhaps Mt. Sinai.

The special problem raised by v. 25 is well-known. It arises in
part because of the manuscript variants. Two major readings are
involved: (*a*) " Now Hagar is Mount Sinai in Arabia " (*to de
Hagar Sina oros estin en tēi Arabiai*) appears in A, B, D, and elsewhere; (*b*) " For Sinai is a mountain in Arabia " (*to gar Sina
oros estin en tēi Arabiai*) is found in Χ, C, and elsewhere. It may
be noted that Χ adds *on* following *estin*, an addition which, as
Burton observes, " there would be no occasion to insert " if *Hagar*
(Hagar) had not been in the original text; thus " the testimony of
Χ is really in favor of the presence of *Hagar* in the text." [8] Other
slightly different forms also exist.[9]

If (*a*) is accepted, a certain ambiguity still remains, for it has
been suggested that the reading refers to the *name* Hagar, not to
the woman herself. (The neuter article *to* with *Hagar,* rather than
the feminine *hē,* may be said to support this claim.) This requires the assumption that Mt. Sinai, or some peak connected with
it, was designated by an Arabic name similar to the name Hagar.[10]
In any case, according to this reading of the text, Hagar (in one
way or another) " is Mount Sinai."

The present writer is inclined to accept this reading since it
has the best manuscript support and since, by association of ideas,

Paul *could* have pictured Hagar as Mt. Sinai. If Ishmael represents the Jews and if Hagar represents the covenant "from Mount Sinai" (v. 24), then there is a sense in which it could be said that the Jews are the children of the covenant, since Ishmael is the child of Hagar. But the association of the covenant with Mt. Sinai easily suggests the idea that the Jews are then the children of Mt. Sinai. The point intended to be emphasized is that whereas the Christians are children from above (the "Jerusalem above . . . is our mother," v. 26), having been given the promise directly by God (compare ch. 3:15-20), who is certainly "above," the Jews, on the other hand, are children, not from above, but from an earthly geographical location, namely, Mt. Sinai *in Arabia*. "In Arabia," therefore, far from being an unnecessary and hence irrelevant insertion, is thus intended as a contrast to "above" (v. 26). Since the more immediately comprehensible contrast would be between the "present Jerusalem" and the "Jerusalem above," Paul adds the words "she [Mt. Sinai] corresponds to the present Jerusalem," in order to make clearer the real contrast that is intended, i.e., between Mt. Sinai in (the earthly) Arabia and the realm that is "above."

But Hagar not only represents the covenant from Mt. Sinai (v. 24), Mt. Sinai itself (v. 25a), and the Jews ("the present Jerusalem," v. 25b), but she is apparently also thought of as the "mother" of the Jews. At least this is the implication that may be drawn from v. 26; for if the "our" in this verse is intended to be emphatic,[11] referring to the "Jerusalem above" as the mother of the *Christians*, then Hagar, as the "present Jerusalem," must be *their* (i.e., the Jews') mother. This representation is also suggested by the last clause in v. 25 ("she is in slavery with her children"), although the language at this point is more likely determined by the practice of referring to the inhabitants of Jerusalem as the "children" of that city (as in Matt. 23:37 and Luke 13:34).[12] If Hagar is thus conceived as representing the mother of the Jews, then she is made to "correspond" in four different ways. Furthermore, if she represents both the Jews and also their mother, there is found here another example of reversal in analogical usage.

Sarah, like Hagar, is a figure used representatively in more

than one way, although on the whole the points of correspondence are implied rather than stated explicitly. In fact,
Sarah is not even named. At first she obviously represents the
second of the " two covenants " mentioned in v. 24, even
though Paul does not say this. The covenant involved here
may be assumed to be the " new covenant " of I Cor. 11:25,
which, viewed in a different manner, however, may also be
said to be the original covenant (see the discussion of Gal.
3:15-18). In v. 26, on the other hand, Sarah apparently " corresponds " to the " Jerusalem above," presumably the community of those who are now united through faith in Christ
(compare Heb. 12:22-24). Both the fact that the " Jerusalem
above " is " free " and the fact that " she is our mother "
agree with the representation of Sarah in v. 22 as " free "
and also as a mother. If this implication is intended, then
it is possible to draw the further implication that Sarah is
not only thought of as the Christian community itself but
also as the " mother " of that community, in which case a reversal in analogical thinking is involved, as in the case of
Hagar. Particularly striking, however, is the fact — to be discussed below — that none of this is spelled out.

(2) Several examples may be given of Paul's failure to
develop systematically or carry through to their full conclusions the points of correspondence that he introduces. In
v. 24, for example, he speaks of the two women as two covenants. He begins the application with the words, " One is
from Mount Sinai." The expected parallel, as to whence
comes the other covenant, is entirely absent. If it should be
held that there existed no ready parallel that Paul *could*
have introduced, this would only bear out the fact that he
shows relatively little concern that his analogical material
should be used or developed systematically; rather, he is
content to seize simply upon that which serves his immediate
and momentary purpose.

Again in v. 25a there is introduced a point that is left undeveloped. This is readily apparent if the correct reading
here should be, " Now Hagar is Mount Sinai in Arabia " (see

the discussion of the textual problem above). If it is meant that the *woman* Hagar is Mt. Sinai, not only does she represent no longer the covenant, as in the previous verse, but also the point is quickly thrown in — and dropped — for nothing of a parallel nature is said regarding Sarah. If the meaning should be that the *word* " Hagar " denotes Mt. Sinai (see above), the same absence of development exists, since nothing is said about the parallel word " Sarah." If the correct reading, on the other hand, should be " For Sinai is a mountain in Arabia," the fragmentariness of Paul's presentation is equally apparent, even though it is of a somewhat different sort. If the statement is thrown in simply as a geographical observation, it constitutes a fragmentary statement having little bearing on the thought that is being expressed. If the statement is more than a geographical observation and is intended to suggest a contrast between the *places* of the two covenants,[13] there is also an absence of any development of this idea in the form of some reference to the place of the other covenant.

Indifference to systematic development may be seen, furthermore, in the fact, already noted, that certain points of correspondence between analogy and thought are at best only implied; they are not made at all explicit. The reader may *imply* that Hagar is thought of (among other things) as the mother of the Jews, or that Sarah represents the " Jerusalem above," or that Sarah, as the " Jerusalem above," is thought of also as " our mother," but in all of this no attempt whatever is made to direct the reader's attention to these specific points of correspondence. And what is most striking of all is the fact that in the entire use of the picture concerning Hagar and Sarah, Sarah's name, as parallel to that of Hagar, is not even mentioned. All of this bespeaks a flow of ideas to which certain elements drawn from the Old Testament story may be joined analogically, but it does not indicate any concern on the part of Paul to have the story serve as a useful basis for the understanding of his thought.

These examples of the fragmentariness of Pauline usage

indicate that for the apostle the analogical material does not occupy a really central or determinative position in his thinking. He employs that material loosely, one might say casually, drawing upon it when this or that element within it can be useful for immediate purposes. But the purposes themselves are determined by his own thought as there occur to him certain ideas, ideas arising out of his present experience and out of the vital issue that he is facing.

There are still further evidences, however, of the fact that Paul's thought is not to be defined by the use he makes of analogy, but rather, that his use of a given analogy is determined by his most immediate thought. Earlier it was seen that he represents Hagar and Sarah as the "two covenants," presumably the "old covenant" (as suggested by II Cor. 3:14) as over against the "new covenant" (of I Cor. 11:25). While the allegorical usage now under consideration reinforces effectively the contrast between those who are enslaved under the covenant based on law and those who are free under a covenant based on faith, this usage simply does not agree at all with Paul's thought in a different context, even though that different context is removed by only one chapter in this letter to the Galatians. For in Gal. 3:15-18 the apostle argues that the covenant given "by promise" and based on faith *preceded* the giving of the law and hence is the one and only true or valid covenant. The picture of Hagar and Sarah as representing *two* seemingly rival covenants, even granted that one is superior to the other, would be thoroughly inappropriate. Furthermore, even if the idea of two covenants *could* be read back into Gal. 3:15-18, the story of Hagar and Sarah would still not be applicable in that context, since, according to Gen., chs. 16 ff., the promise of a child by Sarah *follows* the birth of a child by Hagar, whereas the main emphasis in Gal. 3:15-18 is on the fact that the covenant by promise *precedes* that which is based on law.

Finally, one finds in Gal. 4:21-31 yet another possible indication that Paul's own experience and thought determine his use of analogical material rather than that the latter provides clues to his thought. Verse 29 reads: " But as at that time he who was born according to the flesh persecuted him who was born according to the Spirit, so it is now." The parallel that is drawn here can hardly have been suggested to Paul by the Biblical account that he is allegorizing, for that account contains no reference to Ishmael's persecution of Isaac. It is often suggested, it is true, that Paul here has in mind Gen. 21:9, which the King James Version renders: " And Sarah saw the son of Hagar the Egyptian, which she had borne unto Abraham, mocking." Lightfoot agrees that the meaning must be " mocking " or " jeering," adding that the " anger of Sarah taken in connection with the occasion, a festival in honor of the weaning Isaac, seems to require it.[14] It seems unlikely, however, that mockery would in itself suggest to Paul the stronger idea of persecution and hence lead him to draw this parallel. It is much more likely that Paul's thought, beginning with his own knowledge of the persecution of the Christians by the Jews, would lead him to make the comparison. Furthermore, it is far from certain that Paul's Old Testament text contained even the idea of mockery. If he was relying on the Septuagint, which elsewhere he seems to quote,[15] that text has simply, " playing with her son Isaac " (as in the RSV). This, certainly, would not have suggested the comparison. It is true that in certain rabbinical interpretations of the story of Ishmael and Isaac the former is described as taking up bow and arrow against the latter.[16] If Paul had such interpretations in mind,[17] it is possible that the comparison might have been suggested by the older story. Against this, however, is the fact that in introducing this section in Galatians (ch. 4:21) Paul explicitly appeals to the authority of " the law," probably meaning, in this context, the Scriptures;[18] and the rabbinical interpretations lie outside this source of authority. If it *is* the law in this sense to which Paul is referring, then it must obviously be his own thought and experience that leads him to make the comparison, not the story itself, since the law upon which he is drawing contains no real basis for it. Finally, if, as Burton observes, " the apostle may also have had in mind the mutual hostility of the nations supposed to have descended from the two brothers," [19] this also would only bear out the contention that the analogical material itself is not determinative for the progression of the Pauline thought; rather, it would be another case where an element in his own thinking has led him to shape the analogical material to serve his purpose.

The preceding analysis has brought to light these characteristics in Paul's allegorical interpretation of the story of Hagar and Sarah and their respective sons: (1) The apostle does not move systematically from the story to his ideas. The fragmentariness of his application, involving sudden shifts in comparison and also incomplete development in given points of comparison, shows that it is his own thought and experience, not the story itself, that determines his language and his form of expression. (2) There is evidence that the analogical application may have relevance only for the issue or argument immediately under consideration and may be entirely inappropriate to another context. (3) Paul's own experience and thinking takes such precedence over his analogical material that he shapes it freely in order to adjust it to his purpose. This means, altogether, that, as Paul seeks to give effective and forceful expression to his ideas, he reaches out — in a series of sudden thrusts, as it were — and grasps at this or that element in his analogical material which might be useful. Even then he shows no inclination to make full use of such elements; instead, he moves quickly to a different, though perhaps related, idea that, again, springs from his own mind, not from the material that he is using.

This study of Gal. 4:21-31 has shown the essential validity of an observation made by Lightfoot in his note comparing Paul and Philo in their respective allegorizations of the story of Hagar and Sarah: " With Philo the allegory is the whole substance of his teaching; [20] with St. Paul it is but an accessory. He uses it rather as an illustration than an argument, as a means of representing in a lively form the lessons before enforced on other grounds. It is, to use Luther's comparison, the painting which decorates the house already built." [21] There is a sense, therefore, in which Paul's use of the story of Hagar and Sarah is not true allegorization at all. Although he treats allegorically certain elements in the story, he manifests little interest in careful allegorization as such.

3.

The First Letter of Paul to the Corinthians

I Corinthians 2:11

An analogy is introduced in I Corinthians as part of the larger discussion in which a contrast is drawn between the "wisdom of God" and the "wisdom of this age" (ch. 2:6 f.). The wisdom of God, hitherto hidden or kept secret (v. 7), God has now revealed to us in the person of Jesus Christ (ch. 1:30). But since it is God's wisdom that is thus revealed, Paul emphasizes that it is God himself who has made this known through his Spirit, for it is the Spirit that "searches . . . even the depths of God" (ch. 2:10); that is, it is the Spirit that throws light "upon the deep things of God"[1] for those who love God (v. 9). In order to bring out the full force of the idea that only divine agency can know (or "comprehend") and hence reveal "the thoughts of God" — literally, "the [things] of God" (v. 11) — the apostle writes: "For what person knows a man's thoughts except the spirit of the man which is in him? So also no one comprehends the thoughts of God except the Spirit of God."

The purpose of the analogical usage here is quite clear. It is to reinforce the idea that the "wisdom of God," "the depths of God," can be understood by man only through divine revelation, since only God himself comprehends the "things" of God. Just as no one really knows a man's thoughts (the "things" of a man) except that man himself, so also no one comprehends or knows the thoughts (or the "things") of God except the Spirit of God.

According to Paul's language, it is the "spirit" of a man which knows the thoughts (or "things") of that man. As Bultmann has

76

shown, however, the use of " spirit " in this way really means " the person." When Paul speaks of the *pneuma* (" spirit ") of man " he does not mean some higher principle within him or some special intellectual or spiritual faculty of his, but simply his self." [2] As Bultmann emphasizes, this usage of *pneuma* by Paul must, of course, be carefully distinguished from the predominant use of the word to refer to the Holy Spirit or the Spirit of God. In fact, in this discussion in I Corinthians the word is employed in both senses, first as referring to the human " person " (v. 11a) and then to mean the Spirit of God (vs. 11b-13).[3] Thus, to say that only the " spirit " of the man knows the " things " of that man is in reality to assert that only the man *himself* really knows the " things " that pertain to him.

The analogy is one that cannot be carried through or developed completely. While it may be said that the " things " of God are comprehended only by the Spirit of God just as the " things " of a man are known only by the spirit of the man himself, the idea of the divine Spirit as that which can be " received " by Christians (v. 12) has no parallel with respect to the spirit of a man. In other words, the picture of a man's spirit involves no element that corresponds to the thought of God's Spirit as being bestowed upon Christians. There is seen here, therefore, an example of Paul using a picture to reinforce an idea — " a case of conclusion by analogy " [4] — although the analogy itself is not fully appropriate.[5]

It should also be noted that this picture of man does not seem to represent accurately the Pauline view of man which is expressed elsewhere in the letters. In this particular context there appears to be ascribed to man a fuller comprehension or understanding of himself than other passages will allow. If the picture of man found here is to have analogical significance at all, it must be assumed that a man *does* comprehend fully his own thoughts (or " things "). Particularly in his letter to the Romans, however, Paul writes as though he did not believe this to be true. In Rom. 8:26, for example, he says that " we do not know how to pray as we ought." If his meaning is that " we know too little of our own needs

. . . to pray aright," [6] or that "we are so weak that we do not even know how to pray," [7] then it is clear that according to his thinking man's self-understanding is certainly limited (and as such, of course, could provide no proper analogy for God's self-understanding). And when he says in Rom. 7:15, "I do not understand my own actions," limitations in man's self-understanding seem also to be indicated.

This is obviously true if the thought in Rom. 7:15 is that "man acts, so to speak, blindly: he is not a fully conscious agent." [8] It is less obvious if Paul means, "not, 'I do not know what I am doing,' for Paul knows only too well, but 'I do not recognize and approve.'" [9] Even in this case, however, there lurks the suggestion that man is very definitely limited in his understanding of the "things" that pertain to him.

It is not to be denied that a certain case can be made for the claim that Paul is *not* ascribing to man full self-understanding in I Cor. 2:11. In the reference to a man knowing his own thoughts, Paul's word for "know" is *oiden*. In the reference to the Spirit of God comprehending the thoughts of God, the word is *egnōken*. Since, upon occasion, the latter may be employed where the idea of "thoroughness" is involved,[10] it might be argued that the apostle intended to suggest, through his choice of verbs, that man's knowing of his own "things" *is* limited in contrast to God's knowing.[11] It is extremely doubtful, however, that such a distinction is intended. Some passages seem to indicate that in the New Testament the two verbs are "nearly interchangeable." [12] And it is especially important to note that if this distinction were intended in the choice of verbs, then much of the force of the analogy would be lost, for then God's knowing of his own "things" could not very convincingly be likened to a man's (inferior) knowing of the "things" that pertain to himself.

Even if a distinction existed in Paul's thinking at this point, the purpose may have been, not to suggest that a man's knowing is less thorough than that of the Spirit, but rather, that the things of

God are "a degree more out of reach"[13] than are the things of man.

It is extremely interesting to observe in this connection that certain manuscripts introduce variant readings for I Cor. 2:11. In some of them the second *tou anthrōpou* ("of the man") is omitted,[14] so that the first part of the verse may be translated, "For what person knows a man's thoughts except the Spirit [of God] which is in him?" It seems likely that this change was made precisely because it was felt that according to the general Pauline thought man did *not* fully know the "things" of man; only the Spirit of God could know them. Thus it appears to have been recognized quite early that Paul's words in the original text introduce a picture of man which is not strictly in harmony with the actual Pauline thinking about man. Hence the text was altered even though the alteration destroyed the analogy!

Altogether, since the picture of man here is of one who *does* comprehend or know himself in an apparently thoroughgoing way, and since this picture does not properly represent what is otherwise seen to be Paul's thought concerning man's self-understanding, it must be concluded that we have here a case where the picture has been adjusted in such a way as to serve an immediate purpose in a particular context. It is not a picture that can be taken as providing a reliable clue to the apostle's thinking generally.

I Corinthians 3:5-17

As Paul addresses himself to the problem of factionalism or party division within the Corinthian church he attempts to alleviate the situation in part by establishing an understanding of the Christian ministry which leaves no room for personal or party rivalries. It is in connection with this attempt that he relies heavily upon analogical usage in order to present his position. An examination of this section of I Corinthians (ch. 3:5-17) brings to light certain characteristics in his use of analogy.

There is introduced, first of all, the picture drawn from agriculture: " I planted, Apollos watered, but God gave the growth " (ch. 3:6). As the following verses make more explicit, neither the one who plants nor the one who waters " is anything " in comparison with God " who gives the growth " (v. 7); hence both are " one " (KJV), that is, " equal " (RSV), in their common subordinate position insofar as the growth of the crops is concerned (v. 8a). The analogy is presented, obviously, to suggest the wrongness of the rivalry and factionalism which, in Corinth, mistakenly presupposes the superiority of one leader as over against another.

It may be noted that the Greek text of v. 6 brings out more clearly than do the English translations the kind of contrast made more explicit in v. 7. In the Greek the first two verbs are in the *aorist,* the simple past tense, whereas the verb for which " God " is the subject is in the imperfect — the tense denoting *continuing* past action. Men's actions " come and go," and hence are vastly inferior to God's action " which goes on for ever." [1]

Verse 8b should be given special attention insofar as it throws light upon the nature of Paul's use of analogy. Having said in v. 8a that the person who plants and the person who waters are " one," or " equal," the apostle adds that " each shall receive his [own] wages according to his [own] labor." This addition can hardly have been suggested by the analogy itself, for, if it has just been said that the performers of the two functions in agriculture are " one " or " equal " in their labor,[2] it would be blatantly contradictory to add immediately the suggestion that the wages earned by the labor of the one might *differ* from the wages earned by the labor of the other. This contradiction is to be avoided only if, in v. 8b, Paul no longer is thinking of the agricultural analogy as such. His thought is dominated, rather, by the problem or situation at Corinth which he is facing, where he and Apollos, as laborers for God, are the subjects. *Before God* a distinction may exist between them even though before or among men neither is superior to the other.[3] This means, therefore, that Paul throughout v. 8 continues in his use of the *language* of his agricultural analogy, but the thought conveyed (at least in v. 8b) in actuality has nothing to do with the analogy. In other words, there is found here a case where the analogy itself cannot be used as a key to an understanding of Paul's thought on the issue under consideration. Rather, it is his thought on that issue which determines his analogical language.

If, even in v. 8a, Paul's thought has *already* shifted from the analogy back to the situation involving himself and Apollos, this means that the analogy itself is even *less* important as a key to his thought.

In ch. 3:9 is seen a further example of the use of analogical language where the thought is dominated, not by the analogy itself, but by the situation for the sake of which the analogy has been introduced: " For we are fellow workmen for God; you are God's field, God's building." [4] In the first two clauses the agricultural picture continues to provide the language, but the thought is completely determined by the Corinthian problem. The triple use of *Theou* in the sentence shows that the emphasis is upon *God* as over against the " fellow workmen." [5] The Corinthians are *God's* field, not the field of either Paul or Apollos. The agricultural analogy that provides the language here, however, had nothing to do with the ownership of the land on which the laborers worked; it concerned only the differing functions of those laborers. As above, therefore, there is also here a case where the picture provides only the vocabulary, so to speak: it is impossible to begin with the picture and use it as a basis for understanding the Pauline thought. To put it differently, the analogy is adjusted or used freely to conform to the thought. *It has no independent significance.*

All of this means, therefore, that the analogy itself must be recognized as having only limited application. It is introduced primarily for the sake of the idea that in agriculture men may perform different functions, but they occupy a common or equal position under God, who himself " gives the growth." As just observed, a further element in the analogy is applicable partially: the "field" in which the men work is a field belonging to *someone*. The question of *ownership of the field*, however, is not developed or applied fully; God's ownership is suggested, not to contrast God with some other possible owner, but rather, to emphasize the contrast between God as owner and men as workmen. And it has been seen that while this particular idea of ownership may be related to the agricultural picture that has been used, and the language may have been drawn from it, the *idea* involved in Paul's statement (v. 9b) appears to be introduced, not as a part of the application of the analogy at all, but rather, as the idea is suggested by the situation at Corinth.

Even less is the reference to "wages" (v. 8b) introduced as a part of the application of the analogy. While the picture of laborers *might* have suggested the idea of wages, in this instance such was not the case, for, as seen above, what is said about the wages actually is quite inconsistent with the picture of laborers who perform equal, though different, functions. In other words, the idea of wages *suggested by the picture in the analogy* not only *is not* applied by Paul; it *cannot* be applied, for Paul's statement with reference to wages (v. 8b) stands in contradiction to what would have to be said if the ideas suggested by the picture were applied.

There are also further ideas associated with the agricultural picture which are not developed or applied. *What* Paul planted is not stated. Nor is it said *how* Apollos watered (v. 6).

It has sometimes been urged that "planted" refers to the conversion of the Corinthians and "watered" refers to their baptism.[6] On the basis of ch. 3:10 ff. it might be argued that Paul established the Christian community and that Apollos cared for its members. J. Weiss has suggested, however, that to emphasize such a contrast is to do violence to the picture, and that the terms employed are here intended only to suggest temporal sequence.[7] Straub suggests that planting and watering are specified only as examples of different kinds of work, noting that not all of the activities of the farmer are enumerated and that in the Pauline usage the field and the lord of the work are more important than the individual worker and his work. It seems quite unlikely, therefore, that Paul intends " planted " and " watered " to be given specific application or to have particular significance as defining a distinction between the work of Paul and that of Apollos. The picture, after all, is introduced, not at all for the sake of emphasizing contrast in function, but rather, to stress the fact that they both serve under God. They stand *together*, "servants through whom you believed " (ch. 3:5). It may be noted, finally, that if the analogy is applied strictly, conveying the idea that Paul won the converts and that Apollos nurtured them or cared for them, this could mean that the latter made no new converts at all — he only " watered." It is highly unlikely that this is the case.[8] Simply to state this quite unlikely possibility, however, is to show the danger involved in giving to the Pauline analogies applications beyond those which the apostle himself makes explicitly.

At ch. 3:9c the picture changes suddenly: " [You are] God's building." While the joining of the architectural with the agricultural picture is by no means unique with Paul, since the same combination is found elsewhere (Jer. 1:10; 18:9; 24:6; Ezek. 36:9 f.),[9] it should nevertheless be noted that the apostle does, upon occasion, move rapidly from one picture to another. In this particular case he does so rather than develop further or fully the former picture drawn from agriculture. This suggests, of course, that Paul's thought is dominated by the situation and the ideas with which he is concerned rather than by a given analogy.[10]

A casual reading of I Cor. 3:10-15 may give the impression that here is a passage in which the apostle has taken as an analogy the picture of a building and then has developed and carried through the application with unusual thoroughness. He seems to move somewhat systematically from one element in the picture to another, applying each to the subject under consideration. After saying that the building is *God's,* and that it is (represents) the Corinthian Christians (v. 9c), he then turns to the builder who lays the foundation, the other workmen who add the superstructure, the materials used in the building, the durability or permanence of the construction, the reward that comes to the builder. Here, it may appear, is a case where the apostle intends the reader to take each element in the picture and see in it that which provides a clue to his religious thinking. It is like an allegory, as over against a parable,[11] where each element is intended to have relevance and significance. One should therefore be able to say: As this fact or that fact is true in regard to the analogical picture, so, correspondingly, this or that is true in regard to the issue at hand.

Upon closer examination, however, it becomes evident that such a procedure is not wholly justified. It must be granted that at a few points what is true in the case of the picture *is* intended to suggest what is true concerning the issue under discussion. For example, just as a building belongs to the *owner* and not to the workmen who are employed, so the Corinthian Christians "belong" to God, not to Paul, nor to Apollos, nor to someone else (I Cor. 1:12; 3:9c). Or, it may be said, perhaps,[12] just as one workman may lay the foundation and another (or others) may build upon it, so Paul has served God in setting forth Jesus Christ as the true foundation of the church while others have served in other ways (ch. 3:10 f.). (This, of course, is parallel to the "planted" and "watered" in vs. 6 ff.) In these cases, as has already been stated, Paul seems to mean that what is true in regard to the analogy provides a clue as to what is true in regard to the subject under consideration. In interpreting Paul's thought *at these points,* therefore, one may begin with the "fact" that is found in the analogy, and interpret Paul's thought correspondingly. *At other points, however, this is not possible.* For although, as seen above, Paul does mention other elements in the picture, he does not do so in such a manner that they can be taken as a clue as to what is true in the apostle's thinking, primarily because in his allusions to these elements what he says is actually *not* true insofar as the picture itself is concerned. In other words, Paul *refers* to various other elements in the picture as he expresses first one and then another idea in regard to the situation under discussion, *but the ideas do not correspond to what is true in the picture;* rather, the ideas are allowed so completely to dominate the references to the elements in the picture as to create an unreal picture, one that does not correspond at all closely to the architectural reality.

In v. 12 is given a list of building materials: " gold, silver, precious stones,[13] wood, hay, stubble." Just as the " foundation " is intended to correspond to Jesus Christ, or the preaching concerning Christ (v. 11), so also the various building materials represent the various teachings that are added. Following the listing of the materials there is expressed the further idea that the kind of work that has been done will become manifest as it is tested by fire. This seems to mean that just as the quality of the work on a building is brought to light by the fact that it either survives the test of fire or is burned up, so also the teachings of this or that leader will be revealed on the Day of Judgment as sound or as unsound. Finally, it is stated that the builder's receiving of his " reward " ("wages ") is determined by the survival or nonsurvival, presumably in the testing by fire, of the work that he " has built."

Insofar as Paul's use of analogy is concerned here, it is not enough to say, as does Moffatt, that " Paul's corporate and figurative description is more impressive than lucid." [14] It must be recognized that Paul, in several specific ways, has created with language drawn from his original architectural analogy a further picture that does not conform to architectural reality.

(1) The use of nothing but noncombustible building materials can hardly be regarded as the determining criterion of sound workmanship; yet this must be assumed in this section if the language is taken seriously. If such a criterion

were generally accepted, this would mean that no good builder would ever use wood for purposes of construction. The present-day idea of a "fireproof" building may not be a wholly modern concept, but the inclusion of some wood in the building is not, even today, accepted as the sign of unacceptable workmanship.

(2) In actuality the quality of work done on a building is not, normally at least, tested by fire. Fire, of course, may occur, and in such an event the survival of the building may then be considered as evidence of sound workmanship. But even if noninflammability should be regarded as a primary criterion as to quality (see above), actual testing by subjecting the building to fire would obviously be both unnecessary and wholly impractical. The fact remains, therefore, that in building practice the test by fire is neither planned nor presupposed.

(3) When workmen are employed, their compensation is *not* dependent upon — and does not await — the test of survival through fire.

(4) The list of materials given in v. 12 is not such as would be expected if Paul were thinking of actual building procedures.

(*a*) Even if, by some stretch of the imagination, it should be assumed that judgment as to the quality of the work were determined by the test of fire, then the list of building materials given is wholly unrealistic. While it is true that the last three items mentioned (wood, hay, stubble) are inflammable, while the first three (gold, silver, precious stones) are not (supposing that such a contrast is intended), only a little reflection brings to light the meaninglessness of such contrast. Gold, silver, and precious stones may be noncombustible, as over against wood, hay, and stubble, but as building materials they have no survival value in case of fire. As Lietzmann has observed, these, in a fire, would be melted or fused into a shapeless mass. One would therefore expect the mention of such good materials as stone or brick.[15]

(*b*) Lietzmann is of the opinion that gold, silver, and

precious stones are listed, not in contrast to the inflammable wood, hay, and stubble, but rather, with the intent of suggesting the " costliness " of the materials used. He admits, however, that in this case these are chosen for mention without careful reflection as to their use in actual construction; otherwise, more suitable materials would have been included.[16] Furthermore, the costliness of the materials used can hardly be regarded, in actual building processes, as assuring sound and enduring construction.

(c) Straub denies that there is intended either the idea of costliness in the reference to gold, silver, and precious stones, or the idea of inflammability in the reference to wood, hay, and stubble, contending that the entire list is offered merely to provide evidence of the manifold possibilities that exist in regard to materials for further building, once the foundation has been laid.[17] He agrees with Lietzmann, however, that, in presenting the list in v. 12, Paul shows little concern for authentic building practices.[18]

(d) Deissmann, especially, has attempted to justify the apostle's language here. On the one hand, he contends strongly that *lithous timious* should be given the meaning " costly (building) stones," rather than " precious stones," noting that the former meaning is to be found for this Greek expression in the Septuagint version of I Kings 7:9 ff. (LXX, III Kings 7:46 ff.).[19] He argues also that even though modern men may not build with gold and silver, yet to such a " Septuagint-Jew " as Paul the idea of building with these materials was not foreign or strange.[20] This point may have some validity. Tobit 13:16 (LXX, ch. 13:17) reads:

" For Jerusalem will be built with sapphires and emeralds,
    her walls with precious stones,
    and her towers and battlements with pure gold." [21]

This does not alter the fact, however, that gold and silver add little if anything to the soundness and durability of a structure, and it is precisely this quality of the building to which Paul refers in v. 14. Deissmann himself seems to suggest that the gold and silver serve a decorative purpose primarily.[22] Therefore, even though *lithous timious* (if interpreted as "costly [building] stones") should refer to material that does make for soundness and permanence in actual building procedures, this cannot be claimed for the gold and silver. Undoubtedly Deissmann is correct in tracing Paul's usage of terms here to certain literary references (see above). He seems to have missed the full significance of this fact however. This significance will be discussed below.

The foregoing treatment indicates clearly that in at least four respects Paul's statements do not "ring true" insofar as architecture is concerned, even when allowance is made for possible variations in the interpretation of specific expressions. Furthermore, it is impossible to plead for him a state of ignorance with regard to actual architectural procedures, for none of those which are under consideration involves technical knowledge of any sort.

Since the architectural picture that Paul presents includes elements that are thus *not* true to actual fact, the purpose in Paul's use of the analogy, therefore, cannot have been to say, in effect: What is true in architecture is also true in regard to the subject under consideration. This must be ruled out by the simple fact that much that has been said is *not* true in architecture.

On the other hand, it is equally apparent that the (unreal) architectural picture that he presents *does correspond to the message that he is setting forth,* involving (in regard to the "superstructure" built upon the "foundation") the following points: (1) The soundness of the teachings proclaimed by the various leaders in the church will "become manifest" on the Day of Judgment.[23] With *this* thought in mind it may be said that the quality of the workmanship (the teaching) *is* to be determined by the fact that the materials used (the teachings presented) do, or do not, withstand and survive the testing that that "Day" brings, a testing frequently associated with, and likened to, a burning fire (see below). It is therefore appropriate to say that the noncombustibility of

the building materials is the criterion of sound workmanship, *so long as the words are taken as having eschatological
rather than architectural significance.* (2) A divine testing is
to occur on the Day of Judgment and each man's teaching
will be approved or condemned. In saying that the Day will
be revealed with fire Paul is simply employing familiar eschatological terminology, for fire was frequently associated
with the divine Judgment.[24] The inevitability of this Judgment is indicated by the fact that the verb *apokaluptetai*
(" is revealed ") appears in the present tense, for such a present form is often employed with reference to a future event
when its occurrence is anticipated with certainty.[25] Again,
therefore, if the *eschatological* idea prevails, it is understandable that Paul can say that the quality of work done on
the building will be tested by fire. (3) A man (a leader or
teacher) will receive his " reward " if that which he has done
" survives "; that is, if he is approved by God in the Judgment.[26] With this eschatological thought in mind Paul can
thus declare that a workman's receiving of his wages depends upon the survival of the work when it has been tested
by fire, even though this is not the basis for recompense in
actual construction. (4) The reference to gold, silver, and
precious stones — which, as seen above, raises serious problems if it should be assumed that those materials are to be
related to actual building practices — is entirely appropriate
if related to the apostle's eschatological thought. In the case
of gold and silver this is especially true. Since, in the refining process, such metals are separated from the dross by fire,
the testing of men by God was often likened to the " trying "
of gold and silver.[27] Particularly relevant are those Old Testament passages in which such refining is mentioned in an
eschatological context, involving the divine testing and judgment [28] on the Day of the Lord.[29] It is therefore Paul's eschatological thinking — in reference to the ultimate divine
judgment to which the leaders in the church and their teachings will be subjected — that leads him to include gold and
silver among those materials which must stand the test of

fire. As gold and silver are distinguished and separated by
the fire of the furnace, so the sound teachings will be distinguished from the unsound on the Day which " will be revealed with fire " (v. 13). Paul speaks of *building* with gold
and silver in order to relate this thought to the architectural
analogy that he employs, but it is his eschatological thought
rather than the analogy itself that determines the inclusion
of these materials in the first place. Thus understood, the
inclusion of gold and silver becomes intelligible even though
they are not really relevant to the architectural picture that
Paul is using.

It is possible that the reference to gold and silver is appropriate for an additional reason also. This reason, furthermore,
helps to account for the reference to precious stones. The anticipated Day was not only thought of as the occasion of
testing and of judgment; it was also thought of as the time
when there would be inaugurated a new age, an age of glory
and splendor. It is not surprising that eschatological procla-
mations should describe that age in those materialistic terms
which were practically synonymous with glory and splendor
on this earth. Thus, in Hag. 2:7-9 gold and silver are mentioned in connection with the splendor that is to be.[30] And in
Isa. 54:11 f. there is the promise that in the new age founda-
tions, pinnacles, and walls will be made of precious stones.
Particularly pertinent is the passage in Tobit 13:16 (LXX,
ch. 13:17):

> " For Jerusalem will be built with sapphires and emeralds,
>   her walls with precious stones,
>   and her towers and battlements with pure gold."

Paul's thought could well be that that which " survives "
(I Cor. 3:14) is that which corresponds to the new age. And
if the analogy of building is to be employed, it is only natural that the nature of that building should be described in
language drawn from architectural pictures that were associated with the new age. As stated earlier, Deissmann is undoubtedly correct in his contention that Paul would have

been familiar with this kind of description. He fails, however, to bring out clearly the significance of this fact for an understanding of the apostle's analogical usage, namely this: *Paul shows that, upon occasion at least, he allows ideas associated with the thought he is attempting to convey* (in this case the thought that a teacher's work will be vindicated if it survives the divine Judgment) *to determine the form of his analogy even though that form is not then consistent with actuality in the situation from which the analogy is drawn.*

The foregoing statement applies not only to the Pauline mention of gold, silver, and precious stones but also to each of the other elements in the passage which have been shown to be untrue in actual architectural practice but entirely intelligible when those elements are taken, not for their literal but for their figurative and associational significance. This means that when Paul uses and develops the analogy of a building and of the building procedure, the resulting picture is not to be understood as indicative of Paul's thought or belief about such building. In other words, he draws his picture so that it may conform to the message that he wishes to convey. The picture itself has no independent significance as indicative of Paul's thought or belief about the subject material of the analogy itself. A final observation may be made in regard to this section of the material. There are two further elements in it which involve a certain measure of inconsistency. (1) A question may be raised, for example, concerning the appropriateness of the term *architektōn* ("master builder," I Cor. 3:10) in the analogy as it is otherwise presented. In this word, the prefix (*archi*) is that which, when found with the name of an office, generally designates "the one who is placed over the rest that hold the office." [31] The idea of a superior position is certainly suggested by the usage of the word in II Macc. 2:29: "For as the master builder [LXX, *architektoni*] of a new house must be concerned with the whole construction, while the one who undertakes its painting and decoration has to consider only what is suitable for its adornment, such in my judgment is

the case with us." [32] In view of this, the term does not fit
easily into the Pauline picture, for when he says that he
himself " laid a foundation," and that " another man is building upon it," he appears to be restating the idea that one
person is *not* superior to another simply because the function of the one is different from that of the other (compare
vs. 5-8a). (2) Also, v. 11 seems to alter the picture. " He has
just said that he laid the foundation in a skilful way. Now
he says that it was lying there ready for him, and that no
other foundation is possible." [33]

It seems probable that the use of the word *architektōn*
("master builder") and the inclusion of v. 11 serve a common purpose. The latter stresses the centrality and fundamental significance of Jesus Christ, an emphasis that Paul
makes repeatedly in this part of the letter, both indirectly
and directly (chs. 1:13; 1:30; 2:2; 3:23). And the former,
especially when combined, as it is in v. 10, with the adjective
sophos (" skilled," or " wise "), tends to suggest that this emphasis is of particular importance since it constitutes the
groundwork that is laid by the expert, the highly qualified
workman. These elements, therefore, are in full agreement
with the Pauline proclamation concerning Jesus Christ. Furthermore, they are not, taken alone, inconsistent with the
general picture of building practices, as was the case of the
four points previously discussed. Nevertheless, since they do
not agree entirely with other *specific* aspects of the picture
that has been drawn, Paul shows, by their inclusion, that the
details in his analogical material are of little significance in
and of themselves. Each must be recognized as having importance only in respect to that aspect of the Pauline
thought and message for which it has immediate relevance.

Verses 16 and 17 appear, at first glance, to continue the
analogy of a building (compare v. 9c with v. 16a): Paul
" thinks of the Building under the aspect of God's temple,
for the sin of these party-leaders is the sin of sacrilege." [34] It
is true that the temple is a building, and it is certainly possible that the picture of a building may have suggested in a

general way the picture of the temple. If this is true, then several observations may be made. The difference in meaning is greater than the architectural difference between "building" and "temple." In v. 9c — "[You are] God's building" — the emphasis is on "God's," on the fact that the Corinthian Christians belong to God, not to Paul or Apollos or someone else. In the use of "temple" in v. 16, however, the emphasis is upon the idea of that which is "*holy*," as is shown not only by the use of *hagios* ("holy") in v. 17b and by the use of the verb *phtheirei* ("destroy") with its connotation of "defile" or "corrupt,"[35] but especially by the clause, "God's Spirit dwells in you," for it is the presence of the divine Spirit which gives to the temple the quality of holiness.

There is also a further difference. As Robertson and Plummer have pointed out,[36] v. 17 presupposes a situation that is not the same as that of vs. 10-15. In vs. 14 f. the picture concerns the builder of the superstructure: "A good superstructure wins a reward for the builder. A bad superstructure perishes but the builder is rescued." In v. 17, however, the building of the superstructure is not involved. Rather, "he who, instead of adding to the edifice, ruins what has been built, will himself meet with ruin." The subject, therefore, has nothing more to do with the place and the function of the workmen in the construction of a building, as was the case in vs. 9c-15. This means that while the word *naos* ("temple") may have been *suggested* by the "building" of vs. 9c ff.,[37] what is said in vs. 16 f. cannot be regarded as due to further development of the original analogy.[38] That analogy in and of itself hardly gives rise to the idea of an owner's "spirit" dwelling in his "building." This means that Paul is not actually applying further the original analogy in any serious way. We have here, therefore, another example in which Paul makes a connection with a picture that he has previously drawn, but the picture itself has not provided the basis for his thinking and hence cannot be taken as a clue to an understanding of his thought. Once again an analogy is made to conform to the author's religious thinking. It has significance only as it provides a part of the vocabulary with which that religious thinking may be expressed.[39]

I Corinthians 4:9; 15:30-32

The picture of the gladiatorial arena is introduced both in I Cor. 4:9 and in I Cor. 15:30-32. In the former passage the picture concerns the prisoners, doomed or " sentenced to death," since such prisoners generally did not survive the fights with the wild animals.[1] They are a " spectacle," as Paul suggests. In the apostle's use of the picture he is seeking to reinforce the contrast that he is making (in irony) between those Corinthians who act like kings (ch. 4:8) and the apostles, who are placed at the opposite end of the social scale. The picture is introduced for the sake of the idea of the lowly and condemned state in which the prisoners in the arena find themselves. No attempt is made by Paul to apply the picture in any further way. At least one element in the picture would be entirely inappropriate for application. The condemned persons who engaged in the fights in the arena did so because of external compulsion only. Their role was not one that they would have chosen; nor was it one in which they could have found any satisfaction. Paul indicates clearly in this letter that his own lowly position, which he compares to that of the men in the arena, is one that he has assumed voluntarily; he has deliberately chosen that which led to condemnation by men. (See I Cor. 2:2; 1:22 f.)

Of course it might be said that condemned criminals had also deliberately chosen the course of action that led to their conviction. It is unlikely, however, that their choice was deliberately made because they believed it to be ultimately good and right. In any case they would not have chosen the role of the fighter of the beasts in the arena. Paul seems to mean here that he is content to remain in the state or condition in which he now finds himself (assuming that the last part of v. 8 is written in irony).

Especially significant is his use of the word *apedeixen* in v. 9, where the meaning seems to be " exhibited " – " as if being doomed men was an office of distinction." [2] The lowliness and the condemnation of men which Paul experiences is quite different from that of the ill-fated fighters who are on exhibit in the arena, for he can believe that his role is in harmony with the will of God (I Cor. 1:27 f.).

The picture of the arena appears again in ch. 15:32: "What do I gain if, humanly speaking, I fought with wild beasts at Ephesus?" It is generally agreed among interpreters that these words have analogical rather than literal significance. The Greek phrase (*kata anthrōpon*), here translated "humanly speaking," is apparently intended to indicate that metaphorical usage is involved.[3] Even if the phrase does not have this meaning the statement must nevertheless be metaphorical, for otherwise "Paul would not have omitted this most terrible of all perils from the catalogue in II Corinthians 11:23 sqq."[4] Furthermore it is unlikely that as a Roman citizen the apostle would have been compelled to fight with the beasts in the arena, at least while he remained a Roman citizen,[5] and there is no hint anywhere that his citizenship was ever revoked.

In this context the picture of the arena is introduced, not for the sake of the idea of the lowly and condemned state in which the prisoners in the arena found themselves (as in ch. 4:9), but rather, because it provided an image of the savageness and ferocity of the beasts, an image that served to make vivid the nature of the human animosity and opposition that had confronted him at Ephesus.

Thus it appears that the same picture is introduced in ch. 4:9 and in ch. 15:32, but for quite different purposes. The element in the picture which is relevant in ch. 4:9 is quite irrelevant in ch. 15:32, and vice versa. It is clear that no detail in the picture can be regarded as having significance for the Pauline thought and message except that which is suggested by the immediate context.[6]

I CORINTHIANS 5:6-8

Brief use of the analogy of leaven is made by Paul in Gal. 5:9: "A little yeast leavens the whole lump." Since his wording in the Greek is exactly the same as that which he employs in I Cor. 5:6,[1] it seems likely that the apostle is quoting a familiar proverb. Certainly the use of the picture of leaven working in dough was not uncommon, either in Jewish or non-Jewish circles, usually to suggest or illustrate the idea of something that corrupts.[2] It is in this sense that the analogy is introduced in Gal. 5:9. It is possible that the leaven represents here the corrupting teaching on the part of the Judaizers regarding the necessity of circumcision,[3] since the subject in the immediately preceding verse is this "persuasion." This teaching threatens to affect the entire body of Christians. It is also possible that the leaven represents the Judaizers themselves, who are tending to corrupt the Christian community,[4] since Paul's attack is directed in part (see especially I Cor. 5:12) against *persons*. In view of the fact, discussed below, that in I Cor. 5:6-8 Paul gives first one and then another application to certain elements in the same analogy, it is likely that both ideas may have been in the apostle's mind here.

More fruitful for a study of Paul's analogical usage are his references to leaven in I Cor. 5:6-8. Here, as in Gal. 5:9, leaven is taken as something that corrupts.

It is to be observed, first of all, that the leaven is intended to have twofold significance. On the one hand, it represents the incestuous man whose presence threatens to weaken the moral and spiritual fiber of the Corinthian church.

Although this point is ignored by the many commentators who place exclusive emphasis elsewhere (see below), it is justified by the total context. Paul shows very clearly that he is deeply concerned about the effect of the man's presence in the community — so much so that he asks for the man's expulsion from the church not only in I Cor. 5:2c but also in v. 5.[5] The admonition, "Cleanse out," in v. 7, suggests so clearly this idea of expulsion that it is impossible not to relate the two requests. If the connection is thus made, then the "old leaven" of v. 7 must refer, in part at least, to the incestuous man. And if this is so, then the "leaven" in the intervening v. 6 probably has the same significance.

On the other hand, the leaven also stands (v. 8) for the "malice and evil" — or, better, perhaps, "wickedness and evil " — which was in evidence at Corinth. (In v. 8 it clearly does not stand for the sinful man himself.)

Moffatt interprets the " old leaven " in v. 8 as referring to " any immoral practice " inconsistent with Christian principles.[6] Robertson and Plummer regard Paul as having in mind in v. 6 " a vitiated public opinion," an indifference on the part of the church members to the evil conduct that was in their midst.[7] Verse 6a suggests this. It is necessary, of course, to recognize this kind of meaning in v. 8. And interpreters are undoubtedly justified in seeing something of this meaning in v. 6 also. In view of what is said above, however, this must not be taken as the exclusive meaning intended in this section.

A twofold application, similarly, is found in regard to the " lump " (of dough). On the one hand, it represents the body of Corinthian Christians. In the second clause of v. 7 this connection is made explicit.[8] On the other hand, it stands, in v. 8, for " sincerity and truth " (or " purity " and " integrity "), qualities standing over against the leaven of " malice and evil."

It is true that the word " lump " (*phurama*) does not appear in v. 8. There is present, however, the adjective *azumois* (" unleavened "), used substantively, and generally rendered " unleavened bread." Since that which is unleavened, as bread, is the *same* body as the " lump " of dough — at a different stage — it may properly be said that in v. 8 the " lump " stands for " sincerity and truth."

Thus both " leaven " and " lump " are given double analogical significance. At first glance this might suggest that Paul has taken the picture of leaven working in the dough and attempted rather systematically to apply as fully as possible the separate elements in the picture to the situation that he is discussing. Further analysis reveals the fact, however, that this is not the case. It appears, rather, that instead of using the analogy systematically he has actually allowed his mind to move freely from one idea to another, simply using, here and there, language involved in the analogy in such a way as to give to the reader the semblance of systematic application. There are various considerations that justify this conclusion.

(1) Absence of systematic application is seen in the fact that a striking inconsistency appears in the total picture that is drawn. In v. 6b the Corinthian Christians are represented as the "lump," subject to the corrupting influence of the "leaven." In v. 7a, however, they are no longer the "lump" at all, but are rather the members of the household who are admonished to remove the "old leaven." In v. 7b they are the "lump" once more. Finally, in v. 8 they are again the members of the household, asked to "celebrate the festival" *with* the lump, which now is given the form of the "unleavened bread." This feature in the passage is quite different from the twofold application of the "leaven" and of the "lump." The "leaven" and the "lump" are elements in the analogy itself, and it may be argued that the writer moved from these elements to their (twofold) application. Here, however, it is not an element in the analogy which is applied in a double way to the Corinthian situation. It is precisely the reverse: an element in the Corinthian situation (the body of Christians themselves) is being analogically represented in a double way. The movement of thought is not, as in the case above, from the analogy to the situation, but rather, from the situation to analogies. In other words, there is indicated here not a systematic application of the analogy, but rather, the dominance of an idea concerning the Corinthians to which the language drawn from the analogy is very loosely adapted.

(2) Verses 7 and 8, although using language derived from the picture of leaven in dough, actually are based upon a different picture, the picture of a Jewish family observing a practice of the season of Passover. This practice, commemorating the exodus, when the departing Israelites " took their dough before it was leavened " (Ex. 12:34), was intended to fulfill the Priestly injunction: " Seven days you shall eat unleavened bread; on the first day you shall put away leaven

out of your houses" (Ex. 12:15; compare Ex. 12:19 and 13:7). Hence it included the ritual of searching through the house to find and "cleanse out" any leaven that might be found.[9] That this picture of the Passover observance was in Paul's mind is made certain by his addition in v. 7: "For Christ, our paschal lamb, has been sacrificed." Both in Exodus and in Deuteronomy the command to eat only unleavened bread is closely related to that pertaining to the sacrifice of the Passover animal.[10]

The Greek text of Paul's letter has simply *pascha* ("a passing over"). This does not specify explicitly a lamb, though apparently a lamb was generally offered. The important consideration here, however, is the fact that both the noun and the verb that Paul uses are those which are found together in the above-mentioned passage (in the Septuagint).

It can hardly be doubted that Paul is making the same connection. If this is so, then it is clear that the original picture of leaven working in dough has been superseded by the picture of the Passover ritual. Verse 7a becomes much more intelligible when this is recognized: "Cleanse out the old leaven that you may be fresh dough." These words in reality are unintelligible if they are taken as a development of the original analogy of leaven working in the lump of dough (v. 6b), for in actual practice it is quite impossible to remove the leaven once the fermenting process has begun. It is the new picture alone that gives meaning to the words. It is true, of course, that the two pictures are related, and the second was undoubtedly suggested by the first. The fact remains, however, that the two pictures are essentially different, so much so that v. 7a has meaning in the light of the second but not in the light of the first. This replacement of one picture by the other points clearly to the fact that Paul is not here developing a given analogy, but rather, is adjusting his analogical language to the new (though not unrelated) idea.

(3) The statement that "Christ, our paschal lamb, has been sacrificed" is significant in another way also. Not only

does the reference to the sacrificial animal indicate that there was in Paul's mind the essentially new picture of the Passover ritual; the representation of *Christ* as that animal introduces yet another picture. One may say that Paul here presents an analogy within an analogy. The picture is useful, apparently, because it provides "a reason for the practical summons at the beginning of the verse: ' It is high time for you to purge out the old leaven; for the Lamb is already slain and your house is not yet fully cleansed: you are late! ' " [11] In introducing this picture, Paul shows how widely his thought was ranging beyond the narrow limits of the original picture.

(4) Finally, in v. 8 there are words that show that Paul once more is not developing the application of the original analogy, but, instead, is introducing yet another picture, though still continuing to employ language derived from the first picture: " Let us, therefore, *celebrate the festival.* . . ." Although some interpreters regard the apostle's expression here (*eortazōmen*) as an allusion to the Passover observance,[12] Moffatt contends that Paul is using the " festival metaphor " as it was familiar in Greek circles. He produces considerable evidence to show that the living of the good life was likened to the keeping of true festival by numerous persons in the Greek world, noting that the " Corinthians themselves in days gone by had once praised the Athenians for their indefatigable temper, by declaring, ' they consider doing their duty to be their sole festival.' " [13] Paul's admonition to them — that they " celebrate the festival, . . . with the unleavened bread of sincerity and truth " — certainly suggests this common figurative use of " festival," whether or not he happened to be acquainted with the particular case just mentioned.

Thus there emerges from this examination of these three verses considerable evidence that Paul uses his analogical material with much freedom and looseness. He moves rapidly from one idea to another and from one analogy to another. Even his continued use of language drawn from the original analogy (as in v. 7 and again in v. 8) does not mean that that analogy is being given further application, for, as in v. 7, especially, that which is said is actually inconsistent with the original picture. All of this suggests that in his writing, Paul's thought moved rapidly from one idea to another, as one idea suggested another. Certainly it cannot be said here that he gives evidence of any serious attempt to develop or apply fully the various elements involved in any one of the pictures here drawn in such rapid succession. Nothing is said, for example, as to the fact that leaven may also serve a useful purpose in the dough. No application is made of the fact that the Passover ritual is one of decidedly limited practice, during a very few days in the year. No careful application is made of the picture of the " paschal lamb," nor of the "festival" metaphor. All these pictures are introduced, not because each is intended to indicate in any detail what the Pauline thought is, but rather, simply because they involved *some* elements that are relevant to the issue under consideration.

I CORINTHIANS 9:4-14

In I Cor. 9:4-14, Paul offers a series of analogies in order to strengthen his contention that he and Barnabas [1] possess certain rights as apostles. The emphasis is especially on the right to expect provision for their physical needs. In a series of three questions, first of all (v. 7), there is reference to the fact that (1) the man in military service receives his supplies, (2) the man who plants a vineyard eats from its fruit, and (3) the man who tends a flock partakes of the milk from the flock.[2] Here the analogies are not merely illustrative. They are obviously intended to constitute an argument: what is true in these areas of activity ought also be true for Paul (and Barnabas). To strengthen his argument further Paul then appeals to the "law of Moses" (v. 9), quoting Deut. 25:4: "You shall not muzzle an ox when it treads out the grain." In presenting this quotation the apostle not only brings to his support the authority of Scripture; he also introduces a further analogy, that of (4) the workmen on the farm where grain is raised, workmen who plow or thresh (v. 10), or who, by implication, sow or reap (v. 11).[3] Superficially also there is suggested the analogy of the ox, conveying the idea that just as the ox is not to be denied the right to eat from the grain being threshed, so the apostles should not be denied their provisions. The total context, however, indicates that this is not precisely Paul's meaning, for, as he shows in vs. 10 and 11, he regarded the quotation as having, in reality, little, if anything, to do with oxen: " It was written for our sake." Paul, in other words, looked upon the Deuteronomic prohibition as having allegorical rather than literal significance, primarily if not exclusively.

The thought is not entirely clear. Paul's Greek word, *pantōs* (v. 10), can mean either "altogether" ("entirely") or "certainly" ("surely"). He can be saying, therefore, either that the quotation is to be understood "entirely" (exclusively) allegorically, or that it "surely" is to be given an allegorical meaning (as well as a literal one). There is ambiguity also in the preceding question: "Is it for oxen that God is concerned?" If an unqualified negative answer is implied, then it must be true that for him "the literal sense of the injunction had no significance at all."[4] Robertson and Plummer, on the other hand, contend that Paul "does not mean that God has no care for the brutes. . . . Nor does he mean that in forbidding the muzzling God was not thinking of the oxen at all. He means that the prohibition had a higher significance, in comparison with which the literal purport of it was of small moment."[5] Even if the latter view should be accepted, the fact still remains that Paul is *here* concerned with the allegorical meaning of the quotation.[6]

Since it is only the allegorical meaning with which Paul is now concerned, then his thought in this context concerns, not the (literal) picture of the oxen, but rather, the picture of the plowman and the thresher which it represents: "Because the plowman should plow in hope and the thresher thresh in hope of a share in the crop" (v. 10).[7]

A further appeal to Scripture (and to Jesus) is seen in vs. 13 and 14, where, again, another (final) analogy is involved: (5) just as those who serve at the temple receive a share of that which is offered,[8] so also "those who proclaim the gospel should get their living by the gospel," as Jesus himself had ordained.[9]

It is perfectly clear that each of these analogies is relevant to the subject under discussion insofar as in each there is found a common idea: for one who is engaged in an activity there is the expectation that physical needs will be supplied. A further question, however, must be raised: is it intended that the pictures thus introduced should be applied in further respects or in greater detail?

It is sometimes suggested that the first three pictures of men who serve (the soldier, the planter of a vineyard, the shepherd) "are analogous to the Christian minister, who wages war upon evil, plants churches, and is a shepherd to congregations." [10] Although this kind of application might be possible, there is no hint in the text that it was intended by Paul. It is true that elsewhere he does employ metaphorically the figure of the soldier and that of warfare, but nowhere is the soldier representative of the Christian minister "who wages war upon evil."

His word here (*strateuetai*, "serves as a soldier") appears (in different forms) also in II Cor. 10:3 f., but there the warfare that is mentioned seems to be that which characterizes the Christian life,[11] and is not related specifically to that of the Christian minister. Furthermore, the warfare is directed, not against evil as such, but rather, against those "arguments" or "imaginations" (KJV) or "theories" with which men "fortify themselves against God." [12] And where Paul uses other terms suggesting military life he never does so in a context that makes that military life a metaphor for the Christian leader's warfare against evil.[13]

Earlier in this letter (I Cor. 3:6-8), it is true, Paul refers to himself as a Christian leader who "plants." Nowhere else, on the other hand, does he employ the (otherwise well-known) metaphor of the shepherd to represent the apostolic care of the Christian congregations.

The word *poimainō* (to "tend a flock") is not used at all by
Paul outside the passage now under consideration (I Cor. 9:7).
The same is true for *poimnē* ("flock"). Never does he use *poimēn*
("shepherd"). Only once (Rom. 8:36) does *probata* ("sheep")
appear; there it is given metaphorical significance, it is true, but
it is introduced in a quotation (Ps. 44:22) and in a context that
has nothing to do with the relationship between pastor and people.

Altogether, therefore, of the first three metaphors found
here only the figure of the one who plants is used elsewhere by Paul in such a way as to suggest that it represents
a corresponding form of activity on the part of the apostles.
Hence it seems unlikely that they were chosen because they
suggested the different kinds of labor analogous to those of
the Christian minister.

If a reason is to be sought for the selection of this particular combination of figures, a more likely explanation may be
offered, namely, that Old Testament material may have suggested it. Deuteronomy 20:6 [14] reads, "And what man is
there that has planted a vineyard and has not enjoyed its
fruit?" Several extremely interesting facts pertain to this
quotation. Not only (in the Septuagint) are the verb and the
direct object (forms of *phuteuō* and *ampelōn*) the same as
those found in I Cor. 9:7. Especially significant is the fact
that in both places the form of expression is a question, both
introduced by *tis*. Even more striking is the further fact
that immediately preceding the reference to the man planting the vineyard are words pertaining to a right that a soldier
should have — once more in the form of a question beginning
with *tis* — just as with Paul. It is true that the soldier's right
in Deut. 20:5 is that he be allowed to dedicate the new
house that he has built rather than have his needs met while
in the army, but this difference does not reduce the impression, created by the more numerous points of similarity, that
Paul's wording may have been suggested by the Deuteronomic material. Since the verse concerning the man planting the vineyard served Paul's purpose admirably, the larger
Deuteronomic context may very well have suggested the
analogy of the soldier.

Proverbs, ch. 27, may also be relevant here. Proverbs 27:18 reads, according to the Septuagint, " He who plants a fig tree will eat its fruit." Here again is a verse that could, at least, have served the apostle's purpose. The first verb, once more, is a form of *phuteuō* (" plants "); and the second, *phagetai* (" will eat "), is a form of the second verb that Paul uses (*esthiei*) in his corresponding sentence. Of special interest is the fact that later in Prov., ch. 27 (vs. 26 and 27), there appear these words: " The lambs will provide your clothing, and the goats the price of a field; there will be enough goats' milk for your food [literally, " life "]." Hence, in this chapter, a reference to one who plants is followed by the mention of those who tend flocks, just as in the case of I Cor. 9:7. In both cases the idea of receiving a return from the work corresponds closely to the Pauline emphasis. The original purpose in Prov. 27:23-27 was apparently to recommend the advantages of life in the country, which, of course, is different from that of Paul. Also, the Septuagint word rendered " milk " is not the same as the term used by Paul. On the other hand, the similarities are such as to suggest at least the possibility that the apostle was influenced by this Old Testament material.

Combining these features observed in connection with Deut., ch. 20, and Prov., ch. 27, similarities with I Cor. 9:7 are so numerous as to suggest that they can hardly be accidental. And since these two passages, taken together, involve precisely the figures of the soldier, the one who plants, and the shepherd, just as Paul introduces them, it seems likely that Paul's choice of metaphors may well have been influenced by those passages. This conclusion is decidedly preferable to the idea that Paul chose them because he saw in the work of each of them that which was analogous to the various activities of the Christian leader.

With all the foregoing considerations taken into account, there is little reason to believe that Paul intended significance to be attached to that element in the analogies which concerned the *type* of work done by each of the figures. All three were chosen for the sake of the major point only.

Similarly, in the fourth analogy, that of the workmen on the farm, only the one idea seems to have relevance. There is no clear indication that specific details in the picture are intended to be applied to the Corinthian situation. In I Cor. 9:11, it is true, the reference to the sowing of "spiritual good" (literally, "spiritual things") suggests the kind of seed which a workman may scatter, and the mention of the reaping of "material benefits" (literally, "things pertaining to the flesh") suggests the kind of crop which is gathered. It is obvious, however, that the words in this verse cannot involve a development or application of the idea of seed and crop, for in agriculture seed and crop are of the same kind.[15] Hence the reference to the sowing of "*spiritual* good" followed by the reference to the reaping of "*material* benefits" shows that the thought here is not to be construed as involving further application of details in the analogy, but only as the use of language suggested by the analogy.

It is also unlikely that the *acts* of plowing, threshing, sowing, and reaping (vs. 10 f.) are intended to have significance in this context. If such significance *were* intended, the order of these acts would be different; the threshing should then appear in fourth place rather than second.

As to the separate acts, Paul nowhere shows that he was inclined to use the idea of plowing analogically, though such usage was not uncommon.[16] Since this is also true of the idea of threshing, there is little reason for believing that here the threshing "may represent the separation of the true converts from the rest."[17] Of course threshing was a common metaphor in the Old Testament (II Kings 13:7; Isa. 28:27 f.; 41:15 f.; Jer. 15:7; 51:33; Amos 1:3; Micah 4:12 f.), and it came to be used to describe the final separation of the good and the evil (Matt. 3:12; Luke 3:17). Only in I Cor. 9:9 f., however, does Paul use the verb *aloaō* ("to thresh"). Nowhere does he use *ptuon* ("winnowing fork" or "fan") or any of the other terms that might suggest threshing, such as *achuron* ("chaff"). While all of this does not prove that Paul *could not* have intended significance to be attached to the picture of threshing here, it *does* mean that he nowhere gives any evidence to support the claim. The references to plowing and threshing, therefore, are undoubtedly to be understood simply as providing examples of the kinds of labor performed by the workmen on the farm, kinds of labor from which some return may be expected. No further analogical significance seems to be involved in the mention of these acts.

The pictures suggested by "sown" and "reap" obviously do have analogical significance (v. 11). Since the pictures themselves are not directly introduced, but only presupposed in the application, however, it is probable that Paul is here merely using common forms of expression to mean "acting" and "receiving in return." Elsewhere (II Cor. 9:6; Gal. 6:7 f.) he uses them in this manner wholly apart from any reference to the larger picture of workmen on a farm. Although the *words* may have been *suggested* here by the larger picture, the acts of sowing and reaping cannot be regarded as having been introduced as part of the *development* of the larger picture. If conscious development and application of the analogy of the workmen on the farm had been involved, then, as already suggested, the order of the acts would not have been given as they are here: plowing, threshing, sowing, and reaping.

As to (5) the picture of "those who are employed in the temple service" (I Cor. 9:13), once again it appears to be unlikely that analogical significance extends beyond the idea that just as those who minister in the temple "get their food from the temple," so also the apostles have a claim to their provisions. It is not impossible, perhaps, that a further point *might* have been in Paul's mind: just as those who serve in the temple are priests, so also we are priests. It is true that in Rom. 15:16 the apostle speaks of his ministry in terms of priesthood. But if this thought *had* been in Paul's mind here, it is strange that he did not give it explicit expression, for it would have served admirably to strengthen his claim upon provisions for sustenance: we, as priests like them, should also get our living from our service! The absence of any such assertion suggests that at this point he attaches no more analogical significance to the service of those who are employed in the temple than he has attached to the work of the soldier, the planter of the vineyard, the shepherd, or the workmen on the farm.

It appears, therefore, that all five of the pictures introduced in I Cor. 9:4-14 are employed simply for the sake of the one idea that they have in common: those who labor should receive their living from that labor. In no case is there evidence that further elements involved in the pictures are intended to have relevance or significance.

I CORINTHIANS 9:24-27

In these few verses Paul draws upon the field of sports for analogical material. In view of the proximity of Corinth to scenes of athletic contests and games it was perhaps particularly appropriate for him to do this in a letter sent to the church there, although he does the same in other letters as well.[1]

The larger context may be noted briefly. In dealing with the problem of the eating of meat that had been offered to idols, Paul had set forth the principle that while the eating of such meat in itself was not wrong, yet it was better that it be avoided if it threatened the spiritual well-being of a fellow Christian (ch. 8). This meant that although one had a right to eat the meat, it was better, upon occasion at least, to forego that right for the sake of others. In ch. 9, Paul develops this theme, showing how he himself has attempted to abide by this principle. He and Barnabas, for example, had a right to their maintenance as a return for their labor,[2] but this right was not claimed; in fact, it was purposely rejected for the sake of a greater good (ch. 9:12b-18). As he continues (vs. 19-23), he centers further attention upon the purpose of this renunciation of rights. It was "that I might win the more" (v. 19) — "that I might by all means save some" (v. 22). Thus he develops the principle established in ch. 8.

There is also involved another purpose, however: rights are relinquished not only for the sake of others, but also for one's own ultimate well-being. This is touched upon in vs. 15-18; but it is given renewed emphasis in v. 23: "I do it all for the sake of the gospel, that I may share in its blessings." [3]

It is at this point that the analogies of the race and the boxing match are employed. Through them Paul presses further the idea just expressed. *In effect* he says: As I do for the sake of the gospel — that I may share in its blessings — so also ought you do. The reward is beyond compare. It is of such value that self-control and self-discipline (including, in the light of the total context, the renunciation of certain rights) ought certainly be exercised in order to receive it. As for me, this is what I attempt to do.

There may now be considered this question: How does Paul use his analogical material in the saying of this?

The apostle employs primarily here the picture of those who run in a race (literally, "in a stadium"), observing first of all, that, when they all run, "one" receives the prize awarded to the victor. It is clearly apparent that Paul does not intend the picture to be applied in all respects. Even the fact that is explicitly mentioned, that "only one receives the prize," can have no relevance here, for the reward or prize about which Paul is really concerned is not thought by him to be given only to "one."

The apostle recognized that those who achieved their goal might be few (see I Cor. 10:5; compare Matt. 22:14). It would be absurd, however, to suppose that he thought the "imperishable [wreath]" was to be received by only one Christian. The Lord "bestows his riches upon all who call upon him. For, 'every one who calls upon the name of the Lord will be saved'" (Rom. 10:12 f.). The suggestion has been made that this element in the picture can be made applicable by making "one" represent the "one body" (the church), "and there is a prize for each of its members." [4] There is nothing in the text, however, which even hints that this was in the apostle's mind.

The application, as Paul expresses it, is this: "So run that you may obtain it" (or, "lay hold of it"), referring, of

course, to the "prize," which is salvation. Here the relationship between the analogy (as it is presented) and its application can be seen only as one "reads between the lines," as
Lietzmann suggests: [5] as all who run in a race devote their
full energy to that running (this is implied, though not expressed) in the hope of being the "one" who "receives the
prize," the same should be true of the Christians as they
pursue their course. The noteworthy feature here is that the
element in the picture which does have relevance is not specifically mentioned, while the element which *is* noted ("only
one receives the prize") is not applicable at all!

It is also true that a further idea associated with the picture cannot be intended to have significance for the Pauline
thought. As is brought out by the Revised Standard Version ("all the runners compete"), an inevitable factor in a
race is that of competition. The very nature of the event, including the awarding of the prize, presupposes the idea of
rivalry. It is quite unthinkable that Paul should intend this
idea to be given application. In the total discussion of which
this is but a part he has been emphasizing the need for placing the well-being of others above one's own rights.[6] He
hopes that he *and* the Corinthians may receive "an imperishable [wreath]" (*hēmeis*, "we," v. 25), but he has turned
to this subject only after he has dealt much more extensively
with the salvation of *others*. He certainly thinks of his own
salvation as that which he, as a "joint partner" (*sunkoinō-
nos*), *shares* with others (v. 23). Thus, the element of competition in the picture is not only irrelevant; it is entirely inappropriate.[7]

In v. 25a, Paul's words are literally, "Everyone who is
contending exercises self-control in all things." The allusion
is clearly to the fact that while in training the athletes limited themselves strictly in diet and in other matters. The
general idea expressed here is quite relevant, for not only in
these verses but also in the larger context there is advocated
for the Christian the practice of self-control or self-restraint
(including the giving up of some things which in themselves,

in ordinary circumstances, were acceptable). Although the general idea is relevant, however, there is one detail that is not appropriate. In the case of the athlete the self-control or self-restraint is normally understood as exercised during the period of preparation and training rather than during the running of the race. In Paul's *use* of the picture it is the race itself — the living of the Christian life — with which the self-control is associated. The apostle has thus shaped the analogy to fit the subject under discussion. His meaning cannot be derived accurately from an analysis of all details in the analogy.

In v. 25b reference is made to the " wreath " (or " crown " — " that which encircles ") given to the successful runner. Here the picture is introduced for the purpose of contrast. The intended meaning may be expressed thus: the runners in the games race in the hope of receiving an award that is " perishable " or destructible; [8] we, however, are concerned about an award that is not corruptible.[9] Since the analogy itself does not suggest the value of one kind of wreath as over against another, the sentence cannot be understood as expressing an actual application of an element in the analogy. Rather, it represents the assertion of a Pauline conviction to which an element in the analogy has been adapted.

The picture of the runner is introduced again in v. 26a: " I do not run aimlessly." The meaning is generally understood to be: just as the one who races directs his course steadily toward the finish line, so also Paul runs with singleness of purpose — " not uncertainly " (*ouk adēlōs*) — toward his goal.[10] This, it must be noted, seems to create a change in the picture. Whereas earlier it was the " prize " (v. 24) — the " wreath " (v. 25) — that represented the object of his endeavor, now it is suddenly, at least by implication, the finish line. Once again there is observed, therefore, an adaptation of the total picture to the thought being expressed, not a systematic application of the picture itself.

If the above interpretation of v. 26a is accepted, then the words " I do not box as one beating the air " (v. 26b) are apparently intended to convey essentially the same meaning. In the Greek the constructions are closely parallel.

V. 26a: *houtōs trechō hōs ouk adēlōs*
V. 26b: *houtōs pukteuō hōs ouk aera derōn*

The thought, therefore, must be: just as the boxer does not beat the air at random, but directs his attack "with sure aim and effect,"[11] so also Paul aims steadily at the object of his attention and concern. The fact that he can thus shift suddenly from the picture of the runner to that of the boxer indicates that the idea to be conveyed, rather than an analogy itself, is determinative for his progression of thought.

To the present writer this line of interpretation for v. 26 does not sufficiently take account of the total context. Throughout much of chs. 8 and 9, Paul has been emphasizing the renunciation of the rights of the individual for the sake of a greater good. In the more immediate context (ch. 9:25a) he centers attention upon the idea of "self-control," which also involves the idea of limitations imposed upon oneself for the sake of a given end. In v. 25b he turns briefly to the importance of that end. Is not v. 26 best understood if interpreted in the light of v. 25a: "Every athlete exercises self-control in all things"? In v. 26, Paul seems to be saying in effect: Similarly, I do not run about hither and yon in an uncontrolled or undisciplined way, but rather, in a manner that serves the end or purpose at hand. I do not box as one who thrashes about in my rightful freedom, but I control my actions in a manner that best contributes to the victory that I hope to achieve. Taken thus the words involve, it is true, the idea of the goal at which he aims, but the central emphasis is upon the idea of disciplined action. In this way it is consistent with the main purpose of the entire section of the letter. It is also consistent with v. 25a. In fact, it applies to himself the idea of self-control which is expressed there. This interpretation, furthermore, contributes to a clearer understanding of v. 27a, as will be seen below.

Insofar as the characteristics of the Pauline use of analogy

are concerned, both of these interpretations point to the
same conclusions. Since the idea of goal or purpose is involved also in the view just presented (though only sec-
ondarily), it is still true that Paul has been adapting his pictures to his ideas rather than developing and applying the
pictures systematically. Furthermore, although v. 26a may
now be considered as an application to himself of the picture (of self-control) in v. 25, there remains also the distor-
tion of the picture to suit the idea, since (see above, on
v. 25) the self-control and self-restraint of the athlete is normally associated with the period of training rather than with
the race itself.

The language of pugilism is retained in v. 27: " But I pommel my body and subdue it,[12] lest after preaching to others
I myself should be disqualified." The wording here, too,
lends itself to different interpretations: (1) It is often assumed that the picture of the boxing contest is here intended.
Since the word rendered "but" (*alla*) can suggest a contrast, the first clause here may be combined with the preceding words, giving the meaning: I am "no air-smiter,"[13] but
I "beat and bruise my body."[14] If this represents correctly
the Pauline meaning, then it is true that the picture of the
pugilist striking blows is carried from v. 26 into v. 27. In this
case, however, the picture is not correctly drawn, for the
pugilist does not direct his blows against his own body. If
this *is* the intended meaning, therefore, it can only be said
that Paul is not engaged here in applying further his analogy, but, instead, is using only the idea of striking blows.
Beyond this the picture is actually distorted in the service of
his own thought. (2) To the present writer a different interpretation is to be preferred. It is to be granted that *alla*
(" but ") indicates a contrast. It seems likely, however, that
the intended contrast is not that which is mentioned above.
The words " I pommel my body " may stand in opposition,
not to the picture of " one beating the air," but rather, to the
common *idea* expressed in both parts of v. 26. The thought
may be phrased in this way: I do not run or box in an un-

controlled or undisciplined manner. To the contrary! I exercise the most severe discipline upon myself; [15] I " subdue " myself (that is, I treat myself " to stern and rigid discipline ").[16] It is true that Paul specifies " my body " (*to sōma*) as the object of treatment. And in the light of the pugilistic picture there is immediately suggested the physical body. Often, however, the apostle uses the term " body " to mean the " self," the " person as a whole," [17] so that here he can be saying, " I control *myself* with stern treatment." In view of the fact that Paul otherwise uses his analogies quite loosely in this section, it seems more likely that he is, in v. 27, thus setting his discipline of *himself* in contrast to the idea of an absence of such discipline mentioned in the preceding verse.[18] Thus what he says is in line with the purpose of the entire context. This means, insofar as analogical usage is concerned, that he employs, in v. 27a, language perhaps suggested by the picture of the pugilist, but his meaning is not to be found primarily in that picture.

The closing words here — " lest after preaching to others I myself should be disqualified " — allude once more to the purpose in the light of which he determines his own conduct. He acts as he does lest he " not stand the test " — " not be approved." [19] It has been proposed that this clause may involve still further elements taken from the public games. When Paul refers to " preaching " to others, his word *kēruxas* suggests the *kērux*, the " herald," at the games, who announced the various contests and called the participants to the competitions.[20] If the figure of such a herald was in Paul's mind, the picture is not drawn very accurately, for ordinarily, at least, the herald was not also one of the competitors. This would therefore be another case of the free adaptation of the analogy to suit the apostle's own thought.

Finally, the use of the term *adokimos* (" disqualified ") may, or may not, have been influenced by the picture of the games. If it was, then, as applied by Paul to himself, the word must represent disqualification insofar as receiving the award is concerned. It can hardly be used with reference to the right to participate in the contest, for, with Paul, the contest is already in progress.

The results of the examination of this passage may now be summarized:

A. Throughout this section there are but few elements in the analogical usage which are relevant and which can be applied without qualification. One such element is clear: the athlete " exercises self-control in all things "; so also self-restraint or self-discipline is desirable — and necessary — for Christians. Along with this may be listed the idea that participants in a race devote their full energy to their running, although this is only implied; so also the Christians are admonished to " run."

B. There are several elements in the pictures which have some relevance, *but only in a limited way:* (1) The notion of the athlete's self-control or self-restraint is applied (vs. 25a and 26), especially if the present writer's interpretation of v. 26 is correct; but the fact that this is associated with the period of preparation or training of the athlete is not adaptable to the Pauline idea. (2) A wreath may properly represent the Christian's award, but Paul actually emphasizes *contrast* here, rather than likeness. (3) The striking of blows by the boxer may suggest a picture of disciplined action, but the boxer does not aim his blows at himself. (4) The herald at the games may (possibly) correspond to Paul as preacher, but the herald is himself not normally a competitor also. Insofar as all of these pictures must be somewhat distorted in order to make them applicable, it is evident that Paul has not endeavored to apply them carefully or systematically to the considerations under discussion. The analogies themselves do not provide a basis for a clear understanding of his thought.

C. Two aspects of the pictures are not only irrelevant, but are actually such as would suggest, if applied, ideas quite contrary to those which Paul is known to hold. One of these is that " only one receives the prize." The other involves the element of competition. As has been shown, neither of these ideas is consistent with Paul's thought.

In the treatment of this passage attention has been given to the use of pictures taken from the field of sports. These pictures provide much of the language that Paul employs. It should be noted that in vs. 26 and 27 he uses this analogical language with reference to himself rather than to the Christian whom he is addressing. It is possible to regard this as a case where Paul is " preaching to himself." [21] It seems more likely, however, that the apostle is here adding analogy to analogy. That is, he uses analogical language taken from the athletic contests in order to speak about himself. *In addition to this* he uses his own conduct or endeavor as representing the kind of conduct or endeavor which he is urging upon the Corinthians.[22] In a sense this in itself is a form of analogical usage. This type of usage is not being considered at length, since the correspondence between analogy (himself) and others obviously would reflect the common humanity that he shared with them and would therefore be complete.

I Corinthians 12:12-30

The most extensive use of an analogy by Paul is that which is found in I Cor. 12:12-30, where the apostle employs the picture of the human body. Insofar as this picture provides the language for the larger part of this material it may be said that it dominates the entire section of the discussion of which it is a part.[1] This discussion concerns spiritual gifts (chs. 12 to 14). Although the exact nature of the situation at Corinth, in this regard, is not very clear, Paul's words seem to indicate a condition in which some members of the community were attaching particular and undue significance to the " gift " of speaking in " tongues." [2] Apparently those who possessed this gift were assuming an attitude of superiority over those who did not. Conversely, those who did not possess the gift were inclined to feel that they lacked something that they ought to have if they were to share fully in the Christian life and experience. Paul's purpose in writing was, in part, to convince the Corinthian community that the various Christians, regardless of the gifts that individually might be theirs, must understand the proper place and function of these gifts both in relationship to the larger Christian community and also in relationship to one another. It is in connection with this objective that he introduces the analogy of the human body. The analogy is employed, therefore, (1) to reinforce the idea of unity in diversity, and (2) to indicate the proper relationship between the various factors in the diversity.

(1) *The idea of unity in diversity* is stated from both sides, so to speak. From the standpoint of the body, it is " one " yet it " has many members " (v. 12a); and again, " the body does not consist of one member but of many " (v. 14). From the standpoint of the members, " all the members of the body, though many, are one body " (v. 12b); and also again, " there are many parts,[3] yet one body " (v. 20). The application is stated both at the beginning (" so it is with Christ," v. 12c) and also near the end (" Now you are the body of Christ and individually members of it," v. 27).

The words in v. 12c, " so it is with Christ," do not in themselves express this application directly, for it is not Christ as the historical Jesus that Paul is likening to the human body. One must presuppose the thought that is stated only later (v. 27): " Now you are the body of Christ." In the light of this the apostle's meaning must be: so also the various members of the Christian community constitute a unified body — the body of Christ.[4] In reality more than *likeness* is involved here, for there is a sense in which the Christians *are* the body of Christ. " For Paul it is no simile but a spiritual reality." [5] Or, in Lietzmann's terms, " For Paul this is not merely a comparison but rather a mystical truth." [6] The Christian community, from this point of view, is not *like* a body; it *is* a body. This does not alter the fact, however, that Paul nevertheless draws a comparison between the two (actual) bodies — the human body and the body of Christ. It may be noted that the thought is similar to that which is expressed in I Cor. 6:15; 10:16 f.; Rom. 12:4 f.[7]

In I Cor. 12:15-20 the idea of unity in diversity is developed in two ways: (*a*) It is argued that *since there is unity in diversity, therefore each element in the diversity belongs to the unity:* the foot is still a part of the body (literally, " is of the body "), though it is not a hand; and the same is true of the ear, though it is not an eye (vs. 15 and 16).

The thought in vs. 15 and 16 is probably: the *condition* of being a foot or an ear instead of a hand or an eye does not make either member any less a part of the body. Less likely is the meaning: the " discontented grumbling " of the foot or the ear does not make either member any less a part of the body. Robertson and Plummer in expressing this view add: " In each case it is the inferior limb which grumbles, the hand being of more value than the foot, and the eye than the ear." [8] There is nothing to indicate, however, that Paul placed such value judgments on these members of the body. That he would have done so is unlikely in view of v. 17, where seeing (" eye ") and hearing are given parallel positions.[9] It is true that in vs. 22 and 23 Paul attaches to some (unnamed) parts of the body the adjectives *asthenestera* (" weaker "), *atimotera* (" less honorable "), and *aschēmona* (" uncomely " or " unpresentable "). It is important to observe, however, that there he uses forms of the verb *dokeō* (to " seem," or to " suppose ") in connection with each of the first two of these adjectives, and the construction is such that the force of the second usage of the verb should be carried over to the third adjective. (Compare the use of *dokeō* in Gal. 2:6.) Thus Paul designates some members of the body as only " reputed to be " or " supposed to be " on some lower level.

In the same way, Paul implies, no individual in the Christian community is any less a part of the whole because his function is different from that of someone else, or because the " manifestation of the Spirit " vouchsafed him is different from that of another (see vs. 7-11). The more specific application appears in the words that follow the restatement of the general application (v. 27). There it is stated (v. 28) that " God has appointed *in the church* " (the " body," the unity) a variety of offices or gifts, and a list is given. Though these may differ, they all, like the members of the body mentioned in vs. 15 and 16, " belong to the body," the church.

Verses 17-20 continue the development of the idea of unity in diversity. Along with the claim that the various elements in the diversity belong to the unity, there is the further thought (*b*) that *the unity (the body) needs or requires the diversity*. If the whole body were only an eye or an ear, then other (presumably necessary) bodily senses would be lacking (v. 17). But this really means that if the whole were only a single member, then the body *as a body* would not exist (v. 19), for God himself chose to create [10] the body as a body in which the various *members* had their appointed place (v. 18). The relevance of this for the Corinthian situation is obvious, though the actual stating of the application is postponed to vs. 29 and 30. Just as the "whole body" requires the various members (vs. 17-20), so also the "body of Christ," the church, needs the different offices and functions that God has appointed for it. There is a particularly close parallel between v. 17, on the one hand, and vs. 29 and 30, on the other. The questions in v. 17 might well be rephrased: "Is the whole body an eye? Is the whole body an ear?" The answer, of course, is "No." Fundamentally the same kind of question is found in vs. 29 and 30: "Are all apostles? Are all prophets? . . ." That is, "Is the whole body of Christ made up of apostles only, of prophets only . . . ?" The (implied) answer here, too, is "No." The parallel nature of the thought is made all the more clear by the fact that in both places the expression of that thought is in the form of questions, whether such identity of form was the result of conscious intent or not. In any case, the application is made: That which is true of the human body is true in the Christian community. In *both* there is needed diversity for the existence and the full functioning of the body.

(2) *The relationship between the various factors in the diversity* is discussed in vs. 21-26. Here, again, the idea of need is involved. But whereas in the previous statements it was the need of the various members *by the body* that was emphasized, now it is the need of one member *for another member:* the eye needs the hand; the head needs the feet

(v. 21). Even those (unnamed) parts of the body which
"seem" to be inferior are necessary (v. 22).

Paul's word here, *asthenestera*, is generally translated as
"weaker" (RSV) or as "more feeble." In view of the larger
context, however, "inferior" seems better. Compare the use (v.
24) of *husteroumenoi*, where the reference is to that which is
"inferior," or which is "lacking" in some respect. Paul uses
esthenēkamen (a verb form of *asthenēs*) in this sense in II Cor.
11:21a; there again "weak" is often given in translation (KJV,
RSV, American Translation), but the context is such as to indicate that "inferior" is meant (see especially the immediately following words, II Cor. 11:21b-23).

I Corinthians 12:23 may be taken as an explanation of the reference to the parts that seem to be inferior. Instead of the "and"
at the beginning of v. 23 one may read "namely," or "for example." [11]

Although we may "think" (or "suppose") some members
to be "less honorable" or "unpresentable," we actually ele-
vate them to a position no less honorable or presentable by
giving them special attention (vs. 23 and 24a),[12] so that there
may be no (basis for) "discord" or dissension among the
members, but rather, that there may be equal ("the same")
attention and concern of one for another (v. 25). In reality
two ideas are thus blended: (*a*) the members of the body
need each other, and (*b*) those members which are "supposed" to be inferior or lacking in some way are given (by
the special attention granted them) an honorable position
among the others. (Although Paul does not designate the
latter members, it is not difficult to guess some, at least, of
those which he must have had in mind. And it is certainly
true that some parts of the body which are treated with the
greatest "modesty" or "seemliness" [*euschēmosunēn*, v. 23]
are those parts which perform particularly essential functions.) One final point is then added by Paul regarding the
relationship between the various factors in the diversity:
(*c*) the experiences of each one affect all the others (v. 26).
The application of these points is not spelled out, so to

speak, but the relevance of each is obvious. (*a*) The " members " of the Christian community exist in a state of mutual dependence. The fact that some of them possess a particular spiritual gift or serve a particular function does not justify an attitude of exclusiveness on their part toward those who possess a different gift or who serve a different function, since each needs the others. (*b*) Even those who might be regarded as occupying an inferior position should be treated with equal respect, for God has invested them with such " honor " that they are not, in fact, inferior. Thus there should be no " discord " or rivalry. (*c*) In the Christian community each shares the experiences of the others. In all of this section (vs. 21-26) the words are directed, apparently, at those who were taking undue pride in their own gifts, assuming an attitude of superiority — if not more than this — toward those whose activity in the church was different from theirs.

Thus far there has been considered the way in which Paul has used certain aspects of the picture of the human body in order to reinforce the ideas that he wished to impress upon the Corinthian community. Attention may now be given to some further facts that this usage discloses.

Perhaps the most important point to be noted is this: although the picture of the human body is retained and used throughout most of this section of the material, Paul shows by what he says that it is his thought regarding the Corinthian situation which determines his use of the picture; it is not the picture itself that provides the important key to an understanding of his thought. This may be seen in two ways: (1) There are numerous aspects of his presentation which can hardly have been suggested by the picture but which *are* intelligible if understood as inspired by the circumstances at Corinth. (2) There are elements in the picture which are not developed or applied. These two points may now be treated.

(1) There are numerous evidences of the influence of the situation upon the use of the analogy: (*a*) The inclusion of the sentence (v. 13) found immediately after the initial analogical statement (v. 12) shows that it was something other than the picture of the human body which occupied the central position in Paul's mind, for the content of the sentence seems to have no relationship to the picture of the physical body: " For by one Spirit we were all baptized into one body — Jews or Greeks, slaves or free — and all were made to drink of one Spirit." Certainly the idea of being baptized into one body has no parallel in the picture.

Of course the term " body " is used. It does not seem to have analogical significance here, however, since for Paul (as seen above) the Christian community is not only *like* a body: it *is* a body; and it is in this sense that the word is employed here.

It might be suggested, it is true, that a parallel can be drawn between v. 18 and v. 13: as God has arranged the members of the physical body into a unity (v. 18), so also he has, through his Spirit, " baptized [all] into one body " (v. 13). To use v. 18 in this way, however, is to do violence to it. Not only is it too far removed from v. 13 to suggest an intended relationship, but (more important) v. 18, *in its context*, emphasizes the fact of diversity (and the need for diversity) rather than the fact of unity. Thus the parallel cannot be drawn, for in v. 13 it is the fact of unity which is stressed.

It is solely the idea of the Christian community as the body of Christ which could have elicited the statement found in v. 13. It is included, apparently, as an explanation as to how or why *this* unity in diversity came to be.

(*b*) Reflection upon the physical body would hardly suggest even the possibility that one member or another might not " belong to the body." The fact of such belonging is too obvious to allow questioning. Such a suggestion, therefore, as found in vs. 15 and 16, must have arisen from the Corinthian situation, in which some persons apparently wondered if they were participating fully in the Christian life, since they did not share in the gift of " tongues." [13] Similarly, the picture of the human body would itself hardly suggest either the thought that the " whole body " might consist of only one member (v. 17) or the notion that one member might exist without others (v. 21). What is said here appears, again, to have been suggested by the circumstances at Corinth. In these verses Paul seems to have had in mind those who were attaching undue — or even exclusive — importance to the gifts that they claimed.

(c) The idea that " there may be no discord in the body " (v. 25) must definitely have been suggested by the issue under consideration rather than by the picture that provides much of the language, for in the human body discord or rivalry simply does not exist. Inner discord or conflict may occur, as Paul elsewhere shows, especially in Rom. 7:13-25. And the apostle refers to the " members " of the body in his discussion of such conflict (Rom. 7:23). It is clear from the Romans context, however, that this discord is quite different from that which is mentioned in I Cor. 12:25, for in Romans it does not involve a conflict or rivalry between different members of the physical body. Such discord simply does not occur. Paul must have been led to speak of it only because the state of affairs at Corinth suggested the idea.

It is possible, of course, that Paul may have been familiar with the story of Menenius Agrippa, told in order to bring about the return of the plebeians, who had withdrawn from Rome in 494 B.C. The story concerned the discontent on the part of the members of the body because the belly profited from the activity of those members, but did nothing in return. They therefore refused to contribute to the belly, only to discover that in refusing to provide nourishment for the belly they were also depriving themselves of that which they required.[14] It is important to note that here, as with Paul, the picture of the body is used because it suggests naturally the idea of mutual dependence and concern. The force of the analogy lies precisely in the fact that it is absurd to think of the body as involving discord and rivalry among its members.[15] In other words, the idea of discord does not spring from thought about the picture of the body, but rather, is introduced because of the nature of the issue under consideration.

Strack and Billerbeck [16] quote at length an account taken from rabbinical literature (*Midrash*, Ps. 39:2) where rivalry among members of the body is described. The thought is different, however. Whereas Paul emphasizes that no priority is to be given to one member as over against others, the rabbinical passage gives to the tongue (which Paul does not mention at all) a position of preeminence. Even if a story of this sort were known in the apostle's time, it would have had to be the rivalry at Corinth rather than reflection upon the body as such which could have brought it to mind (just as it was Ps. 39:2 rather than any knowledge of the body which inspired the rabbinical account).

(*d*) Still less can the individual members of the physical body "have the same care for one another."[17] Nor, strictly speaking, do the separate members of the physical body "suffer together," or "rejoice together" (I Cor. 12:26).

In dealing with v. 26, commentators sometimes note the statement of Plato (*Republic,* v. 462): "The best ordered polity resembles an individual. For example, if one of our fingers is hurt, the entire community of the physical organism feels the pain as a whole, although it is only one part that suffers. So we say, a man has pain in his finger."[18] It is true that in this statement, as in Paul's, there is the use of the analogy of the physical body to express the idea that the experience of one member of a community affects the entire community. However, the language of Plato is closer than that of Paul to the actual case of the human body. Whereas Plato says "a man" has pain, Paul says, "all the members" suffer. Ordinarily, at least, it is the *man,* and not the individual members of his body, who suffers the pain. Paul's form of expression must therefore reflect the fact that he is thinking primarily of those in the Corinthian body (the church) who share *individually* the experiences of the separate members; he has adjusted his picture of the human body accordingly.

(*e*) It is perhaps possible to regard the very personification of the members of the body as evidence that Paul has transferred to those members certain attributes of personality suggested by the *persons* involved in the Corinthian situation. The members of the body are described as though they may have the *experience* of discord, or of suffering, or of rejoicing (vs. 25 and 26). Furthermore, they are represented as speaking (vs. 15 f. and 21). This point cannot be pressed, however. There are evidences that such personification was not unique.[19] And speaking on the part of non-self-conscious entities was not uncommon.

Straub speaks of it as a "fable-motif."[20] It may be noted further that it is found in the fable of Jotham in Judg. 9:7-15 and in other Old Testament passages.[21] Speech is also ascribed to various parts of the body in the *Midrash* on Ps. 39:2, discussed above.

In view of Paul's undoubted familiarity with some such examples of personification it is conceivable that his use of it *might* have occurred naturally as he thought about the body and its members.[22] One cannot eliminate the possibility, however, that at least the ascribing of speech to various parts of the body may have been influenced by his thought about the utterances of the rival elements in Corinth.

All these considerations point to the fact that Paul's use of the picture of the body has been determined by the Corinthian situation rather than by ideas associated with the picture itself.

(2) As a kind of corollary to the above is the fact that Paul has not developed or applied all the elements in the picture or all the ideas associated with it. There is no attempt at thoroughgoing allegorization. Although numerous members of the body are mentioned specifically (foot, hand, ear, eye, [organ of] smelling, head, feet), none of these is made to represent a corresponding element in the Corinthian community. Elsewhere in his letters Paul does introduce statements in which some of these parts of the body are used metaphorically. In Rom. 3:15, " Their feet are swift to shed blood," and in Rom. 10:15, " How beautiful are the feet of those who preach good news! " the " feet " must be understood as referring, not simply to parts of the body, but rather, to the *persons* under consideration. (It is persons — and not " feet " — who " shed blood," in the former reference. And, in the latter, the allusion is clearly to the messengers who pro-

claim the good news.) In Rom. 3:18, "There is no fear of God before their eyes," the "eyes" must refer similarly to *persons*. Quite similar is the use of the "head" in Rom. 12:20, "For by so doing you will heap burning coals upon his head," where "head" again denotes the *person* himself.[23] It is obviously impossible to transfer this metaphorical meaning of "feet" and of "eyes" and of "head" to the "feet" and "eye" and "head" in I Cor., ch. 12, for there the context involves a clear *distinction* between the person (the "whole body") and these members of the body. This observation has an important bearing upon the problem of the interpretation of the Pauline material generally, for it shows that the meanings attached to expressions in one context cannot, as a matter of course, be transferred to those same expressions in other contexts.

A certain qualification is in order here. In all of the passages just mentioned Paul is quoting, either exactly or freely, from the Old Testament.[24] Thus these metaphorical usages may be said not to be Paul's own; hence there may be a *special* reason for ruling out the transference of meanings in these cases.

Particularly noteworthy is Paul's metaphorical use of "head" in I Cor. 11:3, "The head of every man is Christ, the head of a woman is her husband, and the head of Christ is God." Here "head" stands for that person or Being which occupies a position of superiority or supremacy. That the "head" was often employed to convey the idea of supremacy is well attested.[25] This idea is wholly inappropriate in the use of "head" in the analogical section of I Cor., ch. 12, since (as emphasized above) the passage emphasizes the *absence* of superiority or supremacy in connection with *any* member of the body.

The references to Christ as the "head" of the body (the church) in Ephesians and Colossians [26] are not taken into account here because those letters cannot be regarded with certainty as Pauline.[27] If they were to be accepted as Pauline compositions, the meaning of "head" found in them would be even less appropriate in I Cor. 12:21, even though the "body" in I Cor., ch. 12, does represent the Christian community.

All of this means that it is impossible to read into Paul's thought (in I Cor., ch. 12) all the ideas that may elsewhere be associated with the whole or with parts of his analogy. Thus it must be recognized that where Paul himself fails to develop and apply all the elements in his analogical material it is improper for his interpreters to do so, even when his words in other contexts suggest such development. In this particular part of his letter it is evident that the analogy is to be applied only insofar as that application is made explicit or insofar as it is clearly implied.

I CORINTHIANS 13:12

The analogy of the mirror is introduced very briefly in I Cor. 13:12a: "For now we see in a mirror dimly."

The King James Version has "through a glass [margin: "in a riddle"], darkly." The same Greek word is also translated "glass" in James 1:23, where the context indicates that "looking glass" (mirror) is intended. Though experiments with glass mirrors may have been made by the time of Paul, polished metals were the common materials used.[1]

The words appear in that well-known chapter in which Paul is emphasizing the supremacy of love among all the spiritual gifts.[2] He closes the chapter with the thought that this love never comes to an end. Other gifts belong to the present "imperfect" world order and "will pass away" (v. 8). This is true even of our gift of "knowledge" (vs. 8 f.; see ch. 12:8). Thus the contrast may be drawn between the present "imperfect" knowledge and that future knowledge or understanding which will be ours "when the perfect comes" (ch. 13:10). This contrast may be likened to the difference between a child's and a man's thinking or reasoning (v. 11). It may also be compared to the difference between what is seen in a mirror and what is seen in direct and immediate confrontation.

The main idea involved in the analogy is to be recognized only as the entire verse is taken into consideration. " For now we see in a mirror dimly, but then face to face." Since the latter phrase has to do with *direct* observation, therefore to " see in a mirror " must be intended to express *indirect* vision, for a mirror shows not the face itself but only a reflection of it. Paul's words here are strongly reminiscent of Num. 12:6-8, where God is represented as saying that to a prophet he makes himself known indirectly (" in a vision," speaking " in a dream "), whereas with Moses he speaks " mouth to mouth." The possible influence of this Old Testament passage upon Paul's statement is suggested not only by the identity of contrast between indirect and direct confrontation and by the similarity of the expressions " mouth to mouth " and " face to face," but also by the fact that Paul inserts the phrase *en ainigmati* (" dimly," literally, " in an enigma " or " in a dark saying "), which is practically the same as the *di ainigmatōn* (" in dark speech ") of Num. 12:8 (Septuagint).

It is possible that the analogy of the mirror is introduced solely for the sake of the idea of indirect knowledge.[3] The picture does lend itself to further application, however. In the Wisd. of Sol. (ch. 7:26), Wisdom is called " a spotless mirror of the working of God," and in Ecclus. (ch. 12:10 f.) an enemy's wickedness seems to be likened to rust on a (copper) mirror. These usages suggest the idea that a reflection in a mirror may be somewhat distorted because of blemish or rust;[4] and this idea would be consistent with the statement that in this present life " our knowledge is imperfect " (or, more literally, " we know in part," I Cor. 13:9). It would be consistent also with the *en ainigmati* (" dimly," or " in an enigma ") in v. 12 itself. In application this would mean: as one sees an image unclearly in a mirror because of stain or rust, so we understand God only " in part." One objection to this interpretation is that Paul designates simply " a mirror," giving no hint whatever that he was thinking of a *faulty* mirror. Furthermore, although the larger context does involve the contrast between imperfect vision as over against the perfect, the *immediate* context — in v. 12 itself — has to do, rather, with seeing indirectly (in a mirror) as over against seeing " face to face." Finally, the inclusion of *en ainigmati* (" dimly," " in an enigma ") by no means requires the notion of a faulty mirror; in view of the similarities (see above) between Num. 12:6-8 and I Cor. 13:12 it is possible that the inclusion of this phrase may have been due to the use of *di ainigmatōn* in the Old Testament passage. The objection, that Paul does not specify a *faulty* mirror, may, of course, be avoided by emphasizing the idea that *all* mirrors provide images that fall short of accurate reproduction: " The best of them would give an imperfect and somewhat distorted reflexion." [5] Altogether, one cannot eliminate entirely the possibility that the picture of the mirror is intended to convey the thought of imperfection as well as that of indirectness in the apprehension of an object.

There are other facts or ideas associated with the analogy of the mirror, however, which cannot be intended to have relevance for Paul in this context. Particularly inappropriate for application here is the fact that (normally, at least) one looks into a mirror in order to see the reflection of oneself, not that of someone else. Paul uses the analogy with reference to man's knowledge or understanding of *God* (v. 12b). One may, of course, think of reflections that may be seen upon a smooth surface of water,[6] but this is hardly suggested by the simple phrase *di esoptrou* (" in a mirror ").

Similarly out of place here is the not uncommon idea of that period that some mirrors possessed a magical quality that enabled a person to see or foresee events beyond the normal range of vision.[7] In Paul's usage, however, he is referring to the *limitations* involved in looking into a mirror, limitations that stand in *contrast* to that which is to be. It is unlikely, therefore, that this idea can be involved here.

I CORINTHIANS 14:6-12

During his discussion of the place of "speaking in tongues" in the life of the Christian community, Paul suggests that such a practice serves no constructive purpose if it is unrelated to revelation, or knowledge, or prophecy, or teaching (I Cor. 14:6). If the church is to be edified or "built up" (v. 12), then that which is uttered must be intelligible and meaningful (vs. 9 and 11). This he illustrates in several ways, first of all with reference to musical instruments: "If even lifeless instruments [literally, "lifeless things"], such as the flute or the harp, do not give distinct notes [literally, "do not give a difference in the sounds"], how will anyone know what is played [literally, "what is piped or harped"]? And if the bugle gives an indistinct sound, who will get ready for battle?" (vs. 7 and 8).

In the case of the flute (or pipe) and the harp, the thought probably pertains to the melody that is played,[1] although the translation, "distinct notes," does not properly convey this meaning.

The Greek word (*phthoggois*), here rendered "notes," may be used with respect to melody in the Wisd. of Sol. 19:18 (Septuagint), which can be translated, "as in a psaltery, notes (*phthoggoi*) change the name of the tune." It is true that instead of "tune" one may read "rhythm," since the Septuagint *hruthmou* may refer either to form or to motion. (Compare the reading in the RSV.)

The idea appears to be that unless there is the proper "difference in the sounds," the result will not be recognizable or meaningful.

Much the same is true in the reference to the "bugle" (or "trumpet"). Its sound, in order to be meaningful as a signal, must be "distinct" in the sense that it can be recognized and understood.

When Paul speaks of a sound as "indistinct," his word, *adēlos*, is the negative form of *dēlos* ("evident"), which he uses twice (I Cor. 15:27 and Gal. 3:11), in both cases referring to "what is known and understood."[2] Therefore *adēlon* must refer to something *not* known or understood. In the only other New Testament usage of the word (Luke 11:44) it obviously means "not recognizable."

In all of this Paul is not precise. In actuality it is a *pattern* of sounds (not the sounds themselves) which creates a recognizable melody or rhythm or signal, and this, though implied, is not stated. The apostle's meaning, therefore, is expressed in his use of the pictures only in a very general way.

The application is given in I Cor. 14:9: just as the sounds given by the instruments serve no real purpose if they do not produce a recognizable — and hence meaningful — melody or rhythm or signal, so also, " speaking in tongues " does not make a contribution if the sounds are not intelligible.

On the basis of language v. 9 may be interpreted, not as providing an application of the foregoing analogies, but as introducing a new analogy. In Paul's Greek the article " the " stands with " tongue," so that this part of the sentence may be translated, " if you . . . [with *the*] tongue utter speech that is not intelligible." Thus " the tongue " can refer to the organ of speech in the body and not to the " speaking in a tongue." If this is the case, then v. 9 adds a new picture, parallel to those in vs. 7 and 8: the human tongue, like the " lifeless instruments," does not serve its proper function if it does not produce something that is recognizable or intelligible.[3]

In support of the view that the tongue refers here to the bodily instrument of speech (rather than to the phenomenon of " speaking in a tongue ") is the fact that the language is similar to that in which the other instruments (musical) are mentioned (vs. 7 and 8, immediately preceding): not only is there the continued use of a *question* as a form of expression, but also the same verb (*didōmi*, " to give ") is used to indicate the bringing forth of the sounds made by the instruments.

On the other hand, numerous considerations seem to indicate that v. 9 presents an application of the previous analogies rather than a new one: (1) Although it is true that Paul generally omits the definite article when he refers to " speaking in tongues," [4] there are two other instances (chs. 13:1 and 14:22) besides this one where the article *is* used. In both of these the context requires the meaning " speaking in tongues." Hence the presence of the article here does not necessarily change the meaning. (2) The use of a *question* means no more than that the application of the analogies is given a form parallel to the form in which the analogies themselves are stated. (3) It would be entirely unnecessary to insert the words, " with the tongue " (referring to the organ of the body), for *all* speaking is "with the tongue."[5] (4) Finally, the words at the beginning of v. 9, "So with yourselves," presumably indicate that now the analogies are applied, since exactly the same words have this meaning at the beginning of v. 12.

It seems to the present writer that v. 9 is intended to express the application of the previous analogies, though it is difficult to avoid the impression that "the tongue" here refers to the organ of speech. Perhaps the two views may be reconciled if the language is regarded as a way of saying this: "So with yourselves; if (in speaking in tongues) you utter (or give) with the tongue (i.e., with the tongue only, and not with your mind or your understanding)[6] speech that is not intelligible, how will anyone know what is said?" Such a meaning allows not only for the evidence that application is intended, but it also allows for the reference to "the tongue" as a part of the body.

It should be noted that in at least one respect the pictures of the playing of musical instruments cannot be applied to the issue under consideration. Even though instruments of this kind may produce patterns of sounds which are recognizable and which, in this sense, convey a meaning, this meaning cannot really be compared to that which Paul is emphasizing and which he finds lacking in the speaking in tongues. Melodies or rhythms may "speak" to the hearer, in that they may suggest, by association, different kinds of moods or experiences, but they do not serve to communicate ideas or thoughts that can be apprehended or grasped by the mind. Strictly speaking, therefore, one cannot say: instruments *not* properly played can be likened to speaking in tongues, but instruments *properly* played can be likened to speaking that edifies or builds up. For even that which is properly played does not communicate the corresponding thoughts or ideas.

This statement needs to be qualified somewhat with reference to the bugle. Insofar as certain sounds played upon it constitute specific signals, these sounds do communicate intelligible ideas. Since Paul does not indicate that the bugle is different from the other instruments in this respect, however, it is to be assumed that he had not given direct attention to this feature in the analogy, and hence he must not have intended it to be given application.

As already stated, what is properly played, conveys (at best) *impressions* suggesting or creating moods and experiences. The application of this fact would actually compel a *recommendation* for "speaking in tongues," for it was precisely *with* moods and experiences that such speaking was concerned. This, of course, would be contrary to the major point that Paul is making, although it would be consistent with his recognition that speaking in tongues does have a certain value (vs. 18 f.).

Altogether it is apparent that the analogies can be applied as relevant in some respects only. To apply them in all possible respects would distort greatly the author's meaning and intent.

The final analogy introduced in this section concerns the diversity of languages (vs. 10 f.).

Here Paul uses forms of the noun *phōnē*, translated in vs. 7 and 8 as "note" or "sound." Verse 11 indicates that now it must be given the meaning "language," a meaning that was quite common.[7] Although *glōssa* ("tongue") was frequently employed to designate "language,"[8] Paul reserves it largely for use in connection with speaking in tongues (see above).

Turning to the use of the first person singular, the apostle emphasizes the fact that speech in a language is meaningless unless the language is understood (v. 11). In the following verse the application is stated somewhat indirectly: "So with yourselves; since you are eager for manifestations of the Spirit [literally, "for spiritual things"], strive to excel in building up the church." It should be noted that the relationship between the analogy and its application is evident only as the reader supplies the implications: where language is not understood — and the speech in it is therefore meaningless — there can be no edifying or "building up" by means of its use. And since the objective *is* to "build up" the church, therefore the Christians must not be content with unintelligible "speaking in tongues." Thus Paul can then move on (v. 13) to express the need for interpreting what is spoken in a "tongue."

I CORINTHIANS 15:35-50

A combination of pictures is found in Paul's discussion of resurrection in I Cor., ch. 15. In the first part of this chapter the apostle presents the testimony concerning the resurrection of Christ himself (vs. 3-11). He then directs his attention to a refutation of the claim that "there is no resurrection of the dead" (v. 12), emphasizing especially the fact of Christ's resurrection as the crucial consideration in this regard (vs. 13 ff.). The next question to which he addresses himself is expressed in two ways: "How are the dead raised? With what kind of body do they come?"

The latter form of the question expresses more specifically what the former presents in a general way.[1] This interpretation is preferable to that which makes of the two forms essentially different questions. Robertson and Plummer give as the meaning for the former, "Is it possible for the dead to be raised?"[2] It is extremely doubtful that this is the intended meaning, partly because the following verses are concerned, not with the *possibility* of resurrection,[3] but with the kind of body that is involved, and partly because Paul has actually dealt with this question earlier (vs. 12 ff.).

In attempting to answer the question as to the nature of the resurrection body Paul introduces first of all the analogy of the seed (vs. 36-38). In view of what is actually said, three ideas are suggested: (1) That which ought to follow the sowing of the seed (that is, the stalk or plant) does not "come to life" except on the condition of the death of the seed (v. 36). (2) The seed that is sown ("a bare kernel") is quite different from that body (the stalk) which is later to come into being (v. 37). (3) God has chosen to give to each kind of seed its appropriate or proper kind of body (v. 38).

Since the analogical material involved in these verses

must be analyzed in the light of the purpose for which it is employed, it should be noted at once how the application is made. This application, given in vs. 42-44, emphasizes the contrast between the body with which man first appears on earth and that other body which will be his at resurrection (vs. 42-44a).

It is evident from v. 44a that the contrast is between two kinds of bodies. The one that "is raised" is obviously the resurrection body. That which "is sown" is the body of "flesh and blood" (see v. 50). The thought intended by the verb ("is sown") is not clear, however. Numerous interpreters regard the expression as referring to the burial of this body (the corpse) in the grave.[4] This is a natural assumption, since such burial corresponds to the planting of the seed in the soil. Furthermore, to speak of the body as sown *en phthorai* ("in corruption"), *en atimiai* ("in dishonor"), and *en astheneiai* ("in weakness") would be consistent with this view.[5] On the other hand, the total context suggests that Paul is contrasting to the resurrection body, not simply the dead body (the corpse), but rather, the body that man has as a living being (vs. 44b-49). Although the picture of sowing seed may suggest burial of the corpse, Paul shows by his usages elsewhere that the verb *speirō* ("to sow") held for him such general metaphorical connotations that it need not necessarily be given literal significance.[6]

In these particular verses there is a special reason why the application of the picture of the sowing of the seed should not be pressed in all details. The words *speiretai* ("it is sown") and *egeiretai* ("it is raised") are strikingly similar in sound. To read vs. 42b-44a aloud in the Greek is to become convinced that the fourfold repetition of the words is due not only to the fact that the former was derived from the analogy of vs. 36-38 but also to the effectiveness of the rhyme. In other words, since it was not simply the use of the word in the analogy that accounts for its use here, its connotation should not be determined by ideas associated with it in the analogy.

Also, the terms found in vs. 42 and 43 are applicable to the body of a living being as well as to a corpse. To be sown *en phthorai* (" in corruption ") can mean " to be subject to corruption "[7] or to be " perishable "; it does not mean that death has necessarily occurred. " Dishonor " (*atimia*) is appropriate with reference to the living as well as to the dead, as Paul himself shows.[8] The same is true of *astheneia*.[9]

It is true that in the picture of the seed being planted (v. 37) the mention of the " bare kernel " (*gumnon kokkon*) has sometimes been interpreted as involving an allusion to the body prepared for burial. " The grain, before being sown, is stripped of all the sheaths which protected it on the plant, as the human body, before burial, is stripped of its usual clothing."[10] J. Weiss believes that the adjective *gumnon* (" bare," " naked ") is intended to allude to the condition of " the dead " before the resurrection, suggesting that a secondary analogy is thus introduced. He thinks that the expression may have been taken from Paul's Jewish heritage, and quotes the following: " If the grain of wheat, which is buried naked, comes forth with many garments, much more (is this true of) the pious, who are buried in their clothing."[11] (Weiss agrees that Paul's thought at this point is quite different from that according to which the soul was supposed, after death, to be entirely dissociated from a body.)[12] It is true that Paul draws a distinction between the " bare " seed and the (later) growing plant, corresponding to the distinction between the body of this earthly life and the body of the future life. In view of the above considerations, however, it is unlikely that the " bare seed " refers only to the bodies of this earthly life which have already died and have been placed in the earth. The adjective *gumnon* (" bare ") is intended simply to heighten this contrast: the seed is " mere grain, not the plant itself."[13]

Altogether, therefore, there is nothing in this section of the letter which invalidates the impression created by the total context. " The argument implies that to be sown is to be born, not to be buried."[14]

In drawing the contrast between the body that is sown

and the body that is raised, Paul prepares the way for his primary emphasis with the lyrical expression of the various antitheses: perishable — imperishable,   dishonor — glory,[15] weakness — power.[16] The central and dominant idea itself is stated in v. 44: " It is sown a physical body, it is raised a spiritual body." The reading of the King James Version is: " It is sown a natural body, it is raised a spiritual body."

The meaning of the adjective *psuchikon* does not, in itself, mean " physical " or " natural," since it is a form of *psuche*, a noun often translated into English as " soul." [17] Since *psuche* means for Paul the " natural life of earthly man," as opposed to his " supranatural life," [18] therefore the *psuchikon* body is that body which is given to him as an earthly human being; it is to be distinguished from that body which is his in his " spiritual " life. The former may be designated as a " physical body," since this is the form that it has for earthy human beings, even though an interpretive factor is involved in the designation. Similarly, the expression may be rendered as a " natural body," since the reference is to that kind of body which is " natural " for man in his earthly state.[19]

It is in this antithesis between the " physical body " and the " spiritual body " that Paul presents his answer to the initial question, " With what kind of body do they come? " (v. 35). It is an answer that may be restated both negatively and positively. Negatively, the resurrection body is *not* the present " physical " body — as he later states in different words: " Flesh and blood cannot inherit the kingdom of God " (v. 50).[20]

Among the varying ideas as to the nature of resurrection which had been presented by the time of Paul was the notion that the very body that had died would be raised. Such a view is expressed with particular clarity in the Apocalypse of Baruch. Though this document in its present form may have been composed shortly after Paul wrote I Corinthians,[21] it seems to incorporate a type of thought current in his time. The question raised is not unlike that with which Paul is concerned:

" In what shape will those live who live in Thy day?
Or how will the splendour of those who [are] after that time continue?

Will they then resume this form of the present, . . .
Or wilt Thou perchance change these things which have been
    in the world,
As also the world? " (Ch. 49:2 f.)

The reply, however, is different:

" For the earth shall then assuredly restore the dead,
Which it now receiveth, in order to preserve them.
It shall make no change in their form,
But as it hath received, so shall it restore them;
And as I delivered them unto it, so also shall it raise them."
                                                      (Ch. 50:2.)

It is true that after the returned dead have been recognized by
the living, a change in their " aspect " will occur, and those who
have been " justified " will be " exalted and glorified " (chs. 50:3
to 51:5).

        " And they shall be made like unto the angels,
        And be made equal to the stars." (Ch. 51:10.)

The resurrection itself, however, involves the raising of the body
that had died.

More positively Paul's answer to the original question is that
there *is* a different kind of body — a " spiritual body." This he
develops in his references to Adam and to Christ (I Cor.
15:45-49). Adam was " from the earth, a man of dust ";
earthly men are in his likeness. But Christ, a life-giving
spirit, is " from heaven," and as such he represents a different order of being; those men who, like him, are " of heaven "
will bear *his* likeness. The argument, therefore, amounts to
this: Christ represents the heavenly or spiritual realm as
truly as Adam represents the earthly. And since earthly human beings bear Adam's likeness now, it must follow that
in resurrection they will bear Christ's likeness, with a body
appropriate to — and corresponding to — his " heavenly " or
" spiritual " existence. Thus, there *is* a " spiritual body," different from the physical body. And it is with this kind of

body that men " come " in resurrection. The exact nature of this body is not defined, either here or elsewhere.

Moffatt observes that in Phil. 3:21, where a similar idea seems to be stated, there is likewise evident a "noticeable reserve" on the part of Paul.[22] The Lord Jesus Christ, he says, "will change our lowly body to be like his glorious body" (or, "like the body of his glory"). Bultmann, however, is probably correct in his contention that the meaning involved in Phil. 3:21 is not the same as that in I Cor., ch. 15. Bultmann provides considerable evidence to show that the term *sōma* ("body") means generally, for Paul, not "body-form," as in I Cor., ch. 15, but rather, the "person as a whole": a man does not *have* a "body"; he *is* "body." Hence, to "change our lowly body to be like his glorious body" (Phil. 3:21) refers, not to a transformation of man's body-form, but rather, to a change of man's *nature*. Of course the idea of such a change of nature lies behind the thought expressed in I Cor., ch. 15, but the primary subject under consideration is that of body-form. Thus understood the statement in Phil. 3:21 is not directly relevant to the immediate issue.[23]

It is possible, now, to examine in some detail the nature of Paul's use of the analogy of the planted seed as this analogy is related to the thought that he is attempting to express.

The clearest point of correspondence between the analogy and its application is this: just as the seed that is sown is not the plant that "is to be" (v. 37), so also the physical body of the present earthly life is to be distinguished from the resurrection body. It may be noted, incidentally, that Paul fails to define the nature of the body (the plant) which comes into being following the sowing of the seed; he does not even mention the plant explicitly. Similar is the fact that he does not define in any precise way the nature of the resurrected body. This point of correspondence between analogy and idea is probably accidental, however. In any case the analogy is used to reinforce the idea that in resurrection the body will be different from that which is known in the present earthly life.

Verse 36 ("What you sow does not come to life unless it dies") must be intended to suggest much the same idea, although the sentence, when taken alone, seems to convey a different meaning. In and of themselves the words appear to emphasize the necessity of death for the seed before the plant can grow. Although certain interpreters ascribe this emphasis to Paul,[24] this can hardly be the apostle's thought. What is said here is true neither in the case of the sown seed nor in the case of Paul's thought concerning resurrection. With the seed, it must be granted, the body (the kernel) that is sown may be said to die, for it becomes decomposed or disintegrated. But if this is what is meant by "what you sow," then it is incorrect to speak of it as coming to life, for this is not true of the kernel. One can speak of "what you sow" as coming to life only if the thought is upon what may be called the "germ of life"[25] contained in the kernel rather than the kernel itself. But in this case it is incorrect to speak of it as dying, for it does not die. In other words, what dies does not come to life, and what comes to life has not died. Similarly, the sentence, as analogy, does not express accurately Paul's thought concerning resurrection. It is not the body that dies that is to be raised, if the body of flesh and blood is meant. Or, to put it differently, it is untrue, insofar as Paul's thought is concerned, to say that what is raised must first die. What is raised is certainly not the "physical" body that has died. Even if what is raised *were* this body, the statement would not be true, for, as Paul shows in v. 51b ("We shall not all sleep, but we shall all be changed," i.e., at the Parousia) and also in I Thess. 5:16 f., he "did not consider that physical death was a necessary prelude to the resurrection."[26] And if what is raised is the self-identity as distinct from the physical body, these passages rule out death, in this case also, as an occurrence that is necessary before the transformation into the new life. Both in vs. 51 f. and in I Thess. 4:17 the new body is to be given while some are yet alive. Of course the question, as formulated ("How are the dead raised?"), concerns those who have already died. For them, therefore, resurrection can occur only after death. In view of the above considerations, however, this fact does not justify the broader generalization, that death is a *necessary* prerequisite for resurrection.

J. Weiss recognizes that v. 36 is incorrect insofar as the picture itself is concerned. He contends that the words can express what is true only insofar as they apply to resurrection — only insofar as they are meant to say that resurrection can occur only after the death and burial of the body. Thus, according to his view, the form of the analogical statement in v. 36 is determined, not by the picture but by the idea that is stated later, in vs. 42 f. It has been shown above, however, that "sown" in vs. 42 f., does *not* refer to the burial of the body that has died, but rather, to the placing of the human being on earth. Thus the idea of the necessity of death is as inappropriate for Paul's thought of resurrection as it is for the picture itself.

If, therefore, the idea of the necessity of death is inappropriate both in the case of the planted seed and in the case of resurrection, then v. 36 must be intended to reinforce a different idea. The verse becomes intelligible if it is understood in the light of the following verse. As already seen, v. 37 emphasizes the fact that the body "which is to be" is quite different from the seed that is sown. Verse 36 serves primarily to reinforce this thought, saying in effect: the body that is to be *must* be different from the seed that is sown, for that seed is decomposed, disintegrated. The thought that is given emphasis is not the *necessity* of the death of the seed, but rather, the fact that the seed that was sown (and subsequently died) is itself not restored to its original form. Similarly, the physical body of man is not to be restored in resurrection; rather, a different kind of body is raised (vs. 42-44), since, at least for those whose physical bodies have disintegrated, these bodies have died. According to this interpretation, it is still true that the statement in v. 36 is not accurate, since, strictly speaking, "what you sow" does not *itself, as a seed,* "come to life" even after it dies. In shifting the emphasis, however, from the idea of the *necessity* of death to the fact that the kernel, once disintegrated, does not reappear, there is found a meaning that is consistent with the to-

tal thought of the apostle. In this way v. 37 is to be understood as *re*stating — more accurately! — the idea that v. 36
was intended to convey. The fact that such restatement is involved is suggested, furthermore, by the very structure of
the two sentences: both begin with exactly the same form:
ho speireis ("what you sow").

Verse 38 ("But God gives it a body as he has chosen, and
to each kind of seed its own body") is somewhat ambiguous,
for it is not clear whether "body" refers to the "kernel"
(the seed) or to the plant that appears after the seed is sown.
Interpreters generally accept the latter meaning.[27] When understood in this way the thought is that just as God provides
the proper kind of plant for each kind of seed, so also he will
give to those who are raised the kind of body which is appropriate.

It is possible that "body" here may refer to that of the seed
rather than that of the plant. The subject of the preceding verse
(v. 37) is the seed, not the plant that grows from it. The simple
pronoun (*autōi*) that follows would normally, therefore, refer to
the seed. Furthermore, the next verse (v. 39) continues to center
attention on the *original* form of being: "For not all flesh is alike."
The use of *sarx* ("flesh") shows that the thought pertains to the
realm of the (earlier) "physical" body. This means that v. 38
stands between sentences that concern the "seed — physical
body" form of existence. It may seem unlikely that Paul would
have shifted his subject from "seed" (v. 36) to plant (v. 37) and
then back again to that ("flesh") which is parallel to "seed"
(v. 39) without indicating in some way that he has changed his
subject in the course of writing. On the other hand, Paul's thought
in this section concerns primarily the resurrection body (v. 35b).
It would be natural, therefore, that the plant (representing this
body) rather than the seed would have been so central in his
thinking that it did not occur to him — or it seemed unnecessary
— to indicate explicitly that it was this body which he meant in
v. 38.

The words "God gives it a body as he has chosen" deserve
special attention. Paul is saying, of course, that it is God
himself who brings forth the proper plant from each kind of

seed which is sown. Even though God's decision to do so may be traced to Creation itself (God "has chosen"),[28] nevertheless, the actual bringing forth of each proper plant is regarded as a present divine act (God "gives"). This, obviously, corresponds to the fact that it is God who gives to men the appropriate resurrection body. It is important to observe a limitation in the analogy at this point, however. In agriculture it is to be taken for granted that the life of the sown seed will spring up in the form of the growing plant. Even though the process may have been divinely ordained, the appearance of the plant is assumed to be practically inevitable. There exists what J. Weiss calls "the factor of the spontaneously working nature."[29] This aspect of the analogy might be applied to those notions of the future life according to which the "soul," by its very nature, is immortal or indestructible, but it is quite unsuitable for application to the apostle's thought regarding resurrection. According to Paul's thinking, the giving of the new life is by no means automatic or inevitable. It is bestowed by God only through his merciful and gracious act. Paul can say, therefore, that "God gives" the new body, both with regard to the plant and also with regard to the new form of existence for man. But the idea of practical inevitability involved in the analogy of the sown seed simply cannot be applied to the subject of resurrection.

Additional thoughts are also probably involved. In saying that "God gives it a body," he may well have been opposing "the Hellenistic ideal of immortality without any 'body,'"[30] or the view of the Essenes, who, according to Josephus, anticipated a purely spiritual resurrection, without a body of any kind.[31] In any case Paul is emphasizing the fact that a "body" will be given, for, as in II Cor. 5:1-4, he firmly rejects all thought of disembodied souls. By this emphasis he provides for continuity of personal identity. His assurance of such continuity is indicated in I Cor. 15:49, where the "we" who have been in the form of earthly man are "also" the "we" who will "bear the image of the man of heaven." Thus there will be what may be described as " sameness of being but not sameness of body." [32]

When Paul adds, in v. 38, the statement that God gives " to each kind of seed its own body," he probably means (in the light of the general interpretation placed upon this verse) that God brings forth from each kind of sown seed its own proper kind of plant. As noted earlier, this is probably intended to suggest that just as God provides the proper kind of body for each kind of seed, so also he will give to those who are raised the kind of body which is appropriate for them in their new state. Here there is an element in the analogy which cannot be applied to resurrection. If one were to reconstruct the Pauline thought on the basis of the analogy, one would conclude that just as there are different kinds of plants, so also there are different kinds of resurrection bodies. Such an application of this element in the analogy is obviously impossible. For Paul there are not different kinds of resurrection bodies. Rather, there is one kind only — a " spiritual body." All who are raised are to bear " the image of the man of heaven " (v. 49).[33]

If " body " in v. 38 is made to refer to seed rather than to plant (see above) a similar situation would exist. The picture would then concern differences among the various kinds of seeds. While the diversity among God-given seeds might suggest diversity also in the kinds of bodies given to men, the comparison could be drawn only in a limited way. The general idea of diversity would be relevant, but not the sort of diversity here expressed. Diversity among seeds would have to correspond to diversity among different " physical bodies." This is not Paul's concern. The contrast that he wishes to draw is between a " physical body " and a " spiritual body." In order to be applied fully, therefore, the analogical statement should have emphasized (as *does* the statement in v. 37) the differences between seeds and plants, not the differences between seeds.

Taking the analogy as a whole, it may be noted, finally, that there is yet another element in it that cannot be applied to the subject of resurrection. *In nature* the plant " which is to be," following the sowing of the seed, is just as " perishable " as is the seed itself. It bears fruit,[34] and through that fruit its life is projected into the future. The fact remains, however, that *the plant, as a body, also dies,* even though its body is different from that of the seed. As over against this fact pertaining to the analogy, Paul insists that the otherwise corresponding " spiritual body " is *not* perishable (vs. 42 and 50). Any mention of the transitory nature of the plant must of necessity, therefore, be omitted, for it would destroy at least a part of the apostle's argument.

In his discussion of the resurrection body Paul introduces also certain other pictures. He observes that " not all flesh is alike [literally, " not all flesh is the same flesh "], but there is one kind for men, another [flesh] for animals, another [flesh] for birds, and another for fish " (v. 39).[35] As applied (by implication only), the picture suggests that since such differences are possible among the forms of living creatures, differences of body must also be possible for human beings. Here again the analogy is applicable in a limited way only. The general idea of diversity is of course relevant. But, strictly speaking, the analogy cannot be applied in any detail. In the analogy the creatures named differ from one another in form and shape, but they are all " flesh," as the fourfold use of *sarx* (" flesh ") seems to emphasize. To apply this fact to the Pauline idea of the difference between " physical body " and " spiritual body " would produce the conclusion that the two are distinct only in terms of form or shape, not in terms of substance. Paul shows very clearly, however, that this is not at all what he means. In v. 50, especially, he states emphatically that the " flesh " (and " blood ") of the present earthly life are *not* involved in the resurrection life (" the kingdom of God "). In this context it is precisely in terms of substance that the two bodies are different.

Robertson and Plummer have interpreted v. 39 in another manner: " The difference between our present body and our risen body . . . may be greater than that between men and fishes." [36] If it were true that the purpose of this picture is to set the differences among creatures *over against* the difference between men's physical and spiritual bodies, then the limitation just mentioned would not exist. There is nothing in the material which suggests this intention, however. The entire context gives the impression that the difference between the present and risen bodies is *compared*, not contrasted, to the differences found in the world (and in the sky).

The final analogy here concerns differences among " celestial " (or " heavenly ") and " terrestrial " (or " earthly ") bodies (vs. 40 f.). The connotations and implications of these terms are not entirely clear. The meaning of " terrestrial bodies " would present no special problem except for the fact that their " glory " is mentioned, and this term is not particularly appropriate with reference to earthly things.[37] The celestial (or heavenly) bodies undoubtedly include the sun, moon, and stars, as the mention of these in v. 41 indicates. The Pauline concept of such bodies, however, is uncertain. That they were often worshiped in the early world is well-known,[38] and stars, especially, were sometimes regarded as angelic beings.[39] Whether or not Paul conceived of the heavenly bodies as animate,[40] at least he may be alluding to such ideas.[41] In any case, Paul seems to mean that just as there are these differences among bodies, some being " suitable for existence in heaven, and some for existence on earth," [42] so also it is reasonable to conceive of men's resurrection bodies as different from their bodies here and now (see again vs. 48 f.). In one respect this analogy is more fully applicable than that of the different kinds of " flesh " (v. 39), for here the contrast between " heavenly " and " earthly " corresponds (within limits) to the difference between heavenly resurrection bodies and earthly bodies of flesh and blood. Even here, however, the analogy is not fully applicable, for there is no connection between " celestial bodies " and " terrestrial bodies " as there is, in Paul's thought, between the resurrection bodies and the earthly bodies of men, for whom continuity of personal identity is involved. Nor can one apply the fact of differences (in " glory ") between sun, moon, and stars (v. 41), since, as indicated above, Paul's thought did not involve the idea that one resurrection body differed from another.

Robertson and Plummer write: " It is legitimate to apply these differences in the heavenly bodies to possible differences in the glories of the risen saints, and it is not impossible that the Apostle had this thought in his mind." [43] There is no indication anywhere in the context, however, that Paul was thinking of differences in *status* among the " risen saints." And elsewhere he suggests *likeness* rather than difference in men's future condition (Rom. 8:17). Certainly the idea of justification through faith rules out any notion that a higher or a lower position in the future life would be merited. Even if Paul did anticipate differences in *status* for those who were raised, this would in no way alter the fact that they were all given a common kind of body. Since emphasis in this section of the material is precisely upon the one kind of body which will be given, it is simply impossible to apply fully the reference to *differences* among the celestial bodies.

The only point, therefore, that seems to be relevant in v. 41 is the very *general* idea of multiplicity: as there are differences among heavenly bodies, so also different kinds of bodies are possible for men.

This examination of the various pictures found in I Cor., ch. 15, indicates that all of them serve to emphasize one central and dominant idea: man sees around him *differences* in body-forms; and, since the fact of such differences may be recognized, it must also be recognized that a corresponding contrast exists between the body-form that is known in this life and the body-form that is involved in the resurrection life. It is clearly for the sake of this idea that each of the pictures has been introduced. It is equally apparent that no one picture can be applied in detail to the Pauline thought about resurrection, for in each of them there are elements which, if applied, would present notions regarding resurrection manifestly contradictory to those which Paul is otherwise known to have held.

4.

The Second Letter of Paul
to the Corinthians

II CORINTHIANS 2:14-16

Paul's language in this brief section of the letter introduces at least two pictures, that of a triumphal procession
and that of an aroma or scent.[1] The former is presented in
these words: " But thanks be to God, who in Christ always
leads us in triumph." The picture is that of a triumphal parade, what Moffatt calls a " pageant of triumph." [2]

The King James Version has " God, which always causeth us to
triumph." This may seem to be better suited to the larger context. In this part of II Corinthians, Paul is writing to express his
relief and joy that the conflict between the Corinthians and himself has been resolved and that friendly relations have been restored.[3] It is understandable that in this situation he might say,
" God . . . causeth us to triumph," for the difficulties have been
successfully overcome. On the other hand, there is no extant evidence that Paul's verb here (thriambeuō) was ever used in a
causative sense. Recent interpreters therefore generally favor
the meaning, " God . . . leads us in triumph." [4]

The picture seems to be that of a leader returning victori-
ously from his conquests. Ordinarily, the persons being led
in such a situation would be those who had suffered defeat.[5]
Applied to Paul's thinking this would mean: as the military
leader conducts his captives in triumph, so also God leads us
as his defeated opponents. It is impossible, of course, to
apply the picture with such thoroughness. In ordinary circumstances " the captives had no share in the victory; it was
not only a victory over them, but a victory against them." [6]

This was certainly not true insofar as Paul and his associates were concerned. It is a fact that Paul thought of himself as one who had been overcome by God. In yielding to God (Rom. 6:13), in becoming "slaves of God" (v. 22), men acknowledged — and experienced — God's triumph over them. But this was a triumph in which they too shared, a triumph quite different from that enjoyed by the returning conqueror of the picture, where the defeated captives stand condemned. This means that the analogy is relevant only in a general way. Triumph is involved; and there is a sense in which the triumph presupposes a victory over Paul himself as God's captive; but Paul's status as captive is vastly different from that of the defeated enemy in the picture. " If he is vanquished, he is vanquished willingly, and is aiding with all his might his conqueror." [7]

It has been suggested that the object of the verb refers to those who are led " probably not as captives, but as officers in his victorious army, made to share in the triumph." [8] According to available evidence, however, the direct object following the verb *thriambeuō* invariably denoted those over whom the victory was won, not aides or officers of the victor. It is apparent, therefore, that while the picture has provided the language that Paul employs, it can not be applied in all details. Such application would distort the Pauline thought.

Following the clause that introduces the picture of the triumphal procession are the words that present the metaphor of odor or scent: " And through us spreads the fragrance of the knowledge of him everywhere. For we are the aroma of Christ to God among those who are being saved and among those who are perishing, to one a fragrance from death to death, to the other a fragrance from life to life " (vs. 14b-16).

It is possible that these words express, in part at least, an extension of the previous picture. A certain Appian, a first-century historian, reports an occasion upon which incense was burned as the triumphal procession made its way through the streets of the city. [9] Various commentators have seized upon this report and have assumed that the practice was common. They have then contended that Paul, aware of the custom, is therefore continuing to develop and apply his picture of the victor's parade.[10] Others, however, contend that the burning of incense on such occasions did not necessarily occur frequently, since the above-mentioned reference to it is the only one that is known.[11] It should therefore be concluded that Paul is here suddenly changing the picture.[12] Such mingling of pictures is by no means infrequent with Paul.

It seems likely that the apostle may have been influenced here by earlier literary usage. In Ecclesiasticus, for example, where Wisdom is made to " praise herself " (Ecclus. 24:1), this statement appears:

" Like cassia and camel's thorn I gave forth the aroma of spices,
    and like choice myrrh I spread a pleasant odor." (Ecclus. 24:15.)

A little later men are admonished thus:

" Send forth fragrance like frankincense, and put forth blossoms
    like a lily.
Scatter the fragrance, and sing a hymn of praise; bless the Lord."
                                                        (Ecclus. 39:14.)

The association of Wisdom with scent in the former of these two passages — it is Wisdom who speaks there — is particularly worthy of note, since Paul somewhat similarly represents " knowledge " as " fragrance " (v. 14).[13] Furthermore, in each of these passages are found (in the Septuagint) forms of both *osmē* ("fragrance," "smell," "odor") and *euōdia* ("aroma," "sweet smell"), as is the case in II Cor. 2:14 f. In any event, Paul elsewhere also combines the two words in a context that has nothing to do with a triumphal procession: in Phil. 4:18 he speaks of gifts as " a fragrant offering [literally, "an odor of sweet smell"], a sacrifice acceptable and pleasing to God." The picture is therefore one that had in his mind no necessary connection with that of the triumphal procession.

A distinctive feature in Paul's use of this picture is the shift in the application of the "fragrance" or "aroma." Whereas the "fragrance" in v. 14b represents the "knowledge" of God,[14] in v. 15 the "aroma" is said to be Paul and his associates. This change in meaning is in itself of no great moment, since those who "spread" or make manifest the fragrance may, by association of ideas, be thought of as becoming, themselves, the aroma. The very fact that the shift occurs, however, is indicative of the more important fact that the picture is not intended to be applied systematically. Rather, it is used loosely and freely, having relevance only as it is made to serve the immediate ideas that the apostle wishes to convey.

The same conclusion is supported by a further fact. In v. 16 Paul states that the apostles, as "the aroma of Christ" are "to one a fragrance from death to death, to the other a fragrance from life to life." The meaning that Paul conveys in these words is fairly clear. The apostles confront men with the "knowledge" of God which they "spread" (v. 14b); or they come before men as those who, in their persons, represent the knowledge of Christ (v. 15). That which confronts men, however, produces in them quite opposite results. For those who respond affirmatively ("those who are being saved") the result is life; but for those who respond negatively ("those who are perishing") it is death.

The thought here has been compared to that in II Cor. 4:3; Phil. 1:28; and also to I Peter 2:7 f.[15] It suggests particularly the statements regarding "judgment" in John 3:16-21. The appearance of Christ, as a "light," was intended to bring men to "eternal life." To those who "come to the light" the confrontation brings life; to others it brings condemnation.[16]

Thus Paul's meaning is intelligible. His continued use of the analogy of scent or aroma, however, is subject to question, for the picture itself is in reality not suited to this use of it. In ordinary experience, at least, an odor that is pleasing to some may be displeasing to others; but an odor of such strength or intensity as to suggest " death " would hardly be the same odor that could also be associated with " life." [17] The passage is clearly one where the apostle has used certain elements in his analogy to serve his purposes, but the analogy itself cannot be applied systematically and fully.

There are some who see in these verses the use of yet a third picture, that of sacrifice.[18] This is somewhat debatable. It is true that Paul's words here, *osmē* (" fragrance," " odor ") and *euōdia* (" aroma," " sweet smell "), are found frequently in the (Septuagint) Old Testament references to sacrifice.[19] And the statement that the " aroma " is " to God " suggests sacrifice to him. On the other hand, Paul does not combine his words to form the common Septuagint phrase for such sacrifice (*osmē[n] euōdias*).[20] In any case the " aroma " is said by Paul to have reference both to God (v. 15) and also to men (" to one a fragrance from death to death, to the other a fragrance from life to life," v. 16). If the picture of sacrifice is in the apostle's mind here, he is not applying it consistently; for while a sacrifice " to God " may be said to be efficacious " to [man's] life," it is difficult to understand how it could also contribute " to [man's] death."

II Corinthians 3:1-3

In this brief paragraph is found a somewhat confusing mixture of pictures. The three verses are introduced by Paul as a kind of parenthetical comment [1] on the fact that in the preceding statement (ch. 2:17) he has seemed to be commending himself. There are numerous evidences that when he wrote this letter he was particularly sensitive to the matter of commendation. Apparently some who had opposed him at Corinth had boasted of their position and qualifications.[2] Apparently, also, Paul himself had been accused of self-commendation. His awareness of these circumstances is reflected in the frequent use of the verb " to commend " (*sunistanō*).[3]

As the apostle touches upon this issue here he suggests,

first of all, that he and his fellow workers do not require "letters of recommendation."

Letters or notes of introduction and recommendation were not uncommon. Paul himself wrote in behalf of others on numerous occasions. (See Rom. 16:1 f.; I Cor. 16:10 f.; II Cor. 8:16-19, 22-24; and especially Philemon. Compare Eph. 6:21 f.; Col. 4:7-10; Acts 9:2; 18:27.) Deissmann gives examples of such recommendations from non-Biblical texts.[4]

Seizing upon the picture of such letters, he then writes: "You yourselves are our letter of recommendation, written on your [or " our "] hearts, to be known and read by all men."

The Revised Standard Version has "your" instead of "our" in the second clause.[5] The latter is to be preferred, however. It is much more strongly supported by manuscript evidence. Also, it is unlikely that an original "your" should have been changed to "our," since the former is in reality better suited to the metaphor in its immediate context (see below). Furthermore, Paul shows later in this letter that he thought of the Corinthians as "in our hearts" (ch. 7:3).

The picture is not applied consistently. It is true that the Corinthians may be compared to a "letter of recommendation" in that they are, as Christians, a testimony to the effective labors of Paul and his associates, a testimony "to be known and read by all men." (Compare I Thess. 1:8. A somewhat similar idea — though the picture is different — appears in I Cor. 9:2.) On the other hand, it is confusing to say that the letter is "written on our hearts." While the one who is being recommended may be the bearer of the letter, that which was written on the heart *of the person being recommended* would hardly serve the purpose of such a letter, for it would not constitute the kind of independent testimony that documentary recommendations were supposed to provide. It is no doubt because of the inappropriateness of this comment that the change from "our" to "your" was sometimes made in the manuscripts.[6] Even the change does not wholly remove the difficulty, however, since what is "written on the hearts" of the Corinthians could only indirectly, at best, be "known and read by all men."

In v. 3 the picture of the "letter" is retained, but it is drawn differently: "And you show that you are a letter from Christ delivered by us, written not with ink but with the Spirit of the living God, not on tablets of stone but on tablets of human hearts."

The Greek *Christou* ("of Christ") is probably to be understood in the sense of "from Christ," as translated here. Thus it is Christ himself whose authority stands behind this "letter of recommendation." That the genitive case is used to indicate possession ("Ye are a letter belonging to Christ," i.e., "Ye are Christians") is unlikely.[7]

No longer are the Corinthians a letter written on the hearts of the apostles; rather, the apostles have served as ministers of Christ in the creating of this letter. Furthermore, the letter is now understood as having been written on the hearts of the Corinthians, since, in v. 3 as a whole, it is to them that the final phrase in the sentence must refer. The unexpressed application may involve the thought that just as an amanuensis serves the author of a written document, so also Paul and his companions have served Christ in making of the Corinthians a living testimonial.[8]

If Paul is retaining in his mind throughout v. 3 the picture of letters of recommendation, it must be recognized that he is not drawing it accurately in another respect. Such letters were not written on "tablets of stone," but on parchment (compare II Tim. 4:13) or papyrus (compare II John 12). It is likely that this inaccuracy in the use of the picture of the letters is due to the fact that additional pictures are also in Paul's mind, and these have affected his expression of thought. In the first place the contrast between "tablets of stone" and "tablets of human hearts" suggests the influence of Ezek. 11:19 and 36:26, where "heart of stone" and "heart of flesh" are placed in antithesis.[9] Also suggesting this influence is the parallel between Paul's "with the Spirit of the living God" and the statement, in both of the passages in Ezekiel, that " a new spirit " will be given. In addition, the apostle's language almost certainly reflects not only the picture of the giving of the law at Mt. Sinai but also that which is presented by Jeremiah in his words regarding the " new covenant." Paul shows in v. 6 that he has in mind here the idea of the " new covenant "; and the antithesis in v. 3 between " tablets of stone " and " tablets of human hearts " is closely parallel to Jeremiah's contrast between the covenant made at Mt. Sinai (which was set forth on " tables of stone ")[10] and the " new covenant," which is to be made when the law will be written in men's " hearts." [11] There is created the impression that as Paul wrote v. 3 the picture of the letters of recommendation gradually faded away as new thoughts crowded into the writer's mind.[12]

In summary it may be said that in these three verses Paul has mingled together a variety of analogies. Particularly conspicuous is the fact that the picture of the letter of recommendation, which, more than any other, has provided the language here employed, is drawn neither clearly nor accurately. It is evident that it has not been used with the thought that it is to be carefully and thoroughly applied.

II CORINTHIANS 5:1-10

It has been seen that Paul employed a variety of analogies in order to reinforce his answer to a question regarding the resurrection body in I Cor., ch. 15.[1] Similarly, he introduces a combination of pictures as he discusses the relationship between the present earthly life and the future " heavenly " life in II Cor. 5:1-10.

He offers first of all the picture of the " house." Man's present body is represented as an " earthly house " — more specifically a " tent " — in which he dwells. The future body is represented as a house " in the heavens " — a house " not made with hands " (v. 1).

The Revised Standard Version gives a somewhat erroneous impression in the wording of the contrast between " tent " and "house." The Greek, literally translated, contrasts "our earthly house (namely) tent" [2] and "a house not made with hands, eternal in the heavens." It is true that since the former house is a "tent" there is, in a sense, an antithesis between "tent" and "house." In order to grasp the precise nature of the analogy, however, it must be seen that the contrast is in reality between two different kinds of *houses*. In other words, the body in which man dwells is likened to a "*house*," whether that house (now) be a "tent" or (later) a different kind of structure.

Some interpreters suggest that it was natural for a tent-maker (see Acts 18:3) to use the picture of a "tent-house" as a metaphor for the present physical body.[3] More important, however, is the fact that the word *skēnos*, generally translated as "tent," [4] was a common expression for man's earthly body. Numerous examples of this usage of the term have been cited.[5] Particularly noteworthy is a passage in the Wisdom of Solomon (ch. 9:15):

"For a perishable [*phtharton*] body weighs down [*barunei*] the soul,
  and this earthy [*geōdes*] tent [*skēnos*] burdens the thoughtful mind."

The language here is akin to that of Paul in numerous respects. As already observed, *skēnos* ("tent") is the same word employed by Paul in II Cor. 5:1, 4. The verb *barunei* ("weighs down") appears also in v. 4 (*baroumenoi*, "with anxiety," but literally, "being burdened," as in the King James Version). The adjective *geōdes* ("earthy") is at least similar to *epigeios* ("earthly") as in v. 1. The verbal adjective *phtharton* ("perishable"), although not appearing here, is used by Paul in his related discussion in I Cor., ch. 15 (vs. 53 f.). But *thnēton* ("mortal"), which Paul *does* use in v. 4, is found (as *thnētōn*, "of mortals") in the preceding verse (ch. 9:14) of the Wisdom of Solomon. Furthermore, v. 17 in the Wisdom of Solomon refers to the sending of "thy holy Spirit from on high"; Paul writes that God "has given us the Spirit" (II Cor. 5:5). Verse 10 in the Wisdom of Solomon includes the words "that I may learn what is pleasing [*euareston*] to thee"; [6] Paul writes: "We make it our aim to please him," literally, "to be pleasing [*euarestoi*] to him" (v. 9). (This point of correspondence is especially striking because the adjective is found nowhere in the entire Septuagint except in the Wisdom of

Solomon, chs. 9:10 and 4:10.) [7] There is repeated emphasis on judgment in this chapter of the Wisdom of Solomon (ch. 9:3, 5, 7, 12); and Paul says, "We must all appear before the judgment seat of Christ" (II Cor. 5:10). Finally, the chapter in the Wisdom of Solomon expresses repeatedly a concern for "learning" or "knowing" (ch. 9:10, 11, 13, 17); Paul, twice in this section, emphasizes "knowing" (II Cor. 5:1, 6). (This last fact may not be particularly significant, however, since Paul not infrequently prefaces statements with the expression "We know.") [8]

In this usage of the metaphor of the "tent-house" to represent the body, the "body" ($sōma$)—as also in I Cor. 15:35 ff. — is not the total "self," the "person as a whole," [9] as is generally the case with Paul; rather, it is "a shell for the self." [10] Thus conceived, it can be represented by the tent. Just as this kind of shelter lacks the stability and (relative) permanence of a house constructed of wood or brick or stone, so also the present body is one that may be "destroyed" — as over against that other "building" which is "eternal" (II Cor. 5:1).

In the Old Testament the tent is sometimes mentioned as a symbol of impermanence (Isa. 38:12; Jer. 4:20; 10:20). On the other hand, it did not necessarily have this connotation, for in Isa. 33:20 a tent that can*not* be moved or taken down is a metaphor for the security and inviolability of Jerusalem.

The previous verse (II Cor. 4:18) involves a similar antithesis, contrasting the things that are "transient" (literally, "for a season") and those things which are "eternal." [11]

It must be recognized, of course, that the contrast between a tent and a more permanent type of building can be applied to the subject at hand in a limited way only. In reality *no* house is permanent in such a way that it can represent properly the eternal character of the future body given to man. Paul himself apparently had this fact in mind when he referred to the new "house" ("body") as "not made with hands."

The insertion of the expression, "not made with hands," shows clearly that no ordinary house can serve as a suitable picture here.

The new body is a "building from God." It seems possible that Paul may have been influenced here by Dan. 2:34, 45, where the kingdom to be established by God is pictured as a stone "cut out by no human hand" (or "without hands"). It is true that in Daniel the words have nothing to do with a "body" for man. They do, however, convey the idea of that which is provided or brought about by God alone. The passage may well have occurred to the apostle because of the fact that in it the "stone" is presented in contrast to an earthly *body* — the "image" (Dan. 2:31 ff.), in the form of a man, which represented the various kingdoms destined for destruction.[12]

The picture of the tent has also been understood to suggest that "life here is only a pilgrimage."[13] It is true that earthly life was occasionally likened to a pilgrimage.[14] It is also true that tents were often used for temporary shelter by those who were away from their homes (either for military service or for other reasons). It is not impossible, therefore, that Paul's use of the tent as a metaphor for the earthly body may have been intended to suggest the idea that "Christians are citizens of a realm that is in heaven, and on earth they are only sojourners."[15] It must be recognized, however, that the reference to the tent does not necessarily convey this thought, since for many in Paul's world the tent was not merely a shelter during a temporary absence from their more permanent home: it was the only home they ever had.

Thus both the picture of the house as a tent and also the house as a more permanent type of dwelling cannot be applied *fully* to the subject here under consideration.

Beginning with v. 2 a second picture is introduced and merged somewhat with that of the house. When Paul states that we "long to put on our heavenly dwelling," he employs a verb (*ependusasthai*) that literally conveys the idea of "putting on (a garment) over (something else)." Thus there appears the picture of clothing. Here the picture is incomplete and faulty, however, since what is "put on" is the "dwelling" (a "house") which is "from heaven." In the following two verses the shift to the new picture is clearer (though even in v. 4 the metaphor of the tent is once more included).

As the metaphor of clothing is used in vs. 2-4, the picture is that of further clothing being put on *over* the clothing already worn. The verb (*ependusasthai*) which suggests this — as mentioned above — appears both in v. 2 and in v. 4. When this is applied to men's bodies, the necessary conclusion is that Paul is thinking of those who will still be alive at the Parousia, when the body appropriate to the new age will be " put on over " the present body (and then, presumably, the present body will lose its significance).[16]

In v. 1, on the other hand, Paul seems to have in mind the occurrence of death *before* the Parousia, for he implies, at least, that the new body will become one's " house " only after the present body is " destroyed." The words, " we have," may be taken to mean that the new body is already in existence, awaiting us in heaven.[17] Or the present tense may be used " of a future which is absolutely certain," [18] in which case the thought is that a new body will assuredly be provided. But even if the former idea is in Paul's mind, the meaning seems to be that only after the present body is destroyed will the heavenly body be actually appropriated.[19]

Verse 3 (" so that by putting it on we may not be found naked ") is undoubtedly intended to emphasize the idea that the future life *will* involve a " body "; it will not be a life in which the " naked " soul survives wholly apart from any body, as in some forms of first-century thought.[20]

A third analogy is introduced in vs. 6-9. When Paul writes of being " at home in the body " and " away from the Lord " (v. 6) and later of being " away from the body " and " at home with the Lord " (v. 8), his Greek words (*endēmeō* and *ekdēmeō*) pertain to one's homeland — one's country. One is either *in* his true homeland (*en-*) or away from it (*ek-*). The picture is somewhat related to that of the house (vs. 1 ff.), since the thought of one's house may be closely associated with that of one's homeland. Strictly speaking, however, a homeland is not the same as a house. It is evident that Paul is not using the picture of the homeland carefully or accurately. The very expression, "to be at home *in the body*" (or, later, "to be away from the body"), involves a mixing of the metaphors, of homeland and house, since the body, as a covering for the self, may be represented as a house, but it is hardly to be conceived as a "homeland." (The more accurate use of the new metaphor would have involved some such expression as "at home in this earthly life.")

It is probable that in vs. 8 f. Paul is thinking particularly of men's state or condition *at the Parousia*. Although some of the words — "We would rather be away from the body" — might suggest a desire for death here and now, in order that one might be "at home with the Lord," the total context seems to rule out this interpretation. In v. 10 it is stated that all must "appear" (literally, "be made manifest") before the "judgment seat of Christ." The thought, presumably, is of judgment at the Parousia.[21] Hence a point of time in the future is envisaged. If "to be away from the body" refers to death here and now, this leaves an interval of time *between* such death and this future judgment. In this case v. 9 is unintelligible. Since those who have died (those who are "away" from the body) would be in a state of "sleep" (I Thess. 4:13-15), they could hardly be active in their "aim to please him." Therefore it is perhaps better to state the thought thus: although *now* we are "at home in the body" and "away from the Lord" (v. 6), we look forward to the Parousia, when we shall be "away from the body and at home with the Lord" (v. 8). In any case, whether we are (to be found) "at home" in the body or away from it *at the Parousia*, our (present) aim is "to please him" (v. 9), for when the Parousia does occur we shall be judged according to what we have done here and now (v. 10).

Of course, on the basis of Phil. 1:23 the interpreter is tempted to believe that at some point in his career Paul began to regard resurrection (and judgment) as highly personal and individual, not necessarily to be associated with a future *general* resurrection (and judgment). Verses 6-9 in II Cor., Ch. 5, would be intelligible if this is now the apostle's thought. Verse 10, however, with its reference to the future judgment, seems to rule out such an interpretation, unless it is added as a common form of expression suggesting the certainty of judgment and is not intended to be understood with complete literalness.

In summarizing Paul's use of analogy in this section of the material, we note that two major facts emerge: (1) Particularly conspicuous is the mixing of the metaphors. On the one hand, there is the interweaving of the picture of the house with that of the garment or clothing (vs. 2-4). On the other hand, there is mingling of the picture of the house with that of the homeland (vs. 6-9). Such a mixing or interweaving of pictures indicates that it is not the picture itself that dominates the Pauline expression of thought. Rather, the pictures are to be understood as convenient vehicles, used loosely and freely. Elements in the pictures are employed to convey certain aspects of the apostle's thought, but the thought cannot be defined on the basis of the pictures. Or, to put it differently, the mingling of the pictures shows that no attempt is being made to develop and to apply in detail any one picture.

(2) A further fact also emerges: the analogies employed here are applicable to the Pauline thought in a limited way only. It has already been seen that the picture of the two kinds of houses (the "tent-house" as over against the more permanent "building") is only partially applicable. It is relevant primarily as it corresponds, in a relative way, to the contrast between the present earthly body and the body that is eternal. The picture is not wholly suitable, however, in that *no* house possesses those qualities which correspond completely to the "eternal" nature of the body which is anticipated. But it is even more significant that while both the picture of the house and that of the garment have considerable relevance insofar as the *immediate discussion* of "body" is concerned, neither picture suggests satisfactorily the otherwise predominant and really characteristic Pauline thought in regard to "body." In the discussion of the metaphor of the "tent-house" attention was directed briefly to the fact that the picture could be employed to represent man's earthly body if that body is conceived as a kind of "shell" in which the "self" resides. It was noted, however, that such a concept of the body is not the one that Paul gener-

ally expresses. As Bultmann has shown, the apostle sometimes is led (or "misled") into "*adopting* his opponents'
method of argumentation," using concepts that are not necessarily characteristic of him.[22] This seems to be the case in
II Cor. 5:1-10, at least in part. The metaphors of the house
and of the garment convey the idea that a person "has" one
kind of body or another: he lives *in* it, as in a dwelling; he
puts it on, as an article of clothing. Paul apparently introduced the concept because he could use it to develop the
contrast between the "things that are seen" and the "things
that are unseen" (ch. 4:18), but in so using it he has pictured the body as something less than the "person as a
whole."

Bultmann observes that even here, however, the more characteristic Pauline view of body may be seen indirectly. Insofar as
there is expressed the desire to be "further clothed" and not
"naked," it is implied that the future life is "bodily" life. As
over against certain contemporary notions of the survival of the
soul apart from any body, here it is suggested that the body is
not something that is separable from the true self. By implication,
therefore, the true self (or the true person) *is sōma* ("body");
or, conversely, the body is the "whole person."[23] Primarily in this
passage, nevertheless, is the concept of the body as that which
"houses" or "clothes" the self.

From this it is evident that the pictures of the house and the
garment serve only the immediate purpose of the author.
They are applicable only within the framework of the given
context. To use them fully — as a basis for interpreting the
essential Pauline thought — is quite impossible.

II CORINTHIANS 9:6

The picture of sowing and reaping is introduced briefly in
II Cor. 9:6: "He who sows sparingly will also reap sparingly, and he who sows bountifully will also reap bountifully."[1] The words appear in connection with Paul's appeal
for an "offering for the saints" (v. 1).

The analogy, as presented here, is only partially appropriate and applicable. In agriculture the sowing of much seed does not necessarily guarantee a bountiful return, since numerous other factors are involved. Weather, the nature of the soil, and other conditions are also important.[2] Nor is it true, insofar as the matter of gifts for the needy is concerned, that the giver of the larger amounts will necessarily be assured the greater approval from God, for Paul has stated earlier his conviction that man's readiness to give from that which he possesses is more important than the actual amount given (ch. 8:12). Thus the picture, as introduced, can be applied only loosely. It seems likely that it was suggested to Paul by the Septuagint version of Prov. 22:8 ("He who sows what is of little account will reap what is of little worth"), since in the following verse (v. 7) he reproduces in general Prov. 22:8a (Septuagint): "God loves a cheerful giver."

Paul has written *hilaron gar dotēn agapai ho theos*. The Septuagint has *andra hilaron kai dotēn eulogei ho theos*. It is worth noting that though Paul uses *agapai* ("loves") instead of *eulogei* ("blesses") in v. 7, he does use a form of the latter word in v. 6.[3] Altogether, the similarities between II Cor. 9:6 f. and Prov. 22:8, 8a are too great to be accidental.

One must conclude, therefore, that the picture is introduced, not because it can be applied fully to the subject at hand, but rather, because it was a familiar form of expression suggesting likeness between a cause and an effect.

II CORINTHIANS 10:3-6

A use of analogy based upon military activity is seen in II Cor. 10:3-6. The labor of the apostle is likened to the waging of war (*strateuometha* in v. 3 and *strateias* in v. 4); he employs "weapons" (*hopla*); he lays siege to "strongholds" (*ochurōmatōn*); he takes captives (*aichmalōtizontes*, v. 5).[1]

Although the analogy of warfare is applicable insofar as Paul is attempting to "destroy" those "strongholds" of "arguments" which stand in the way of the "knowledge of

God," it cannot be applied fully. Whereas in warfare the purpose of the protagonist is (normally, at least) to subdue and subjugate the opposing persons, the apostles' warfare is aimed at their own welfare (" for building you up and not for destroying you," v. 8).[2]

Paul also uses the military metaphor elsewhere (see II Cor. 6:7; Rom. 7:23; 13:12 f.; I Thess. 5:8).[3] It is possible that here the apostle may be influenced by Prov. 21:22, not only because a similar picture of a siege is involved, but also in view of the fact that in the previous chapter (II Cor. 9:6) he seems to have borrowed from an adjacent passage in Prov. (ch. 22:8).

II CORINTHIANS 11:2 f.

This analogy is introduced briefly in II Cor. 11:2: " I feel a divine jealousy for you, for I betrothed you to Christ to present you as a pure bride to her one husband."

The picture of betrothal and marriage is common, of course, in the Old Testament,[1] where it is used to represent the relationship between God and Israel. After the time of Paul it continued to be employed, but, as here, to represent the relationship between Christ and the church.[2] As Paul uses it in this passage Christ appears as the bridegroom, the Christian community at Corinth as the bride (*parthenon*, literally, " young woman " or " virgin "), and Paul himself as the person (such as the father)[3] by whom the betrothal was arranged. The primary emphasis is upon the role of the arranger of the betrothal, since the total context concerns the status or position of the apostle.

There are various elements in the analogy which may be regarded as applicable to the situation under consideration. As a third person arranges a betrothal, so also Paul has brought the Corinthian Christians into a relationship with Christ. As an interval of time elapses between bethrothal and marriage, so also there is a period of waiting between the conversion of the Corinthians and the final realization of their relationship with Christ at the Parousia.[4] Like the ar-

ranger of the betrothal, the apostle looks forward to this realization and with " jealousy " watches over the " bride," the
Corinthian Christians, so that they may be pure and un-
corrupted at the Parousia.

When Paul writes *zēlō gar humas theou zēlōi*, the verb *zēlō* and
the noun *zēlōi* can refer either to " zeal " or to " jealousy." There
is no doubt that the apostle was exceedingly " zealous " for the
well-being of the Corinthian Christians. The following verse
shows, however, that the idea of " jealousy " was uppermost in
his mind at this point. He is " jealous " lest his converts be " led
astray " from " single-hearted fidelity " [5] to Christ.

Although the picture is thus applicable in several respects,
there is evidence that Paul is not attempting consciously to
apply it in detail. Rather, his thought seems to be dominated
by the situation at Corinth; and his language, though drawn
from the picture, is actually determined by the issue under
consideration. Even when he speaks of being " jealous," he
does so primarily in terms of this issue rather than of the
picture. While it is conceivable that the arranger of the betrothal might be one " who watched jealously over the bride's
conduct in the interval before the marriage," [6] or one who,
with jealousy " cannot bear any disarrangement of his de-
sign," [7] it would be much more normal, in the case of an actual betrothal, to associate the jealousy with the bridegroom
himself, not with the arranger. Thus, in the case of the Old
Testament usages of the analogy,[8] it is God, as the " husband," who is jealous in regard to his " wife," Israel. When
Paul, therefore, associates the jealousy with himself, the
third party, he seems to be adjusting the analogy to his immediate purpose rather than developing the analogy. This
conclusion is supported, further, by the reference to a " *divine* jealousy " (literally, a " jealousy of God ") on the part
of the apostle. Although the expression is somewhat ambiguous,[9] it seems to suggest a contrast between Paul's (divine)
jealousy and the " sectarian zeal of his opponents." [10] If this
is true, it is without doubt clearly the issue at hand, rather

than the picture itself, which is determinative.

Similarly, the reference to the "one" husband could hardly have been suggested by the picture. In the case of a betrothal the third party would, of course, expect to present the bride to the "one" husband. But this would ordinarily be taken entirely for granted. The insertion of "one" (*heni*) is therefore "probably aimed at those who were distracting the Corinthians from their loyalty to the Christ preached by St. Paul." [11] Thus, again, it is not the conscious application of the picture which is involved here, but rather, the adjustment of the picture to the situation at hand.

Interpreters differ in regard to the relationship of v. 3 to the analogy of betrothal and marriage: "But I am afraid that as the serpent deceived Eve by his cunning, your thoughts will be led astray from a sincere and pure devotion to Christ" (literally, "from the singleness and the purity which is toward Christ"). On the one hand, it is supposed that the analogy of v. 2 is here further developed: "The Church, as a second Eve, is espoused to Christ, the new Adam (I Cor. 15:45). She must beware lest, like Eve, she listen to the voice of the same tempter, who ever lieth in wait to deceive, and so lose the privileges she was destined to enjoy." [12] If the term "purity" (*hagnotētos*) in v. 3 was in the original text, its presence, as parallel to "pure" (*hagnēn*) in v. 2, might suggest that the picture of the previous verse is carried over here. It seems more likely, however, that "purity" is a gloss,[13] added, perhaps, in order to connect v. 3 more closely with v. 2. If this is true, then there is lacking any evidence that this verse is related to the analogy of betrothal and marriage. Instead, a new picture is introduced: Paul fears that the Corinthian Christians may be "led astray" by false teachers (v. 4) as Eve was "deceived" according to Gen., ch. 3, or as she was seduced by Satan, who, according to rabbinical legend, appeared in the form of a serpent, and then of an angel, and brought about her fall.[14]

Numerous writers are convinced that Paul must have been familiar with some such legend. Verse 14 of this chapter ("even

Satan disguises himself as an angel of light") is mentioned by Menzies as showing, when combined with v. 3, its influence upon the Pauline language.[15] Plummer, however, asks if it is "probable that St. Paul would allude to such legends in writing to Gentiles." [16]

Whether Paul is thinking only of Gen., ch. 3, or also of the rabbinical legend, it appears likely that he has turned suddenly from the analogy of betrothal and marriage to the analogy of Eve. If this is true, it is evident that the apostle, in this passage, has not attempted to develop and apply either picture in any detail. Both pictures are apparently employed for the sake of those elements in them which are immediately and directly relevant to the subject under discussion.

II CORINTHIANS 11:8

Although the English translation does not indicate it clearly, a picture of military life is suggested briefly in II Cor. 11:8, where Paul refers once more [1] to the fact that he had not received support from the church at Corinth: "I robbed other churches by accepting support from them in order to serve you."

Two of the words used here were common in connection with the life and activity of the soldier. The verb translated "I robbed" (*esulēsa*) was frequently employed with reference to the "despoiling" of a defeated enemy.[2] The noun rendered "support" (*opsōnion*) was used for a soldier's pay, or allowance. The latter has already been considered as it appears in I Cor. 9:7.[3] It is to be observed here, however, that Paul can apply the former expression ("I robbed") to himself only in a strictly limited way. He apparently means to suggest, as the last part of v. 8 and v. 9 indicate, that as a soldier took from a defeated foe that for which no service had been rendered in return, so also the apostle has received from "other churches" a contribution for which no corresponding service had been given. (The service has been to the Corinthians instead.) The allusion is somewhat clarified by his words in Phil. 4:15 ff., where he mentions the fact that the Christians in Philippi had contributed to his needs while he worked elsewhere. In a sense, therefore, he could say that he "robbed" other churches.

"The Corinthians were just as much bound to support the Apostle when at Corinth as any other churches were when the Apostle was with them. And, therefore, if when at Corinth he availed himself of assistance from those other Churches, he was taking from them what they ought not to have been called upon to supply."[4]

It is quite evident, on the other hand, that the suggested picture of the despoiling soldier is highly irrelevant and inapplicable in numerous ways. Other churches, such as the one at Philippi, certainly cannot be represented as an opposed — and defeated — enemy. Also, that which was given as a "gift"[5] can in no sense be likened to spoils taken by compulsion. Furthermore, the idea of improper conduct which is associated with the expression[6] is entirely inappropriate, hence it is clearly rejected in v. 7. Altogether the picture is one that can be applied in a most limited manner only.

II CORINTHIANS 12:7 f.

In II Cor. 12:1-10, Paul writes concerning "visions and revelations" and also concerning his "weaknesses." He introduces in this discussion two metaphors: "And to keep me from being too elated by the abundance of revelation, a thorn was given me in the flesh, a messenger of Satan, to harass me, to keep me from being too elated."

It is particularly difficult to analyze the apostle's use of analogy in this passage, partly because the precise meaning of some of the words cannot be determined, and partly because the nature of the "weakness" is nowhere indicated.

Paul's word *skolops* is frequently translated "thorn,"[1] but it can also mean "splinter," or "stake." While in the Septuagint the term is used at times with reference to something small, as a "thorn" or "splinter" (Num. 33:55; Ezek. 28:24), in other places a larger "stake" may be meant (Hos.

2:6 = LXX, 2:8; Ecclus. 43:19).[2] It is perhaps worth noting that in the two passages in the Septuagint where the word is clearly used metaphorically (Num. 33:55 and Ezek. 28:24) something small like a " thorn " seems to be meant. It is possible, therefore, that *in metaphorical usage skolops* was taken to mean " thorn " rather than " stake " (although in both of these cases the " thorns " represent people, which is probably not true with Paul).[3]

Even more uncertain is the nature of that which Paul calls a " thorn in the flesh." Suggestions have included temptations of various sorts, persons who opposed him and caused trouble for him, his own impatience, some physical handicap or malady such as a defect of vision, epilepsy, malaria, rheumatic attacks, and others. Literature on the subject has become quite voluminous.[4] If the " thorn in the flesh " is to be identified with the " bodily ailment " (*astheneian tēs sarkos*), literally, " a weakness of the flesh," of Gal. 4:13, then it must refer to some kind of physical condition likely to produce a feeling of repulsion on the part of others (v. 14), and it might have involved his eyes (v. 15b). It is by no means certain, however, that the weakness mentioned in vs. 13-15 is the same as that to which reference is made in II Cor. 12:7-10. And even if the two are to be identified, the allusion to " eyes " in Gal. 4:15 may be purely metaphorical.[5]

It is interesting that in the Septuagint, Num. 33:55 includes the metaphorical expression *skolopes en tois ophthalmois* (" pricks in your eyes "). The word translated " pricks " (*skolopes*) is the same that Paul uses (" thorn ") in II Cor. 12:7, and the word for " eyes " (*ophthalmois*) is used by Paul in Gal. 4:15. If, in both of these Pauline passages, the apostle is referring to the same " weakness," it is possible that he was inclined to think of it in terms of the metaphor of Num. 33:55. But in this case the reference to " eyes " would be definitely metaphorical, and thus would provide no evidence that Paul's ailment involved his eyes literally.

Altogether, uncertainty remains both in regard to the picture itself (the intended meaning of *skolops*) and also in regard to the nature of the " weakness " or condition that it represents. In view of this, it is utterly impossible to arrive at any useful conclusions as to the extent of correspondence between the picture that is employed and the fact that that picture represents. The most that can be said is that here Paul uses analogical language, but its effectiveness is dependent upon a greater knowledge of background and circumstance than is now available.

As a second metaphor Paul introduces the picture of " a messenger," or an " angel " (*angelos*), of Satan. The difficulty or ailment with which the apostle is afflicted is thus represented in personal terms. The idea of personality is reinforced by the words that follow, for the " messenger " is described as one who can " harass " or " buffet " (*kolaphizē*) — literally, " strike with the fist " — and also is mentioned (v. 8) as one who might " leave " or " depart " (*apostēi*).[6] If Paul's " thorn in the flesh " is understood as some kind of physical ailment or malady, then it must be recognized that at least in this instance the apostle is describing in personal terms something that in actuality lacks true personality. If, on the other hand, Paul is referring to a person (or persons), then the term " messenger " does not necessarily involve analogical usage at all.

II CORINTHIANS 12:14

In the course of Paul's discussion regarding his relationship with the Christian community at Corinth the apostle touches again in II Cor., ch. 12, upon his unwillingness to " be a burden." [1] His concern is for *them;* he does not seek their possessions. He observes that " children ought not to lay up for their parents, but parents for their children " (v. 14c).

The picture of the parent-child relationship is relevant and applicable, of course, in certain respects. Paul shows elsewhere that he thought of himself as a kind of " father " to those whom he brought into the world of Christian life and experience.[2] Particularly important is the fact that there rests upon parents the obligation to provide for the well-being of their children. Similarly, Paul suggests, he labors in behalf of the Corinthians, not receiving his support from them, but rather, serving them out of love (v. 15b) and because of his concern for their " souls " (v. 15a).

It must be recognized, however, that here again the apostle appears to be presenting a picture that is limited in its usefulness. When he says that " children ought not to lay up for their parents," the words seem to deny that children have the obligation to provide for their parents. That Paul would really have denied such filial responsibility is quite unlikely.[3] It is possible, of course, that these words are introduced simply to heighten the force of the contrasting statement, " but parents [ought to lay up] for their children."

"Very often one of two alternatives is in form negatived, not in order to exclude it absolutely, but to show its inferiority to the other alternative."[4]

If this is the case in this instance, then it follows that Paul is not intending, in these words, to make his picture conform to actuality. It has also been suggested that Paul's words may be regarded as true insofar as children are still young.[5] There is no indication, however, that this qualification was intended. It has been proposed, further, that Paul's word for " lay up " (*thēsaurizein*) means " to lay up treasure," or " to accumulate money " — *not* " to support " or " to help " — and this Paul might have meant.[6] But if this distinction were consciously made, then the expression becomes quite irrelevant, since the issue under consideration concerned precisely the matter of " support," not the laying up of treasure.

In view of all of this, the following alternative conclusions must be reached in regard to the statement that " children ought not to lay up for their parents ": (1) If the words are to be taken literally, they can hardly represent the apostle's true thought concerning filial responsibility. (2) If the words are intended only to heighten the force of the contrasting statement ("but parents for their children "), and are therefore not intended to conform to reality, then this part of the picture can have no intrinsic significance. (3) If a distinction is intended between "lay up treasure" (which he means) and "support" (which he does not mean), then this part of the picture is irrelevant to the immediate issue. Altogether, therefore, either this element in the picture does not actually conform to what is believed to be true in family life, as (1) and (2), or else it is irrelevant, as (3). Since relevance is to be presumed, the interpreter is left with the probability that Paul has not drawn his picture according to strict actuality, but rather, has adjusted it in the light of the purpose for which it was introduced: Paul has not expected the Corinthian Christians to provide for him. Thus there is found here another case where it is impossible for the interpreter to use the given picture fully as a key to the apostle's thought. Instead, Paul's thought must be accepted as determinative for an interpretation of the analogical material.

5.

The Letter of Paul to the Romans

Romans 4:4

In Rom., ch. 4, Paul appeals to the figure of Abraham in support of his contention that justification is based upon faith apart from works of law (see also ch. 3:28, 30).[1] After quoting in v. 3 the Septuagint version of Gen. 15:6, "Abraham believed God, and it was reckoned to him as righteousness," the apostle writes (v. 4), "Now to one who works, his wages are not reckoned as a gift but as his due." The picture is that of the workman and of the pay that he has earned by his labor.

Insofar as the use of analogy is concerned, the particularly important point to be observed here is that the picture, as drawn, is not actually applied. In the following verse Paul speaks, not of one who works, but of one who does *not* work; and he does so in such a way as to indicate that his thought is not of the picture at all, but of one (presumably Abraham in this context) who "has faith" in God.

Paul uses forms of the verb *pisteuō* in these verses. The Revised Standard Version gives "believed" in v. 3 and "trusts" in v. 5, though in some other passages it offers "has faith" (chs. 1:16; 10:4). The American Translation more consistently uses "had faith" and "has faith," not only in these verses but also elsewhere in Romans (chs. 1:16; 3:22; 4:17, 18, 24; etc.). Here (v. 5) the word "trusts" (Revised Standard Version) is hardly adequate, for while Paul's thought regarding faith does involve trust, this faith is "not just trust-in-God in general; rather, that trust which, by accepting the cross, lays its foundation upon God's deed of salvation." [2]

173

Lietzmann suggests, following Lagrange, that if Paul were to have provided a picture that would be properly applicable he should have continued in some such way as this: " But if one does not work and yet receives a payment, this occurs out of grace or mercy and not because of the work. Such was the case with Abraham." [3] Thus, instead of developing the analogy and making it directly applicable in this way (or in some similar manner), Paul continues with a statement concerning one's status with reference to God (v. 5). It is possible, in a situation of this kind, that the apostle might expect the reader to supply the development and application of the picture. The difficulty here, however, is that the picture as presented in v. 4 – of a workman and his pay – does not, in itself, suggest such development. At least under normal circumstances the picture of a workman and his pay is not usually associated with the picture of one who receives a payment *without* working. In other words, this latter picture might be supplied in the light of a knowledge of Paul's thought concerning justification through faith apart from law; it is unlikely that it would occur to a reader on the basis of the picture of a workman and his pay. Thus it appears that for the reader, as for Paul, the picture offered in v. 4 possesses relatively little significance in and of itself. It is not a picture that, as drawn, can be used as a basis for an understanding of the Pauline thought about justification. It can be made relevant or significant only in the light of the context that in other terms emphasizes justification apart from works of law.

It is worth noting that just as the Pauline idea of justification is determinative insofar as the relevance of the analogy is concerned, so also the same idea dominates the apostle's use (v. 3) of Gen. 15:6. The statement that Abraham " believed God " (Septuagint) does not, in its own context, involve all that Paul means by " faith." It is true that Gen., ch. 15, includes pre-Priestly material, and hence may reflect a prophetic rather than a more legalistic point of view. The meaning intended by *episteusen* (" believed ") may therefore come somewhat closer to the Pauline concept of faith than might otherwise be the case.[4] The fact remains, how-

ever, that Abraham "believed God" when God declared to him,
"So shall your descendants be" (Gen. 15:5). "To believe," in
this context, must consequently mean "have trust" or "have confidence" that God would fulfill this specific promise. A little later
in Romans, strangely enough, Paul himself attaches this meaning
to the Genesis account of Abraham (Rom. 4:16-21). All of this
indicates, therefore, that when Paul uses Gen. 15:6 the quotation
becomes relevant to his discussion in Rom. 4:1-5 only when it is
interpreted according to his own idea of faith. Thus it becomes
clear, as stated above, that the quotation concerning Abraham,
like the analogy of the workman and his pay, becomes useful and
applicable only as the apostle makes it so, adjusting its meaning
to correspond to his own thought. Neither the quotation nor the
analogy, out of Paul's own context, can provide a proper clue to
his theological thinking.

ROMANS 5:7

In Rom. 5:6-8, Paul attempts to bring out the full force of
the fact that "Christ died for the ungodly" (v. 6). His death
occurred in behalf of men who did not — and could not —
deserve such a sacrifice: [1] "While we were yet sinners Christ
died for us" (v. 8). The apostle emphasizes the uniqueness
of this event by introducing a picture of the attitude taken
by man generally in regard to the making of the supreme
sacrifice: "One will hardly die for a righteous man — though
perhaps for a good man one will dare even to die" (v. 7).

In the Greek the words *dikaiou* ("righteous") and *agathou*
("good") can be either masculine or neuter. It is likely that the
former is intended (hence, "righteous *man*" and "good *man*,"
not "righteous *thing*" nor "good *thing*"), since the context concerns *persons*,[2] and "the notion of dying for an abstract idea is
entirely unlike the New Testament, or the age in which the New
Testament was written." [3]

The picture is not entirely clear. Two lines of interpretation
are possible: (*a*) If "righteous" and "good" are to be understood as synonymous,[4] and if "hardly" (*molis*) is taken
as "very rarely" [5] (so as to agree with "perhaps," *tacha*),
then both clauses of v. 7 have identical meanings.

Lietzmann regards v. 7b as having been dictated as an intentional revision or correction of v. 7a.[6] It seems, however, that there would be little need for such revision unless *molis* ("hardly") conveyed so strongly the idea of impossibility that Paul decided against it in favor of *tacha* ("perhaps"). But other usages of *molis* show that the word did not necessarily convey the notion of impossibility (Acts 14:18; 27:7, 8, 16; I Peter 4:18; Wisd. of Sol. 9:16; compare Luke 9:39).

In this case the picture is that of man as one who only rarely will die in behalf of another, and then only if the other is "righteous" or "good." When the picture, thus understood, is applied to the point of issue, it conveys the idea that whereas it is exceptional for a man to die in behalf even of a person of worthy qualities, Christ has died for "the ungodly" — for "us" — who "were yet sinners," possessing no worthiness whatever.

(*b*) If "righteous" and "good" are regarded as having somewhat different connotations, the latter is probably intended to be the stronger term. It may be supposed that the "good" is "something warmer and more genial,"[7] suggesting the "more generous and inspiring type of character."[8] Thus understood v. 7 may be said to present a kind of double picture: there is man as one who will "hardly" die in behalf of a (merely) "righteous" person; there is also man as one who may somewhat more willingly die in behalf of a "good" person. The rendering of the American Translation expresses this interpretation: "A man will hardly give his life for an upright person, though perhaps for a really good man some may be brave enough to die." If this properly suggests the Pauline meaning, then the intended application may be expressed thus: a man may "perhaps" give his life for one who is "good"; a man will "hardly" make this sacrifice for one who is only "righteous"; Christ, however, died for those who were *sinners* — for those who were "not good men, not even just men."[9]

A distinctive feature of this passage concerns the fact that here there is emphasized *contrast* between picture and idea

rather than likeness. In both of the above interpretations —
(a) and (b) — the death of Christ is shown to be unique because Christ, who has died in behalf of *sinners,* has shown
himself to be *different* from ordinary man, who is pictured as
being willing (at best) to make the ultimate sacrifice only in
behalf of someone possessing merit or worthiness. It may be
argued, perhaps, that likeness is in some measure implied.
The reader might supply, between vs. 7 and 8, something
like the following: thus it is unusual for a man to die in behalf of another. Christ has done this unusual thing. This element of similarity is overshadowed, however, by the greater
contrast that yet remains: a man might die for a " good "
person; Christ, on the contrary, has died for *sinners.*

Romans 6:1-14

Several analogical usages appear in Rom. 6:1-14, where
Paul confronts the question " Are we to continue in sin that
grace may abound? " (v. 1b).

The apostle has insisted earlier that salvation for man is
found only through faith, not through "works." By God's
" grace as a gift " it is made available to sinful man (ch. 3:23-
25). Paul can even say, in the course of his argument, that
"where sin increased, grace abounded all the more " (ch.
5:20). He recognizes, however, that from this a false conclusion might be drawn: in order that there may be more
grace, let there be more sin! [1] In ch. 6:1-14 he addresses himself directly to the issue, emphasizing particularly the idea
that man, having entered into a new life " in Christ," must
now consider himself as " dead " to sin (v. 11). The " old
self " (literally, " old man "), the slave of sin, has died (vs.
5 ff.). To suggest, therefore, that one should " continue in
sin that grace may abound " (v. 1) is to overlook this important point. " How can we who died to sin still live in it? "
(V. 2.)

It must be recognized that in this section of the letter Paul
mingles his verb tenses and moods. The death of the " old self "
has occurred (vs. 5-8a). At the same time, the full realization of

the new condition of life is referred to as future (vs. 5b and 8b). And since Paul must still admonish his readers not to let sin reign in their "mortal bodies" (v. 12), it is evident that there is a sense in which they have *not* yet "died to sin." In v. 11 the apostle suggests the way in which the seemingly divergent views may be reconciled: "So you also must consider yourselves dead to sin and alive to God in Christ Jesus." This seems to mean that, insofar as Christians have experienced through faith God's saving act, they have already entered a new realm of existence, and their conduct is to be determined in the light of this fact. In terms of actual achievement, however, they must look to the future. " For on the ideal or purely religious plane, the Christian, by faith and by his solemn incorporation into Christ's people, *has* left the old life behind and entered upon the new. But Paul was realist enough to recognize that it did not by any means automatically follow that the Christian ceased to sin. His letters are full of exhortations to those who, *ex hypothesi*, have died to sin, but who are far from having realized the Christian ideal in practice." [2]

Michel notes particularly the juxtaposition of the indicative and imperative moods in this section of the letter. The former is intended to emphasize that which God has done with reference to one who has been baptized. The latter is intended to show what the one who has been baptized should do. In this way the indicative and imperative form a unity. [3]

Lietzmann directs attention to the fact that the antinomy found here is similar to that which is found elsewhere in Paul. Justification is also described both as present (Rom. 3:24; 5:1-9; I Cor. 6:11) and as future (Gal. 5:5; Rom. 3:30; 6:16-19). In the same way sonship to God is sometimes mentioned as present (Rom. 8:14-16; Gal. 4:4-7) and sometimes as future (Rom. 8:23). [4]

In emphasizing the idea that Christians have " died to sin," Paul employs the picture of baptism. " Do you not know," he asks, " that all of us who have been baptized into Christ Jesus were baptized into his death? We were buried therefore with him by baptism into death." (Vs. 3 f.)

To state that Paul employs the baptismal procedure *analogically* is not to say that the significance that he saw in baptism is limited to its analogical meaning. It may be true that " here, in this sacrament, is something actually done "; [5] in baptism there occurs something that is very real and not merely " symbolic." [6] Bultmann observes that although the act of baptism was less significant than "the word," nevertheless "baptism is an objective occurrence which happens to the baptized, not simply a symbol for a subjective process within him." [7] But even if baptismal procedure *as analogy* should be understood as relatively unimportant insofar as the total Pauline thought is concerned, the nature of the analogical usage is obviously relevant to the present study.

Although the New Testament provides no clear description of the procedure that was followed in early Christian baptism, Paul presupposes here the act of immersion. It may be urged that baptism was not always by immersion, since this form of the rite would hardly have been possible in a prison (Acts 16:33) or in a private home (Acts 10:48). On the other hand, Philip baptized after going down " into the water " (Acts 8:38). Furthermore, early Christian practice was undoubtedly influenced by the baptism of Jesus himself by John the Baptist; and the reference to Jesus coming up " out of the water " (Mark 1:10; compare Matt. 3:16) indicates immersion. In any case it is only this form which is relevant in the Pauline reference now under consideration.

It is true that Paul does not present a carefully drawn picture of the baptismal procedure. Nor does he indicate explicitly that analogical usage is intended. The implications, however, cannot be avoided. Since death and burial are both mentioned, the thought must be that just as the immersed convert disappears from sight beneath the surface of the water, so also the " old self " disappears (" dies "); [8] and just as the body is enclosed by the surrounding water, so also the " self " that was subject to sin is " buried."

It is possible, furthermore, that the analogical thought is intended to be carried even farther. Paul adds, " So that as Christ was raised from the dead by the glory of the Father, we too might walk in newness of life " (Rom. 6:4b). Although the wording here fails to associate baptism explicitly with the new life that follows the death of the old, [9] the reader can hardly fail to make the connection: just as the convert is raised from the water, so also the Christian ex-periences a kind of resurrection, prepared to " walk in new-ness of life," being now " alive to God in Christ Jesus " (v. 11). One may suspect that the picture of Christ's own death and resurrection as analagous to the death of the " old self " and the emergence of the new (see below) has suddenly led him to turn from the further development and application of the picture of baptism with which he began even though it may yet have been in his thought.

It is sometimes suggested that the picture of baptism may still be in Paul's mind as v. 5 was dictated or written: " For if we have been united with him in a death like his, we shall certainly be united with him in a resurrection like his." More literally the verse reads: " For if we have become united in the likeness of his death, we shall also be (in the likeness) of the (his) resurrection." The thought may be, as perhaps in v. 4b, that " baptism, inasmuch as one emerges from the water after being immersed, is a *homoiōma* [" likeness "] of resurrection as well as of death." [10]

If to " be in the likeness of his resurrection " refers to being in the new state in which one might " walk in newness of life," then v. 5 simply restates the content of v. 4. On the other hand, the use of the future tense suggests that " resurrection " in this instance is intended to be understood literally. If this is the case, then Paul has momentarily turned from the main subject under consid-eration here, and, influenced by his mention of Christ's resurrec-tion as analogy (see below) for the new (present) life in Christ, has interrupted his argument to express his confidence that since Christ has been raised, Christians may look forward with confi-dence to resurrection for themselves also (compare Rom. 8:11; I Cor. 15:20, 23; II Cor. 4:14; Phil. 3:20 f.; I Thess. 4:14). The rising from the water in baptism could be said, of course, to pro-vide a picture to which " resurrection " in *either* of these senses could be likened.

The act of immersion in baptism is not the only analogy that appears in this section of the letter. The death of the " old self " and the emergence of the new is also presented in terms of the picture of Christ's own death and resurrection.

We are not to " continue in sin " (v. 1); rather, we should " walk in newness of life " (v. 4c). As Christ was " raised from the dead " (v. 4b), so also we have entered a new sphere of life.[11] Or, as Paul expresses it later, just as Christ, " being raised from the dead," is freed from the dominion of death (v. 9) and from the claims of sin (v. 10a), so also the Christians must consider themselves " dead to sin and alive to God in Christ Jesus " (v. 11).

This picture of the death and resurrection of Christ is clearly relevant insofar as Christ, after this occurrence, lives in such relation to God that sin no longer has any claim upon him.[12] The Christian, likewise, has " died to sin " and stands in a new relationship to God. The picture, nevertheless, is not fully applicable to the issue under consideration. In the picture the new state of existence for Christ follows his *physical* death. Paul's immediate concern in regard to the Christians pertains to the new state of life into which they have *already* entered (ideally at least) while they still remain in this temporal earthly order. In other words, the picture involving Christ is applicable insofar as it points to a change from one sphere of life to another. In the case of Christ and his resurrection, however, the new sphere of life which is involved does not correspond in reality to that with which Paul is immediately and primarily concerned in this part of the letter.

A third analogy — that of slavery — is introduced very briefly in v. 6b: " And we might no longer be enslaved to sin. For he who has died is freed from sin." This picture is developed somewhat further in the following part of ch. 6 (vs. 15-23), and will be treated in the next section.

From the foregoing consideration the following facts emerge:

(1) The picture of the baptismal procedure is not clearly or explicitly drawn. Apparently baptism by immersion is simply taken for granted.

(2) The application of the picture is implied rather than stated carefully. *How* immersion in water corresponds to

death and burial is not indicated. And the language only very vaguely suggests a correspondence between the rising from the water and a " resurrection " involving " newness of life " here and now.

(3) The picture of baptism is combined almost immediately with the picture of Christ's own death and resurrection (vs. 4b ff.) and a little later with that of slavery (vs. 6 f.).

(4) The picture of Christ's death and resurrection is applicable to the issue at hand in a limited way only.

These facts, taken together, point to the conclusion that Paul's thought in this part of his letter has not involved the intention of taking a particular picture and of developing and applying it in a systematic and thorough manner. His pictures are useful only insofar as certain elements within them are relevant to his immediate purpose.

ROMANS 6:15-23

In Rom. 6:15-23, Paul continues to dwell upon the fact that " to sin " is entirely incompatible with the new state or condition in which the Christians now live. Whereas he stressed in the preceding verses (vs. 1-14) that they must not " continue in sin " because they have " died to sin " and should " walk in newness of life " (using the pictures of baptism and of Christ's own death and resurrection), now he presents the argument that they are not to sin because they are no longer under the sway of sin; rather, they are persons whose lives are committed to God.[1] It is in this connection that he employs the analogy of slavery.[2]

The picture is introduced in combination with its initial application: " Do you not know that if you yield yourselves to any one as obedient slaves [literally, " slaves unto obedience "], you are slaves of the one whom you obey, either of sin, which leads to death, or of obedience, which leads to righteousness? " (v. 16).

Although the picture is not drawn in any detail, enough is said to indicate that Paul is thinking of slavery as a condition in which the submission and obedience of the slave to the master is a central consideration. The slave is one who " presents " or " yields " (*paristanete*) himself to his master, and he does so " unto obedience." Furthermore, when the slave is in this condition he owes his master an *exclusive* allegiance, an " *undivided* service." [3] A slave " could not be under obligation to anyone other than his master." [4] That this was the Pauline intent is indicated by the " either . . . or " construction in the latter part of v. 16.

Sanday writes in regard to *ētoi . . . ē* (" either . . . or "): " These disjunctives state a dilemma in a lively and emphatic way, implying that one limb or the other must be chosen." [5] It is true that this construction is in that part of v. 16 which concerns the application of the picture rather than the picture itself (see below), but it is evident that the picture is still in the apostle's mind. The idea of *undivided* allegiance on the part of a slave is brought out with particular force in Lietzmann's translation of v. 16. Before the word " *Sklaven* " (" slaves ") he inserts parenthetically " *ausschliesslich* " (" exclusively ").[6]

The thought expressed here is of course similar to that which is stated in Matt. 6:24 (" No one can serve two masters . . ."),[7] though it does not necessarily follow that Paul was thinking of this particular quotation.[8]

The idea of submission and obedience, involved in the analogy of slavery, is applied repeatedly. As " slaves " Christians have become " *obedient* " to the standard of teaching to which they were " *committed* " (v. 17).

The last clause reads literally " to which you were given over " (*paredothēte*). The notion of submission is undoubtedly intended, since being " given over " to this " standard of teaching " stands in contrast to being " slaves of sin."

Just as they once " *yielded* " their members to that which is evil, now they should " *yield* " their members to righteousness (v. 19).

The dominance of the idea of obedience is also seen in the not altogether satisfactory contrast that is presented in the latter part of v. 16. When Paul suggests that the Christians are slaves either of "sin" or of "obedience," the reference to "obedience" as the antithesis of "sin" is quite surprising; one would expect to find "righteousness" (compare v. 19b, where "righteousness" does stand in contrast to "impurity" and "iniquity") or "God" (compare v. 22).[9] The use of "obedience" is best understood as due to the fact that it was precisely the idea of obedience which was at the center of the apostle's thinking. It may be noted, too, that in the immediately preceding verses (vs. 12-14) the idea of submission and obedience is also central.

The thought of *exclusive* allegiance is included in the application of the analogy, at least by clear implication. The idea that submission and obedience can be to only one master is suggested not only in v. 16, where picture and application are combined, but also in v. 20, where it is stated that slavery to sin means freedom from righteousness, and also in vs. 18 and 22a, where slavery to righteousness or to God is apparently understood as possible only after the securing of freedom from sin.

Thus Paul employs the analogy of slavery for the sake of the idea that a slave is one who "yields" himself to — and "obeys" — his one master only. In the light of the issue that is under discussion (v. 15), this must mean that Christians are *not* "to sin," since "sin" is no longer their master; their submission and obedience is now solely to "righteousness" or to "God."

If the analogy of slavery is relevant and applicable in this way, it is also true that some elements in the analogy are *not* appropriate to the issue under consideration. The picture of a slave suggests not only the idea of submission and obedience but also the thought of bondage, subjection, and even oppression. Although a person might voluntarily become a slave as a last resort, the position of the slave was obviously something less than desirable. In a different context Paul could employ the picture of a slave in order to illustrate a status decidedly inferior to that of a son.[10] Slavery, whether it be to the law or to men, or to something else, constituted

a condition from which freedom was to be sought.[11] It is perfectly clear that slavery *viewed in this way* is entirely unsuited as an analogy in the present context, where Paul can
even offer thanks to God that Christians "have become
slaves of righteousness" (vs. 17 f.). It is worthy of special
note that the apostle himself calls attention to a certain inappropriateness of the picture (v. 19a): "I am speaking in
human terms, because of your natural limitations" (more
literally, "I say what is human, on account of the weakness
of your flesh").[12] It may be that Paul "is conscious that his
illustration is not going very well"[13] or that he felt an apol-
ogy was required "for using the peculiarly earthly image of
the slave-market to enforce a truth of the most exalted spiritual dignity."[14] In any case he apparently means that the
expression, "slaves of righteousness," drawn from the human picture of slavery, has its very real limitations, since in
reality the Christian anticipates for the "whole creation"
the ultimate release from bondage and the realization of the
"glorious liberty of the children of God" (Rom. 8:21 f.).[15]
It becomes abundantly evident, therefore, that Paul uses the
analogy of slavery for the sake of the idea of exclusive allegiance or obedience that the picture may suggest; he makes
it clear that the picture is not to be applied in all respects to
his religious thinking.[16]

It has just been seen that the analogy of slavery is not
fully applicable and that Paul himself directs attention to its
limitations. A related point may also be observed. There is
found in the material here a use of language which indicates
the absence of a conscious attempt on the part of the apostle
to develop and to apply the analogy carefully and systematically. As Paul refers to that which the Christian obeys or to
which he yields — as over against sin — he employs a surprising variety of expressions. In v. 16 the opposite of slavery to
sin is slavery to "obedience";[17] in v. 17 it is slavery (at least
by implication) to "the standard of teaching to which you
were committed"; in vs. 18 f. it is slavery to "righteousness";
in v. 22, finally, it is slavery to "God." If Paul were intending

to apply his analogy carefully and systematically, or if he were expecting his readers to do so, it is quite inconceivable that he would have allowed himself to designate the new master of the Christians in such diverse ways. Since the terms are by no means synonymous, the use of them is hardly consistent with the primary purpose of the analogy of slavery, which is to reinforce the idea of obedience to *one* master.

That the four terms or expressions are not synonymous is of course obvious. " Obedience " is certainly not to be equated with a " standard of teaching " (*tupon didachēs*), whether the latter refers to " ethical teachings of a rule of faith," [18] or teaching concerned with " Christian duty " generally,[19] or " Christianity " as over against Judaism, with its teaching of the law.[20] Similarly, " righteousness " is not to be identified with " obedience " (as may be seen in v. 16, where it is the *result* of " obedience "), nor with a "standard of teaching." In his reference to " God " as the master (v. 22) Paul moves far beyond the previous three expressions and arrives at that more characteristic " level of thought on which the Christian life is essentially a personal relation to God in Christ." [21]

It thus becomes apparent that Paul is reaching in various directions for language that will serve his major emphasis in this part of the letter. Christians are not " to sin." " Obedience " is involved, as is a " standard of teaching," and also " righteousness." Above all, the Christians are committed to God himself. Having introduced the analogy of slavery, Paul can employ the *terminology* of the analogy and speak of the Christian as the " slave " of these various " masters." But a clear distinction must be made between the use of terminology drawn from the analogy and a careful or systematic development and application of the analogy. The latter must be ruled out in this case by the fact that even though the picture of slavery is presented in order to emphasize submission and obedience to one master only, Paul has actually so far departed from the picture itself that he speaks in terms suggesting diversity rather than oneness.

Akin to the fact that Paul does not develop and apply his

analogy systematically is the further fact that in several other respects his thought is seen to be dominated by the issue under consideration rather than by the picture itself. Even before he completes the sentence in which he first presents the picture of slavery (v. 16) he shows that the picture itself plays a decidedly subordinate role in his thinking. He begins by saying that " if you yield yourselves to any one as obedient slaves, you are slaves of the one whom you obey." But he completes the sentence by saying that men are slaves " either of sin, . . . or of obedience." In offering " sin " and " obedience " as illustrative of the alternative masters that the slave may obey, the apostle is indicating already the dominance of the issue at hand over the picture, for " sin " and " obedience " are not at all the masters that are involved in the actual human institution of slavery. Furthermore, the clauses that suggest that sin " leads to death " and that obedience " leads to righteousness " are relevant only to the theological thought, not to the picture.[22] In reality these references to " death " and " righteousness " as the results of slavery to " sin " and " obedience," respectively, do not even contribute to the principal idea that is expressed in this verse — namely, that servitude to " sin " and to " obedience " are mutually exclusive; these results are mentioned only because they are " inseparable from the whole subject." [23] The inclusion of such references (which are thus not relevant to the picture) points clearly both to the subordinate position given to the picture and also to the fact that Paul has relatively little interest here in any careful or thorough development of elements of correspondence between picture and idea.

The same conclusion emerges from an examination of vs. 20-23, where the thought once more concerns the results of servitude. The picture of slavery is still present (at least in the background), as the phrases " slaves of sin " and " slaves of God " indicate. But there is nothing in the picture of slavery as a social institution which suggests — or corresponds to — the results that are specified: on the one hand, " death ";

on the other hand, "sanctification and its end, eternal life." In actual servitude the slave might receive better treatment from one master than from another, but the differences that might be found hardly correspond to the kind of absolute contrast given here: "death — life." It follows, therefore, that although the picture of slavery still remains in the background, it has not been used as a basis for that which is said.

There is yet a further indication that the picture of slavery does not dominate the thought expressed in vs. 20-23. In the course of this brief discussion Paul uses terms that actually introduce two additional pictures. In the Greek the apostle's word for "return" (*karpon*), both in vs. 21a and 22b, is one that normally means "fruit" and suggests the picture of a harvest. And the word for "wages" (*opsōnia*), in v. 23, commonly designated the pay or allowance received by soldiers (compare I Cor. 9:7 and Luke 3:14) and hence introduces a military metaphor.[24] Since Paul thus mingles language drawn from the picture of slavery with that which is derived from the areas of agriculture and military life, he shows that no single analogy is being used and developed as fully illustrative of his thought.

Attention must be directed, finally, to yet another feature that appears in the total passage under consideration. At several points there is emphasized the idea of a *change* of masters (vs. 17, 18, 19b, 22).[25] It may be claimed that Paul is here "pursuing the metaphor of the transfer of a slave."[26] It must be recognized, however, that when the apostle speaks of the Christian as undergoing a change of masters he refers to this change in such a way as to indicate that it does not correspond to the change that might occur in actual human slavery. Here the Christian appears as one who is in a position to make his own choice with regard to the master whom he will serve. This is especially evident in v. 19. Not only does Paul say, "*You . . . yielded your members* to impurity . . . ," but he adds the *admonition*, "Now yield your members to righteousness." A decision on the part of the Christian himself seems to be indicated also in v. 17.[27]

It is true that the use of the passive voice in vs. 18a and 22a tends to create a different impression. In these passages it is stated that the Christians have been " set free from sin," as though they themselves had no active part in the change. It is probable, however, that the use of the passive is due to the intent, not of denying the reality of decision on man's part, but of recognizing that the very possibility of such decision was something done in their behalf, God's gracious act in Jesus Christ (see v. 23, and compare with Rom. 3:24 f.).[28]

The situation in the institution of slavery was quite different. A person might choose to become a slave in the first place in order to receive sustenance;[29] but as a slave he had no right and no influence in regard to a change of master.[30] In view of this difference it must be concluded that here, again, the analogy itself plays a relatively minor role in the apostle's thinking. The fact that a slave in actual practice had no voice in the choice of his master does not prevent Paul from ascribing to men the power to choose between " sin " and " God " (or his " righteousness ").

All of this means that the analogy of slavery can be used as a basis for an understanding of the Pauline thought only within the limits imposed by the context. In this context the idea of exclusive obedience is relevant. Certain other ideas suggested by the picture are quite inappropriate, and the apostle himself notes that limitations are involved. It is evident, furthermore, that Paul has not attempted to develop and apply the analogy thoroughly or systematically.

ROMANS 7:1-6

Paul's use of the analogy of marriage in Rom. 7:1-6 is of special interest for the present study. This is true even though the passage confronts the reader with unusually difficult problems of interpretation. Indeed it may be said that the very presence of these difficulties is particularly illuminating insofar as characteristics of Pauline analogical usage are concerned.

In this part of his letter to the church at Rome the apostle is continuing to emphasize the idea that in justification through faith the Christian experiences divine grace (chs. 3:24; 5:20 f.), and that life which is lived "under grace" is wholly incompatible with sin (see especially ch. 6:1 f. and 6:15). Having employed the picture of baptism to illustrate the thought that the Christian has "died to sin" (ch. 6:2 ff.),[1] and the picture of slavery to reinforce the idea that the Christian is removed from that state in which there is obedience to sin (vs. 15 ff.), Paul now introduces the picture of marriage to show that the Christian lives no longer in that condition where law — and hence sin — prevails.

Superficially it may appear that Paul's thinking has turned from sin to law. And there is a sense, of course, in which the law does now become a dominant subject in all of ch. 7. The relationship between the law and sin is mentioned repeatedly, however.[2] While the apostle denies that the law is to be equated with sin (v. 7a), he argues, nevertheless, that the law served to incite man to sin (vs. 5 and 7b ff.). Moreover, the law, though in itself good, served to make manifest the true character of sin (v. 13b). The operation of the law, therefore, is closely associated with the fact of sin. Indeed it may be said that in Paul's thinking there is a sense in which sin and the law are inseparable. The law was given *because* of the fact of sin, not only in order "that sin might be shown to be sin" (v. 13b) but also in order to restrain it (see Gal. 3:23).[3]

Verse 8b ("Apart from the law sin lies dead") must not be construed to mean that sin was a fact in human life only after the giving of the law. Sin "indeed was in the world before the law was given" (ch. 5:13a), but it was not "counted" (v. 13b), since its true nature had not been known. Sin existed, but it was "dead" in the sense that its power and effect were not yet fully manifest.

Since it was because of sin that the law was given, it may be said that the relevance of the law depends upon the presence of sin. Or, to express it differently, the continued relevance of the law bespeaks the fact that sin continues to prevail. Conversely, freedom from the working of the law bespeaks freedom from the sin that gives to the law its relevance in the first place. From this point of view the law and sin stand or fall together. And man's subjection to — or freedom from — the law is indicative of his subjection to — or freedom from — sin.[4] Thus, when Paul contends that the Christian is free from the law he is in reality continuing his argument (of ch. 6) that the new life of the Christian is one in which sin should have no place.[5]

It is clear that in Rom. 7:1-6 Paul's immediate concern is to show that the Christian is free from the law. His main line of argument is this: the law " is binding " — or " hath dominion " (KJV) — over a person as long as that person is alive (v. 1). The Christian, however, in a certain sense is no longer alive, for he has " died to the law " (v. 4a; compare v. 6a). Therefore the law no longer has dominion over him. Being thus freed from the law the Christian may now belong to Christ (v. 4b) and in this new relationship " bear fruit for God " (v. 4c), serving in " newness " (*kainotēti*) of Spirit (v. 6c). The thought here is closely parallel to that of ch. 6: the Christian has " died to sin " (v. 2), is therefore " freed from sin " (v. 7) and is no longer under the dominion of sin (v. 14). Since he is thus freed from sin he may now be united with Christ (v. 5). In this condition the Christian may now walk in " newness " (*kainotēti*) of life (v. 4). In view of these parallels of thought and expression the interpreter is undoubtedly justified in presupposing in ch. 7:1-6 certain other elements of thought which are given explicit expression in ch. 6. Particularly important is the idea of the " old self," which dies, and the new self, which then becomes alive and " lives to God " (ch. 6:6-11). This idea is necessary, of course, in order to make intelligible the statement that " you " have " died " and yet may " belong to another " (ch. 7:4), or the similar statement that " we " are " dead " and yet may live and serve (v. 6).

The analogy of marriage is introduced in the midst of this argument: " Thus a married woman is bound by law to her [literally, " the "] husband as long as he lives; but if her ["the"] husband dies she is discharged from the law concerning the husband [literally, "from the law of the husband"]. Accordingly, she will be called an adulteress if she lives with another man [or, "if she marries another husband"] while her husband is alive. But if her ["the"] husband dies she is free from that ["the"] law, and if she marries another man she is not an adulteress" (vs. 2 f.).

The analogy is so placed that it must be related both to what precedes and to what follows. On the one hand, it appears as an illustration of the idea that the law has dominion over a person only during his life (v. 1); on the other hand, it provides a picture that is then applied to the idea that the Christian has "died to the law" and hence may "belong to another" (v. 4). The second idea (v. 4) must not, of course, be sharply distinguished from the first (v. 1), for it constitutes a kind of logical development: if the law has dominion only while a person lives, then it follows that after death the dominion of the law no longer prevails and a new state of affairs is then possible. But although the two ideas are closely related, it is nevertheless true that they are expressed differently. A careful analysis of Paul's use of analogy must take these differences into account. It is necessary, therefore, to consider the analogy with reference both to what precedes and to what follows.

The picture of marriage in vs. 2 f. appears to be applicable to the idea of v. 1 in a very general way only. It may be said that just as the provisions that regulate conduct within the marriage relationship [6] become irrelevant and inoperative upon the death of one of the partners in the marriage, so also the law as a whole has "dominion" over a person only until that person dies (the reference being, presumably, to the person understood as the "old self," which was under subjection to sin and hence to law). The analogy may be applied a little further — again in a very general way — with reference to the *implication* in v. 1, that after the person dies the law no longer has dominion over him: [7] just as the surviving partner in a marriage is free from the provisions of marriage regulations upon the death of the other partner, so also the Christian (as the new self) is no longer under the dominion of the law.[8]

While the analogy thus has a general kind of relevance to the thought expressed in v. 1, the picture, as it is drawn in vs. 2 and 3, is quite unsuitable and inapplicable insofar as details are concerned. Particularly conspicuous is the fact that neither figure in the picture — neither the wife nor the husband — can be made to correspond to the "person" of v. 1. The "married woman" cannot properly represent that person over whom the law has dominion only while he lives, for, according to the implications in v. 1, it would have to be *her* death that brought an end to the dominion of the law over her; in the picture (vs. 2 f.) it is not she, but the *husband*, who dies. Nor can the husband represent the one over whom the law has dominion only while he lives, for (again) according to the implications in v. 1, it would have to be *he* who would be free from the dominion of the law when he died; in the picture it is the *wife* who is made free. In other words, according to v. 1 the meaning seems to be that the "person" who is subject to the law while he lives is the *same* person who (by implication) is free from the law when he dies. In the picture, however, the person who becomes free is *not* the person who dies.

It must be granted, of course, that this incongruity between picture and idea is reduced at least partially if the "person" of v. 1 is understood as one who indeed is a single individual and yet as one who may be conceived as having a kind of double self — the "old self," which dies, and the new self, which emerges in "newness of life." Thus interpreted, there is a *sense* in which the person (the old self) who dies is *not* the same person (the new self) who becomes free, although identity of individuality still justifies the wording of v. 1. In this case the relationship between idea and analogy may be expressed thus: the law has dominion over a person (conceived as the old self) only during his life, just as marriage regulations remain in force only while husband and wife both live; but when the person (the old self) dies — as the husband dies — then the person (the new self) becomes free from the law — as the wife becomes free.[9] On the basis of ch. 6 (see above) it is certainly possible that a meaning such as this may have been intended by Paul. It is important to observe, however, that even here the correspondence between picture and idea is limited. To apply fully the picture of marriage to the religious thought in this way is to represent *as a marriage* the relationship between the old self and the new state or condition of the Christian. This seems to be quite impossible. If one is to presuppose in this way the idea of the two " selves," as it is found in ch. 6, one must likewise presuppose the further idea, also found in ch. 6, that the new self emerges as a reality *only after the death of the old self* (see especially ch. 6:4). Both the picture of baptism and the picture of Christ's own death and resurrection point to this conclusion. But if the two " selves " thus do not coexist, then the relationship between them cannot be properly represented as a *marriage*.

Sanday prefers to speak, not of two " selves," but rather of the *one* " self," which " remains the same throughout," but which, nevertheless, " passes through different states, or phases." [10] Even so, the point now being made is not affected, for the " states, or phases," are successive, not contemporaneous, and hence the relationship between them cannot be likened to a marriage.

Romans 7:13-25 may suggest, it is true, that two selves — the " inmost self " and the self that is " captive to the law of sin " (vs. 22 f.) — *do* coexist and are joined together. But what Paul says only *after* he uses the analogy of marriage can hardly be presupposed earlier, especially in preference to the thought expressed in ch. 6. Furthermore, while a kind of coexistence may be found in ch. 7:13-25, that coexistence is one involving *conflict,* not union (as in marriage). Certainly it is not the kind of union in which the law " binds " one self to the other.

Similar conclusions emerge when the analogy of vs. 2 f. is analyzed in connection with the application that is offered in vs. 4 ff. There is to be recognized, once more, a *general* kind of correspondence between picture and idea: just as a wife is freed from subjection to marriage regulations by the death of her husband and may then marry another man, so also the Christian, no longer bound to the law, may belong to Christ. As above (in connection with v. 1) the picture can be made to correspond in *some* detail if the distinction between the two selves is retained: " you " (the old self), like the husband, have died (to the law), so that " you " (the new self), like the wife, may belong to Christ. But this produces still further inconsistencies. In the picture the " law concerning the husband " was not a partner in the marriage, but rather, was law which served to regulate the conduct of the partners. In v. 4, however, the law *is* such a partner: " you " (the old self) have died to the one partner (the law), so that " you " (the new self) may belong to another partner (Christ).[11] Furthermore, according to this application, the wife must represent the Christian who (formerly), as the old self, was obligated to the law (the husband) and who (as the new self) is now free to belong to Christ. But in this case the picture does not agree with the application, since in the former it is the husband who dies, whereas in the latter it is the Christian (the wife) who has died.

A similar difficulty results if the *husband* is made to represent the Christian. In this case there would be correspondence between the death of the husband in the picture and the death of the Christian (" you," i.e., the old self) in the application (v. 4). But then there would be a double inconsistency. In the first place the wife of the picture would have to represent the law, which is *not* true, since in the picture the law is *neither* partner. And in the second place, if the husband represented the Christian, it would have to be the husband (now as the new self) that would be free to " belong to another "; in the picture it is the *wife*, not the husband, who may marry someone else. There is little reason, however, for even considering the possibility that the husband should represent the Christian. In the analogy of vs. 2 f. the subject is clearly the wife, and the interest centers upon her condition. In the application in v. 4 the subject (" you ") is obviously the Christian, since it is the Christian who would belong to

Christ. Presumably the subject of the application corresponds to the subject of the analogy.

Mention should be made, perhaps, of the view that the metaphor of marriage had already dropped out of Paul's thinking by the time he composed the latter part of v. 4: " So that you may belong to another." According to Denney, the apostle is " speaking of the experience of Christians one by one, and though Christ is sometimes spoken of as the husband or bridegroom of the Church, there is no Scripture authority for using this metaphor of His relation to the individual soul." [12] For Denney, therefore, " the marriage metaphor is dropped." [13] Lietzmann, on the other hand, believes that the picture of a marriage plays an important role, not only in v. 4b but also in connection with the larger context. In fact, he accounts for many of the aforementioned inconsistencies on the grounds that after Paul *started* to illustrate the idea of v. 1 with the picture of a wife freed by her death from the dominion of her husband, there suddenly occurred to him a *new* (though related) picture — namely, that of a second marriage (as suggested in v. 4b). The result was a *mixture* of pictures — each distorting the other — which resulted in the lack of clarity and consistency.[14] These opposing views have one element in common: both point to the conclusion that Paul's picture cannot be fully applied, either because Paul himself did not so apply it (Denney), or because the apostle's shifting thought led him to draw a picture that became too confused to be applied consistently (Lietzmann).

Mention should also be made of the attempts on the part of some interpreters to apply the analogy of marriage even further. Paul speaks of the Christians as belonging to Christ " in order that we may bear fruit to God " (v. 4c). Here, it has been claimed, the " metaphor has been carried into detail." [15] Dodd writes: " The idea of a fruitful marriage union suggests this addition, which enforces the point that the reasonable and proper result of conversion to Christianity is a morally fruitful life (and not an indifference to morality)." [16]

This point of correspondence has been pressed even further. Paul adds (v. 5): "While we were living in the flesh, our sinful passions, aroused by the law, were at work in our members to bear fruit for death." If the picture of marriage is still being applied,[17] then v. 5 combined with v. 4c must have this meaning: the law (the former husband) produces in the individual bound to it (the old self, the wife) "fruit for death"; but Christ (the new husband) produces in the individual belonging to him (the new self, the wife in her new condition) "fruit for God." Certain considerations, however, seem to rule out the fact that Paul is here consciously applying the picture of marriage in this way, or that he intended his readers to make such an application. In the picture of a wife who marries a second husband upon the death of the first there is nothing to suggest that the offspring of the second marriage are normally superior to the offspring of the first. If the picture *is* still in Paul's mind, it must therefore be concluded, not that he is applying that picture at this point, but rather, that his religious thought regarding the law and Christ is simply being expressed through language suggested by the picture. In reality it is not even certain that the language *was* suggested by the picture. Paul's Greek verb here, meaning " to bear fruit " (forms of *karpophoreō*), is never used elsewhere in the New Testament with reference to offspring. Nor does Paul ever use the noun "fruit" (*karpos*) in this sense,[18] though he employs it at least nine times. Altogether, therefore, there is no real evidence that the idea of the offspring of a marriage was in the apostle's mind. Even if it were, the contrast between offspring " for death " and offspring "for God" appears as a result of Paul's religious thought, not as a result of conscious application of the picture of two marriages, since, as seen above, there is nothing in the picture of two marriages which in itself suggests such extreme differences in the offspring of such marriages.[19]

The verb " to bear fruit " (vs. 4 and 5) may also be understood as introducing an entirely different metaphor, one that is derived from the area of agriculture. It is to be noted that in v. 6 Paul's expression "held us captive" suggests the picture of slavery also. In a similar way, he employs words suggesting new pictures — agricultural ("return," literally, "fruit") and military ("wages")— in ch. 6:21-23.[20] Such use of terminology suggesting pictures quite unrelated to the primary analogy may be said to point to the absence of a conscious attempt to develop and apply fully that primary analogy.

From the foregoing analysis it must be concluded that in Rom. 7:1-6, Paul has employed the analogy of marriage in a general and limited way only. There are numerous elements in the picture which simply cannot be made to correspond accurately to the ideas that are being conveyed. This is true regardless of the line of interpretation which is followed. It is understandable, therefore, that a commentator may declare the analogy to be " confused from the outset " [21] or say that the illustration " has gone hopelessly astray." [22] At least it is clear that the picture has not been used as a basis for careful, thoughtful, or systematic application. It has been employed for the purpose of reinforcing in a general way Paul's religious thought, but as the picture is drawn it cannot be taken in its details as providing trustworthy clues regarding the nature of that thought.

ROMANS 9:20-24

The analogy of the potter and the clay appears in that part of Romans (chs. 9 to 11) in which Paul attempts to reconcile the idea of Israel's distinctive role as a chosen people with the fact that on the whole the Jews have not come to participate in the way of salvation revealed by God in Christ. He agrees that to Israel the promises were given (ch. 9:4). The present position of the Jews, in their rejection of Christ, does not mean, however, that God's word has failed — that he is unfaithful to his promises, for the true children of Israel are " the children of promise," those whom God has chosen of his own free will. In fulfilling his promises and his purposes, God has always exercised his sovereign free choice. From among the children of Abraham only the descendants of Isaac were selected. And of Isaac's sons Jacob was chosen, but not Esau (vs. 6-13).

At this point Paul directs his attention to certain questions that may be raised. Does this seemingly arbitrary selection by God (see v. 11, especially) indicate injustice on his part? The reply is an emphatic " No." It is not a matter of injustice that is involved, but a matter of mercy. Furthermore (although this does not really answer the question), Scripture has shown that God is One who " has mercy upon whomever he wills, and he hardens the heart of whomever he wills " in order that his purposes might be fulfilled (vs. 14-18). But this leads to another question: If God acts thus, how can he " find fault " with those whose hardness of heart has been determined by him in the first place? [1] Paul's reply consists essentially in the flat declaration that man is one who is in no position to dispute God's will and action: " But who are you, a man, to answer back to God? " (v. 20a).

It is here that the apostle inserts the analogy of the potter and the clay: " Will what is molded say to its molder, ' Why have you made me thus? ' Has the potter no right over the clay, to make out of the same lump one vessel for beauty [literally, " for honor," i.e., " for a noble purpose " [2]] and another for menial use [literally, " for dishonor "]? " (vs. 20b f.).

In a sense the analogy is a double one.[3] A reference to " what is molded " and to its " molder " (v. 20) need not necessarily involve the specific picture of the clay and the potter (v. 21). It will be shown below, however, that Paul's language in these verses corresponds so closely to that of Isa. 29:16 (Septuagint) as to indicate the probable influence of that passage upon the apostle. And since, in Isa. 29:16, the Greek expressions for " what is molded " and the " molder " are closely associated with the potter and the clay, it is safe to assume that Paul is making the same connection.

The analogy is clearly intended to reinforce the idea of the sovereignty of God the Creator over man the creature.

It does so in two somewhat different, though closely related, ways. (1) Just as it is absurd to think of the clay as being in a position to question the action of the potter (v. 20b), so also it is wholly out of place for man to question the decisions or actions of God (v. 20a). (2) Just as the potter has every right to form the clay into whatever vessels he may see fit (v. 21), so also God, in his sovereignty, is free to deal with men as he pleases in order to fulfill his purposes (vs. 22-24).

Although the analogy is relevant to the Pauline thought in this double way, it is also evident that it is not applicable in all respects. While the absurdity of the clay's questioning of the potter may serve to suggest man's impropriety when he presumes to "answer back" to God, real correspondence between picture and idea is of course absent, since clay is a *thing*, while man is a thinking being: "Man is not a pot; he *will* ask, 'Why did you make me like this?' " [4] Furthermore, between the potter and the clay there is neither a bond of love nor a relationship allowing for "wrath," as is true between God and man.[5] Particularly noteworthy is the absence of real correspondence at a point where correspondence is apparently intended. In v. 21 the object formed by the potter is called a "vessel" (*skeuos*). The use of the same word with reference to men ("vessels of wrath" and "vessels of mercy") in vs. 22 and 23 is undoubtedly intended to connect the picture with the thought that is being expressed.[6] But what is said about the vessels of clay is quite different from that which is stated concerning the vessels that are men. In the case of the former, one is made for "honor" or for "a noble purpose"; another is made for "dishonor" or for "menial use." [7] In the case of men, however, some vessels (presumably those men who have rejected Christ) are made for (or, as Moffatt translates, are "ripe and ready" for) destruction; others are prepared for "glory." It can hardly be denied that there is a marked difference between something that is made to serve a dishonorable or "menial" purpose and something that is ready for "destruction." A vessel that serves a lowly purpose may still have its proper place; and to speak of it as *lowly* is not to designate it as suited for *destruction*.[8]

It is possible, of course, that Paul is here anticipating his later thought, that the rejection of the Jews (see Rom. 11:15) is only temporary, and that after " the full number of the Gentiles come in," then " all Israel will be saved " (vs. 25 f.). If this is true, it is conceivable that "made for destruction" is intended to mean " *fitted* for destruction," but not destined to suffer that fate. Hence there is a sense in which the expression might be taken to mean " serve a (temporary) menial purpose," but not *actually* " made for destruction." But for a reader who had not yet reached ch. 11 this qualification would not be taken into consideration. As the passage stands a vessel made " for menial use " simply does not correspond to vessels made " for destruction," as though they could serve no useful purpose whatever.

Thus it appears that the analogy may have provided a part of the terminology (" vessel," *skeuos*) for the expression of the Pauline thought in vs. 22 f., but the picture is not being applied carefully. The most that can be said is that the terminology merely suggested to Paul certain ideas that he elsewhere sets forth quite apart from this particular picture. Human " vessels " can be used by God in his " transcendent power " (see II Cor. 4:7) in the fulfillment of his larger purposes (Rom., ch. 11), and in his dealings with them he manifests " much patience " (see ch. 2:4).

Thus far attention has been given to the picture of the potter and the clay *as Paul draws it* and to the relationship between that picture and the thought that is being set forth. There is considerable evidence, however, that the picture that Paul has in mind — and that he applies — is not simply the picture as he presents it, but involves also the picture as it had been employed by others before him. If it can be shown that Paul is indeed presupposing earlier usages of the picture, then an analysis of his own usage must take this fact into consideration.

That the general picture was a familiar one is attested by numerous passages in the Old Testament and Apocrypha [9] and by other references as well.[10] There is a particularly strong probability that Paul had in mind Isa. 29:16. His Greek reproduces exactly that clause in Isa. 29:16 (Septuagint) which is translated here, " Will what is molded say to its molder . . . ? " And in the same verse are found forms of Paul's words for " potter " (kerameus) and for " clay " (pēlos). Furthermore, as with Paul, the picture is presented in the form of a question; also, the thing that is formed is made to speak. The application is similar to that of Paul in that it illustrates the absurdity of presumptiveness on the part of the thing that is created. Altogether, therefore, the apostle's picture in this instance is very much the same as the one that is found in Isa. 29:16, and he employs it for a similar purpose. (Both in Isa. 29:16 and in Rom. 9:20b there is undoubtedly an allusion to the account of Creation in Gen., ch. 2, where the creatures are mentioned as " formed " or " molded," the Greek verb being the same as that which appears in these passages.)[11]

It is possible that Paul had in mind Isa. 45:9 also. There, too, the analogy of the potter and the clay is employed to stress the sovereignty of the Creator over the creature. A further parallel to the Pauline usage is to be seen if the passage in Isaiah was intended to meet the objection that God, in fulfilling his purposes, is using a foreigner (Cyrus) to serve a Messianic function.[12] In this case Paul, like the writer of Isa. 45:9, is introducing the picture to refute the suggestion that there is injustice in God's seemingly arbitrary choices or decisions.

A rather striking resemblance to the Pauline usage is found in Ecclus. 33:12 f.: as the potter fashions the clay as it pleases him, so also God is one who blesses men — or brings them low — as it suits his pleasure.

A passage in the Wisd. of Sol. (ch. 15:7) is of special interest, since the language found there is so close to that of Paul as to suggest its influence upon the apostle, although the application differs greatly. In this passage there appears the same combination of terms employed by Paul: " potter " (*kerameus*), " clay," (*pēlos*), " vessel " (*skeuos*), and the verb " mold " (*plassō*). Furthermore, several of the ideas expressed are similar to those found with Paul. (1) Out of the " *same* " material the potter makes vessels for quite different uses. (2) Some vessels are for " clean " uses, while others are for " contrary " uses.

This point is particularly noteworthy. Although " for honor " (Paul) is not exactly the same as for "clean uses," and although " for dishonor " is not the same as the opposite of clean uses, nevertheless, the effects of these expressions are much alike.

(3) The potter alone is the judge regarding the use to which the various vessels are to be put. Altogether, the parallels are too numerous to be regarded as accidental. It seems quite likely, therefore, that this passage at least contributed to the form of the picture which is presented by the apostle. It is especially important to observe, however, that although Paul thus seems to have in mind this earlier picture, he does not apply it in the same way. In the Wisd. of Sol. (ch. 15:8 ff.) the potter is one who uses his powers presumptively and basely, whereas with Paul the potter stands for God, who quite properly and rightly thus exercises his sovereign power. It appears, in view of all this, that we have here an example of Paul employing a picture with which he was familiar, but disregarding the earlier application of it for the sake of one that is consistent with his immediate purpose. It is another case, in other words, where (some) former ideas associated with a picture cannot be carried over into the Pauline thought and taken as a basis for defining that thought.

Reference must also be made to the well-known use of the analogy of the potter and the clay in Jer. 18:1-12. The account of the potter at work (vs. 3 f.) does not correspond closely to the Pauline picture (Rom. 9:20b f.). In Jeremiah the report concerns the refashioning of a single piece of clay into a second vessel [13] after the first one had been " spoiled " or " marred." In Paul's picture, on the other hand, *different* pieces of clay (though they come from the "same lump") are designed and used from the outset for different vessels. Similarly, the application in Jeremiah is not closely parallel to that in Romans. In the former it is suggested that as the potter revised his plan for the piece of clay, so also God may change his intentions for a people if conditions warrant such a change.[14] In the Pauline application, however, no such change of intention is emphasized. The impression, instead, is that as the potter has the right to devise and make different vessels for different uses, so God plans and chooses to use different men (or groups of men) for different purposes; and the expression "He has prepared beforehand" (Rom. 9:23) suggests that no alteration in plan or choice has been involved.

It is true that in a sense the usage in Jeremiah might have been adopted by Paul if he had been willing to concede that the rejection of Christ by the Jews warranted an alteration in the divine intention regarding Israel. As already observed, however, the apostle affirms the promises given to Israel (v. 4). Furthermore, such a concession would run counter to his insistence that the word of God has not failed (vs. 6 ff.) and that the divine sovereignty is absolute (vs. 18-21). Above all it would rule out his later contention that "a hardening has come upon part of Israel" as a part of the divine plan in order that the Gentiles might "come in" and that eventually "all Israel will be saved" (ch. 11:25 f.).

As we consider now as a whole Paul's use of the analogy of the potter and the clay, several conclusions emerge. The picture, as he draws it, is relevant to his thought in some respects but not in others. Certain elements in the picture are applicable to his argument. Other elements provide a terminology that he finds useful, although in his employing of that terminology there is absent a real correspondence between picture and idea. Thus it is apparent that he has not intended to apply the picture thoroughly or systematically. In addition, while he gives evidence that he had in mind certain earlier usages of the analogy, those usages are employed somewhat selectively: in part he adopts the earlier

forms and applications of the picture and in part he deviates
from them. One such earlier usage (Jer. 18:1-12) he seems
to have ignored completely. Altogether, the picture is made
useful, but is subordinated to the line of argument which
he presents. Its various forms do not, in themselves, provide
reliable clues as to the nature of his thought; rather, the
thought is determinative for the use to which they may be
put.

ROMANS 11:16-24

Although Paul expresses his deep sorrow over the fact that
the Jewish people as a whole have rejected God's revelation
in Christ, he affirms nevertheless his belief that to Israel was
assigned a unique role in the world's history (Rom. 9:1-5).
In the eleventh chapter of Romans he sets forth his " bold
hope " [1] that after the " full number of the Gentiles " shall
have " come in " as a result of the rejection by the Jews, then
the Jews, too, will turn from their present position and " all
Israel will be saved " (ch. 11:25 f.). In v. 16 the apostle bases
this hope upon the idea that Israel is essentially a " holy "
people, implying that a people uniquely consecrated and
dedicated to God must eventually come to participate in the
divine plan of salvation. The idea is not stated explicitly but
is presented in the form of two metaphors or analogies: " If
the dough offered as first fruits is holy, so is the whole lump;
and if the root is holy, so are the branches " (literally, " If the
first fruit is holy, so also the lump; and if the root is holy, so
also the branches ").

The former of these two metaphors involves undoubtedly
an allusion to Num. 15:19-21, where it is prescribed that the
firstfruit of the lump (of dough) shall be presented as an offering — in the form of a loaf of bread.

Paul's words here, *aparchē* (" first fruit ") and *phurama*
(" lump ") are those which are combined twice in Num. 15:19-21
(Septuagint) in the expression *aparchēn phuramatos* (" first fruit
of the lump "). The apostle's choice of terms here suggests
strongly that he had in mind the usage in Numbers.[2]

The Old Testament passage is apparently interpreted by Paul to mean that through the offering and dedication of the first of the dough (or bread) the whole body of the dough is thereby consecrated and made " holy." In the same way, it is implied, the holiness of the patriarchs served to consecrate the entire people of Israel [3] or even guarantee their ultimate salvation.[4]

For present purposes it is unnecessary to decide whether " first fruit " is intended by Paul to represent Abraham specifically [5] or the patriarchs generally.[6] The latter is suggested by the reference to the "fathers " or " forefathers " (*pateras*) later in this chapter (ch. 11:28). On the other hand, it may be noted that in Judaism an individual (Adam) was sometimes designated as " dough-offering." [7]

In the Pauline usage of the analogy the following points may be noted: (1) As previously indicated, the application of the metaphor is only implied; it is not stated explicitly. (2) The (implied) application appears to have arisen out of the thought that Paul is attempting to convey rather than from the picture itself. At least this must be true if the picture is that of the offering prescribed in Num. 15:19-21, for in that passage there is nothing to suggest that the dedication of the " first fruit " makes holy or consecrates the whole.[8] (3) Even though the implied application arises, not out of the picture itself, but from Paul's own thinking, the picture is not *really* applicable to that thinking. The offering of the "first fruit " (in the picture) does not correspond closely to the dedication or consecration of the patriarchs. In the setting forth of the offering it is *men* who act in obedience to the Pentateuchal command. In the case of the patriarchs, however, it was *God,* in his free will, who chose them; they were set apart according to his election (*kata . . . tēn eklogēn*) (Rom. 11:28). It may be said, of course, that as *men* choose to make the offering that consecrates the whole, so also *God* chose the patriarchs and thus consecrated the entire people of Israel. Even so, however, the correspondence

is not close, for in the latter case the consecration is with
reference to the one who himself does the choosing (God).
That is, *God* chose the patriarchs; they are then consecrated
to *him,* who chose them. In the case of the picture, however,
this is not true. *Men* choose to make the offering. But here
the offering is consecrated to *God, not* to the men who chose
to make the offering. (4) Insofar as the picture *is* applied
(by implication) it is relevant only to the immediate context
and not to the total Pauline thought. As Dodd has written,
this application " depends on the ancient idea of the solidarity of the tribe or nation. . . . Israel is thought of, not
as a series of individuals each with his own personal responsibility to God, but as a solid whole." [9] Elsewhere Paul argues
that solidarity based on physical descent is by no means determinative insofar as any assurance of salvation is concerned.[10] In Rom. 9:6 ff. he indicates his thought that *not all*
who are descended from Israel or from Abraham are to be
reckoned or counted among those in whom the promises will
be fulfilled. And even in the chapter now under consideration he suggests essentially the same view, for he makes the
inclusion of the Jews dependent, not upon the fact of their
partaking in the solidarity of Israel, but rather, upon their
turning from their " unbelief " (ch. 11:23). Hence it is impossible to reconcile fully the implied application of the picture with the total Pauline thinking. To suggest that all Israel (" the whole lump ") is " holy " — and therefore " all
Israel will be saved " (v. 26) — is simply not entirely com-
patible with the conviction that racial descent does not
count and that faith alone is determinative.

Dodd directs attention to the fact that Paul seems to accept an
idea of solidarity (of the family) also in I Cor. 7:14. He states
further that " there is clearly a truth in the idea of solidarity." [11]
But before he concludes his comments upon this point he is forced
to admit that this " truth " must also pertain to the solidarity of
the human race as a whole, and not only to one branch of that
race (Israel). And since the " truth " involved in the idea of
solidarity does not pertain to one people only, one can hardly ap-

peal to that "truth" in order to justify claims that are made in regard to one people. "The fact is," Dodd adds later, that Paul "has argued from the promise to Abraham on two divergent and perhaps inconsistent lines. If the promise means ultimate blessedness for 'Israel,' then *either* the historical nation of Israel may be regarded as the heir of the promise, and Paul is justified in saying that all Israel will be saved, *or* its place may be taken by the New Israel, the Body of Christ in which there is neither Jew or Greek; but in that case there is no ground for assigning any special place in the future to the Jewish nation as such. Paul tries to have it both ways. We can well understand that his emotional interest in his own people, rather than strict logic, has determined his forecast." [12]

This is not to deny that in the immediate context Paul *does* attach some significance to the idea of solidarity. He does so as he attempts to cope with a particular issue. It is not the purpose of the present study to deal with the problem of reconciling his argument here with the thought that is expressed elsewhere. It *is* pertinent to this study, however, to observe that the analogy that is employed is relevant only to the immediate context or line of argument. It cannot be taken as applicable generally to the apostle's total thought and it cannot be employed as a reliable clue to an understanding of that total thought.

Much that has just been said in regard to Paul's use of the picture of the firstfruit and the lump (of dough) is equally true in regard to his use of the accompanying analogy, that of the "root" and the "branches," insofar as the initial statement in v. 16 is concerned. The two pictures do differ from one another in certain respects, however, although both are intended to reinforce the same main idea.

In view of the preceding metaphor one would have expected Paul to say, "If the root is holy, so also is the entire tree." Instead of this he declares that the *branches* are holy. It has been suggested that the combination of "root" and "branches" is introduced in order to provide a basis for the further development of the analogy that is given in the following verses (vs. 17-24). [13] It is also possible that the form of expression here is due to the fact that Paul is simply quoting an earlier saying.[14] In any case the root (like the firstfruit) must represent either Abraham [15] or, more likely, in view of v. 28, the patriarchs as a group. The branches must stand for the descendants.

If, in composing v. 16b, the metaphor, as first introduced, is intended simply as a parallel to the previous one (v. 16a), then the branches (like the lump) must represent the *totality* of Israel.[16] If, on the other hand, Paul was anticipating the further development of the metaphor in vs. 17-24, then only the faithful descendants of the patriarch(s) may be meant, since according to v. 17 it is implied that some branches are *not* broken off and these alone might more appropriately be called "holy." This latter interpretation is unnecessary, however, in view of the notion of solidarity according to which *all* Israel, "whatever the behaviour of individuals, retains something of the 'holiness' of the patriarchs and of the faithful Remnant." [17] In any case Paul's primary concern in the immediate context is in regard to the status or character of those who are descended from the "root."

Israel had earlier been represented as an olive tree (Jer. 11:16; compare Hos. 14:6), as a cedar (Ezek. 17:22), as a vine (Ezek. 19:10 ff.; Ps. 80:8 ff.), and as a "plant of righteousness" (Enoch 10:16; 93:2, 5). Metaphorical use of Paul's term *hriza* ("root") was not uncommon; sometimes it referred to a progenitor (as in Isa. 11:1, LXX), though sometimes, also, to the progeny (as in Isa. 11:10; compare Rom. 15:12). "Branches" often represented offspring or descendants (as in Hos. 14:6 – LXX, 14:7; Ps. 80:11 – LXX, 79:12; etc.), although various Greek words were employed in the Septuagint.

The intended meaning of the metaphor of the root and the branches must be fundamentally the same as that of the firstfruit and the lump, not only because the two figures are introduced side by side, so to speak, but also because they are set forth in practically identical form:

> *ei de hē aparchē hagia, kai to phurama.*
> *ei hē hriza hagia, kai hoi kladoi.*

As the root of a tree determines the character or essential nature of the branches that grow from it,[18] so also the distinctive holiness of the patriarchs is transmitted to those who are descended from them.

Paul's analogical usage here may be compared to that of Isa. 51:1 f. The writer of that passage, anticipating deliverance for the exiles, suggests (though, as with Paul, the metaphor is not spelled out) that as stones taken from a rock or quarry partake of the nature of their source, so also the Israelites may share in the blessing bestowed upon *their* source, their ancestor (Abraham).

The following observations may now be stated in regard to Paul's initial use of the analogy of the root and branches: (1) As in the case of the previous picture, the application of the metaphor is implied only; it is not made explicit. (2) The Pauline thought concerning Israel determines the use that is made of the analogy; the anaolgy itself does not naturally suggest the thought. It is true, of course, that the character or quality of the root of a tree may be supposed to be transmitted to that which grows or springs from the root. At least this supposition is akin to the notion that the quality of fruit produced by a tree is like the quality of the tree itself.[19] Insofar as this is true it may be said that there is close correspondence between the analogy and the idea that the character or quality of the Israelite ancestors may be transmitted to the descendants. But the emphasis in v. 16 is upon the *holiness* that is shared by the root and branches: if the root is holy, or consecrated, so also are the branches. As over against the picture in v. 16a (where the dough can be regarded as holy because it has been " offered "), there is nothing in the analogy of the root and branches that suggests the holiness of the root.[20] Thus there is found here a further example of the Pauline thought about a " holy " people determining the use that is made of the picture; the picture itself is not one that can be taken as providing a clue to the emphasis in thought that is being made. (3) Even in its limited applicability the picture is relevant only to the immediate context and not to the total Pauline thought. The point that must be made here is the same as that which was set forth in connection with the metaphor of the firstfruit and the lump.[21]

In vs. 17-24, the metaphor of the root and the branches is expanded into a kind of allegory, although picture and idea are mingled throughout the passage.[22]

The picture that is drawn, directly and indirectly, may be described as follows: Some branches of a "cultivated olive tree" (v. 24) have been broken off (v. 17) both in order that others, taken from a "wild olive tree," may be grafted in (v. 19), and also because of some defect in them (v. 20).[23] The grafted branches are made to share in the "richness" (literally, "fatness") of the root (v. 17). Later, the branches that have been broken off will be grafted back into the tree if the defect in them is remedied (vs. 23 f.).

The cultivated olive tree clearly represents Israel, the people chosen and nurtured by God. The branches that have been broken off represent those Jews who have rejected the way of faith (v. 20a). The branches that are grafted into the tree stand for the Gentiles who have accepted the way of faith (see vs. 13 and 20b). The root from which the grafted branches receive their sustenance and strength represents the patriarchs, through whom the people of Israel received their distinctive position (see vs. 28 f.).

There is a certain complexity in the application of the analogy, due in part to the fact that Paul is concerned with a double purpose. On the one hand, he is advocating humility on the part of the Gentiles: he warns them against a boastful attitude, reminding them that they receive their strength or support from that to which they are now attached (the root, Israel) and that they are found in their present condition only through faith and the "kindness" of God (vs. 18, 20, 22). On the other hand, he is expressing hope in the ultimate salvation for all Israel: God is able to restore those who have been cut off if they will turn from "their unbelief" (vs. 23 f.).

The picture appears to be applicable in various respects: (1) As some branches have been broken off from the cultivated olive tree and others, from a wild olive tree, have been grafted in and made to share in the benefits derived from the root, so also " some " of the Jews [24] have been removed from their position within the true Israel and in their place have come Gentiles, who now share in the heritage of the patriarchs (v. 17). (2) As the branches cannot claim to bear or support the root, but rather, are supported *by* the root, so also the Gentiles cannot boast of their position, since they do not provide for the partiarchal heritage, but rather, are the recipients of the benefits of that heritage (v. 18). (3) As some branches were broken off because of a defect, and as grafted branches (which, by implication, do not have this defect) now stand in their place, so also Jews have been cut off because of their " unbelief " and Gentiles " stand fast through faith " (vs. 19 f.). (4) Just as branches that, according to nature, belong to the cultivated olive tree may be grafted back into the tree from which they had been broken off, so also the Jews who had been separated from the true Israel because of their lack of faith will be made a part, once more, of God's people, if they turn from their unbelief. If branches that by nature belong to a *wild* olive tree can be grafted into a cultivated olive tree, surely branches that by nature belong to the *cultivated* tree can be grafted back into it; similarly, if Gentiles can become a part of the true Israel — even though by nature they did not belong to it — certainly the Jews, who did, by nature, belong to it can be restored to their proper position (vs. 23 f.).

Particularly conspicuous in this use of the analogy is the fact that in several respects the picture, as it is drawn (or implied), does *not* correspond closely to actual horticultural practice. (1) It is not normal procedure to graft branches of a " wild " tree into a " cultivated " tree. Instead, it is customary to graft the branches of the cultivated tree into the " wild " stock, and it is from these grafted branches that the superior fruit is produced. Garvie writes: " No gardener ever yet grafted a branch of a wild olive tree on a cultivated one; it is a wild stock on which a branch from a cultivated tree is grafted." [25] This may be an exaggeration in view of the claim that occasionally young shoots from a wild tree *were* grafted into a cultivated tree in order to give it new life and strength.[26] As Lietzmann suggests, however, it may well be questioned that Paul would have been familiar with such an unusual practice.[27] (2) While it is true that the grafted branches derive their nourishment from the root of the tree, the emphasis upon this point (vs. 17 f.) hardly corresponds closely to the purpose involved in the normal grafting procedure. In customary practice the grafting is intended, not primarily to enable the new branches to share the "richness" of the original tree (though there is a sense in which this *is* true), but rather, to enable the tree to have the advantage of that benefit which the new branches may provide. This fact is largely ignored here.

It may be implied, from vs. 20-22, that the branches are thought of as providing something beneficial. As faith is associated with the Gentiles, so also some positive contribution may be associated with the grafted branches. This implication can hardly be intended, however, for the context emphasizes the *dependent* role of the branches, not their beneficial contribution to the productivity of the tree.

(3) Particularly incompatible with actual horticultural practice is the element in the picture which involves the grafting in (later) of the branches that had, in the first place, been broken off (vs. 23 f.). J. Albani rightly speaks of "the unheard-of conduct of the gardener."[28] This point requires no further comment.

It is not difficult to explain the presence of these elements in the picture which do not correspond to actual horticultural practice. Paul has undoubtedly allowed his thought concerning Jews and Gentiles — and their relationship to the' true Israel — to determine the nature of the analogy. One may say that at least in the three respects just described Paul has not sought to reinforce his argument regarding God's purpose by showing that the divine plan corresponds to what is known to be true in the realm of horticulture.

Rather, he has adjusted the analogy so that it may correspond more nearly to the ideas that he wishes to convey, creating a picture that illustrates and makes vivid his thought even though it is not a true picture of horticultural procedure.[29] In other words, points of correspondence are found between the Pauline picture and the Pauline thought concerning Israel and the Gentiles, not because the apostle has used what is known to be true horticulturally in order to support and clarify his views, but rather because, in considerable measure, he has created an unreal picture in such a way that it conforms to his views. The picture provides no important clues to his thought; instead, the picture must be understood in terms of his thought.

There has been considerable debate concerning the significance of the phrase " contrary to nature " (*para phusin*) in v. 24. There are some who interpret the expression to mean that Paul consciously and knowingly introduced a picture of " a purely unnatural process " [30] in horticultural procedure in order to say that " if God has the power against all nature to graft in branches from a wild olive and enable them to bear fruit, how much more easily will He be able to restore to their natural place the branches which have been cut off." [31] Garvie, similarly, though with some reserve, writes that Paul " possibly purposely reverses the natural process to suggest how contrary to all probability and expectation was the call of the Gentiles." [32] If Paul did thus *consciously* draw the picture in such a way that it did not conform to actual practice, then it is particularly clear that the Pauline thought, *not* the horticultural practice, is here determinative.

It is possible, however, that " contrary to nature " refers, not to natural or normal horticultural procedure, but rather, to the relationship between branches and stock.[33] The idea, then, is that the branches were taken from a tree to which they belonged by nature (the wild olive) and grafted into a tree to which they did not belong by nature. This interpretation attaches a meaningful significance to the apparent contrast between *kata phusin* ("according to nature") and *para phusin* ("contrary to nature"), making both phrases refer to the relationship between branches and stock rather than making one of them refer to a grafting procedure. If this is the correct interpretation of the phrase, "contrary to nature," then there is nothing left to suggest that Paul knew he was picturing a grafting process that was not customary. In this case one may conclude that the apostle betrays here his "ignorance of Nature," [34] reflecting "the limitations of the town-bred man." [35] If this conclusion is accepted, then Paul may have thought that he was presenting an accurate picture of horticultural procedure in speaking of the grafting of wild branches on a cultivated tree; in such a case it is unnecessary to explain this particular element in the picture as due to the influence of the Pauline thought regarding Gentiles and Jews. This influence is still to be found, however, insofar as the other points are concerned, especially in regard to the idea of grafting in *again* the branches that had been broken off; it is quite unthinkable that even a "town-bred man" would have thought this to be possible.

6.

The Letter of Paul to the Philippians

PHILIPPIANS 3:2

In the letter of Paul to the Philippians there are found no analogical usages as conspicuous and as extensive as some that appear in most of the other letters. There are, however, a number of words or phrases that present pictures briefly to the mind of the reader. The most vivid, perhaps, is the word *kunas* ("dogs") in Phil. 3:2: "Look out for the dogs, look out for the evil-workers, look out for those who mutilate the flesh." Since the picture of the dogs is introduced in a sudden flash, so to speak, without any specific application, its analogical significance is not self-evident. That Paul applies the picture to persons whom he opposes is clear; but the precise identity of these persons is a matter of considerable dispute, and the extent to which ideas associated with the picture are relevant or applicable to the Pauline thought has been variously understood.

Since the readers are told to "look out" for the "dogs," and since the warning [1] is accompanied by references to "evil-workers" and to "those who mutilate the flesh," it is apparent that the apostle is using the picture to suggest wholly negative ideas. In this he seems to be adopting a usage not at all uncommon, for many examples of this type of expression may be cited.

The usage arises out of the low regard in which dogs were held. In general the dog was looked upon as "the most despised, the most shameless and the most wretched creature." [2] Strack and Billerbeck refer to numerous rabbinical

216

passages in which a similarly low estimate of this animal is indicated,[3] an estimate no doubt reached through the observation of the "herds of dogs which prowl about eastern cities, without a home and without an owner, feeding on the refuse and filth of the streets, quarrelling among themselves, and attacking the passer-by."[4] (See especially Ps. 59:6 f., 14 f.) It is important to recognize that apparently "the Orient does not know the dog as the faithful companion"[5] that it has come to represent frequently in the Western world.[6]

It is hardly surprising, therefore, that the picture of the dog was very often introduced in order to suggest some kind of reproach. Indeed, it has been claimed that metaphorical references to dogs were "always reproachful."[7] To call a person a dog was to indicate rebuke or suggest a state of degradation (see, for example, I Sam. 17:43; II Kings 8:13), and the designation "dead dog" conveyed the "utmost contempt"[8] (see I Sam. 24:14; II Sam. 9:8; 16:9). To speak of a person as eaten by dogs was to heap the greatest condemnation upon him (I Kings 14:11; 16:4; 21:23 f.; II Kings 9:10, 36). Thus, the picture of dogs was employed to characterize evildoers (Ps. 22:16 f.), the senseless or the foolish (Prov. 26:11), the ignorant or the gluttonous (Isa. 56:10 f.). It was applied especially to Gentiles, as the New Testament indicates (Matt. 15:26).[9] The designation served particularly to heighten the extreme contrast that was drawn between those who were God's chosen people and those who stood outside.

As Paul thrusts the picture suddenly before his readers in Phil. 3:2, it is apparently with the same kind of thought that was involved when Gentiles were called dogs: the designation points to those who stand opposed to the Christian community, just as Gentiles stood over against the Jews. There is considerable dispute concerning the precise identity of the persons to whom Paul refers here. On the one hand, it has been argued strongly that "Judaizing Christians" are meant.[10] On the other hand, it has been held that the reference is to "genuine Jews," or, perhaps, to former Gentiles who have turned to Judaism or to some form of Jewish Christianity.[11] It should be noted that when Paul adds (v. 3), " We are the true circumcision," there is evidently intended a contrast to " those who mutilate the flesh." This is clearer in the Greek than in the English. In referring to the opponents as the *katatomēn* (literally, the " mutilation "), " Paul sarcastically alludes to the word *peritomē* [the " circumcision "] which follows in verse 3; as though he would say, Keep your eye on that boasted circumcision, or call it by its true name ' concision ' or ' mutilation.' " [12] Since circumcision was associated particularly with the Jews, it follows that those who are opposed by Paul must in some way be identified with (or at least associated with) the Jews. This is assuming that all three clauses in v. 2 refer to the same opponents.[13]

If the persons designated as dogs are those who stand opposed to the Christian community (as Gentiles stood over against the Jews), and if these persons are at least connected with the Jewish emphasis upon circumcision, then two observations may be made: (1) Paul has adopted a familiar Jewish application of the picture of dogs, but he has reversed that application. Now the picture is used to denote the very group that had employed it with respect to others, or at least to those who, by their concern for circumcision, stood close to that group. It may be said, of course, that insofar as Paul thinks of the Christian community as " the true circumcision " (v. 3),[14] this community is now the true Judaism. From this point of view " Gentiles " would then be those who are not *true* Jews (not Christians). In this sense, " dogs " would still refer to " Gentiles " (not true Jews) as in the usual Jewish usage. The fact remains, however, that a reversal is involved in that the picture is applied to the very group that usually applied it to others. (2) By introducing the picture with reference to those who stood over against the Christian community, Paul's intent apparently is to suggest, not that his opponents exhibit characteristics associated with dogs, but rather, that they are to be distinguished from the Christians as dogs are to be distinguished from men. He is saying, in effect, that "thus understood, the adversary can in no way have a connection with the early Christian faith." [15] In this respect Paul's usage is not unlike that which is found in the Jewish designation of Gentiles as dogs, for the latter bespoke a strong sense of separation. As already noted, however, the application is reversed insofar as it has reference to those who were at least associated with the Jewish emphasis.

It is true that some commentators have claimed a relevance for further elements that may be found in the picture. Lightfoot, for example, suggests that Paul intends to say that his opponents are dogs in that "they greedily devour the garbage of carnal ordinances, the very refuse of God's table." [16] This view is based in part, at least, on Paul's use of the word *skubala* ("refuse") in v. 8. It appears indeed possible that this word may have been suggested to Paul by the fact that dogs were sometimes mentioned as eating refuse in the form of "the leavings of the table" [17] (Mark 7:28), but there is no indication that the apostle had this in mind when he first introduced the picture in v. 2. It seems likely that he employed the Greek word for "refuse" either through association of ideas or simply because it was a common word denoting something "worthless and detestable." [18] There is no real evidence that in this usage he was consciously developing and applying the picture of dogs. Similarly, the context provides no indication that any other characteristic associated with dogs is intended to have relevance or significance. In all probability there "is no subordinate reference to shamelessness, greediness, snappishness, disorderly wandering or howling," as has sometimes been suggested.[19] It is particularly obvious that the idea of the dog as man's faithful companion cannot be applied either in the immediate context or in the larger context of the usual first-century usage.

7.

The Letter of Paul
to Philemon

PHILEMON 10

The picture of a son begotten by his father is introduced
by Paul in Philemon 10 as the apostle presents his appeal on
behalf of Onesimus to the slave's owner: [1] " I appeal to you
for my child, Onesimus, whose father I have become in my
imprisonment." More literally the Greek may be translated
" I appeal to you for my child, whom I begot in [my] [2]
bonds."

This picture, which may also be said to be " more than a
picture," [3] is essentially the same as that which is found in
I Cor. 4:15: " For though you have countless guides in
Christ, you do not have many fathers. For I became your
father [literally, " I begot you "] in Christ Jesus through the
gospel." It is also akin to the metaphor of motherhood, which
Paul introduces in I Thess. 2:7 and in Gal. 4:19 as he writes
of the relationship between himself and the Christians to
whom those letters are addressed.

In speaking of himself as one who " begot " Onesimus, the
apostle obviously intended to suggest that just as a father
brings his child into existence, so also he (Paul) has brought
the slave into the Christian life. He is his spiritual father.

There is also a second idea associated with fatherhood
which is probably intended to have relevance: the idea of a
father's loving care and concern for his child. It is true that
this application of the picture is not made explicit. It seems
to be presupposed, however, in v. 12: " I am sending him
back to you, sending my very heart." As Lohmeyer com-

ments, the meaning of these words is clear: " The slave, who has become a child of Paul, is as dear to him as his own life, indeed as the most inward part of this life, the heart." [4] Thus, both the idea of a father begetting his child and also the idea of a father's love for the child must be meant to be applicable to the thoughts that Paul wishes to convey.

There is one element in the picture of a father and his child which does not seem to be relevant in the immediate context. This becomes especially clear as one compares the usage here with that of the same metaphor in I Cor. 4:15-21. It may be said that when Paul writes to the Corinthians, " spiritual paternity suits his purpose . . . as he stresses obedience to the instruction which it was a father's duty to give in the home." [5] In context there, certainly, the idea of a father as teacher is applicable. That usage of the picture on the part of Paul is not unlike that which is reported by Thayer: " If one teaches the son of his neighbor the law, the Scripture reckons this the same as though he had begotten him." [6] As Paul writes with respect to Onesimus in Philemon 10, however, there is no indication that this thought was in the apostle's mind.

It is perhaps possible that v. 11 may *imply* a measure of instruction such as a father would give his son: " Formerly he was useless to you, but now he is indeed useful to you and to me." It is much more likely, however, that this verse may have been inserted for the sake of a wordplay on the name of Onesimus, which means " useful," or " beneficial," or " profitable." [7] (A further wordplay on the name may be involved in v. 20.) [8] That Paul undoubtedly had given instruction to Onesimus may of course be assumed. " To Onesimus himself Paul had no doubt spoken, with urgent faithfulness, of his sin against his master." [9] Indeed, his instruction must have gone far beyond this. There is no real evidence, however, that Paul associates this idea with his picture of a father in Philemon 10.

That Paul does not intend the picture to be developed and applied in detail is indicated most clearly by the fact that very quickly he turns from it and substitutes a new metaphor. In v. 16 Onesimus is no longer the " child " of the " father " who begot him; instead he is " a beloved brother." Since in the life situations from which the metaphors are drawn one cannot be both child and brother of the same person, it is obvious that the pictures cannot be applied in any thoroughgoing way.

8.

Conclusions

The foregoing analysis of a large number of Pauline analogies indicates that there are indeed certain characteristics of the apostle's analogical usage which may be designated as in some measure persistent.

(1) It is evident that for the most part a picture is introduced for the sake of a *single* element in it that serves to illustrate or reinforce the particular idea involved in the immediate context. In a few cases, it is true, more than one element in the analogy is applied, either explicitly or by implication, to the thought that is being expressed. This is the case with respect to the following pictures: the custodian, the minor heir, ransom, and adoption (Gal. 3:23 to 4:7); Abraham and his family (Gal. 4:21-31); the human body (I Cor. 12:12-30); betrothal (II Cor. 11:2 f.); marriage (Rom. 7:1-6); the potter and the clay (Rom. 9:20-24); the grafting of branches (Rom. 11:16-24); father and son (Philemon 10). Such examples are relatively few, however, as over against the large number of pictures that are found in the letters of Paul.

(2) Especially conspicuous is the fact that a great many of the pictures include elements that are quite inapplicable. To apply these elements to the Pauline thought would introduce ideas that are clearly inconsistent with the apostle's thinking as that thinking is expressed either in the given context or elsewhere in his letters. Pictures falling in this category are at least the following: babes (?) (I Thess. 2:7); the thief in the night (I Thess. 5:1-11); a will or covenant

223

(Gal. 3:15-18); the minor heir, slavery, adoption (Gal. 3:23 to 4:7); travail (Gal. 4:19); a man's thoughts (I Cor. 2:11); planting, watering, giving growth (I Cor. 3:5-17); the gladiatorial arena (I Cor. 4:9 and ch. 15:30-32); the footrace and the boxing match (I Cor. 9:24-27); the mirror (I Cor. 13:12); musical instruments (I Cor. 14:6-12); seed and plant, living creatures, celestial and terrestrial bodies (I Cor. 15:35-50); the triumphal procession (II Cor. 2:14-16); houses and garments (II Cor. 5:1-10); sowing and reaping (II Cor. 9:6); warfare (II Cor. 10:3-6); military life (II Cor. 11:8); the death and resurrection of Christ (Rom. 6:1-14); slavery (Rom. 6:15-23); marriage (Rom. 7:1-6); the potter and the clay (Rom. 9:20-24); the firstfruits and the lump of dough (Rom. 11:16-24).

(3) Numerous pictures are applied differently in different contexts: babes (?) (see the discussion of I Thess. 2:7); sleeping (see the discussion of I Thess. 5:1-11); a covenant (see the discussion of Gal. 3:15-18); the custodian (see the discussion of Gal. 3:23 to 4:7); travail (see Gal. 4:19 as well as I Thess. 5:1-11); the gladiatorial arena (see the discussion of I Cor. 4:9 and ch. 15:30-32); leaven (see the discussion of I Cor. 5:6-8); the human body (see the discussion of I Cor. 12:12-30); slavery (see Rom. 6:15-23 as well as Gal. 3:23 to 4:7); father and son (see the discussion of Philemon 10). In several cases a picture is applied differently even within the same general context: sleeping and being awake (I Thess. 5:1-11); Abraham and his family (Gal. 4:21-31); leaven (I Cor. 5:6-8); aroma or fragrance (II Cor. 2:14-16); letters of recommendation (II Cor. 3:1-3).

(4) Although several pictures are applied by Paul – at least in part – in a manner that may be designated as traditional (since similar applications are to be found in other literature), a number of passages involve applications that differ at least partially from the traditional usages. The following pictures are employed traditionally in at least one respect: babes (see the discussion of I Thess. 2:7); a thief in the night, travail, sleeping, the armed soldier (see I Thess.

5:1-11); leaven (see I Cor. 5:6-8); a building (I Cor. 3:5-17); the planter of a vineyard, the shepherd (I Cor. 9:4-14); the human body (I Cor. 12:12-30); a mirror (?) (I Cor. 13:12); aroma or fragrance (II Cor. 2:14-16); houses (II Cor. 5:1-10); sowing and reaping (II Cor. 9:6); betrothal (II Cor. 11:2 f.); the potter and the clay (Rom. 9:20-24); dogs (Phil. 3:2); father and son (Philemon 10). Pictures applied in a manner that differs at least partially from the more traditional applications include: travail, being awake, the armed soldier (I Thess. 5:1-11); the gladiatorial arena (I Cor. 4:9 and ch. 15:30-32); the planter of a vineyard, the shepherd, the workmen on a farm (I Cor. 9:4-14); the human body (I Cor. 12:12-30); a mirror (?) (I Cor. 13:12); betrothal (II Cor. 11:2 f.); the potter and the clay (Rom. 9:20-24); dogs (Phil. 3:2).

(5) In the case of numerous analogical usages the pictures, as they are presented, include elements that do not represent accurately the phenomena or life situations from which they are drawn. Elements that do not correspond to reality appear in the following: sleeping (I Thess. 5:1-11); a building (I Cor. 3:5-17); the footrace, the boxing match (?), the herald at the games (I Cor. 9:24-27); the human body (I Cor. 12:12-30); aroma or fragrance (II Cor. 2:14-16); letters of recommendation (II Cor. 3:1-3); sowing and reaping (II Cor. 9:6); betrothal (at least by implication, II Cor. 11:2 f.); parent-child obligations (probably, II Cor. 12:14); slavery (Rom. 6:15-23); marriage (at least a *confused* picture is introduced, Rom. 7:1-6); grafting branches (Rom. 11:16-24). In these examples it is evident that the elements in the pictures which do not correspond to reality have been introduced because Paul's thinking has been dominated by the issue that is under consideration, not by the picture itself. In other words, the picture is adjusted so that it will correspond to the apostle's thought even though the result does not represent accurately the phenomenon or life situation on which it is based. There are also further examples of the adjustment of the picture so that it will corre-

spond to the thought — or of the influence of the thought upon the use of analogical language — although the result may not be inconsistent with the phenomenon or life situation from which it is drawn. These include the pictures of leaven and the lump of dough (I Cor. 5:6-8), seed and plant (I Cor. 15:35-50), the workman and his pay (Rom. 4:4), the firstfruits, the lump of dough, the root and the branches (Rom. 11:16-24).

(6) Combinations of pictures are introduced in many contexts: a thief in the night, travail, day and night, sleeping and being awake, drunkenness and sobriety, the armed soldier, building (I Thess. 5:1-11); the custodian, the minor heir, slavery, ransom, adoption (Gal. 3:23 to 4:7); planting, watering, giving growth, a building (I Cor. 3:5-17); leaven, lump of dough, the Passover observance, the paschal lamb, a festival (I Cor. 5:6-8); the soldier, the planter of a vineyard, the shepherd, workmen on a farm, service in the temple (I Cor. 9:4-14); the footrace, the boxing match, the herald at the games (I Cor. 9:24-27); musical instruments, languages (I Cor. 14:6-12); seed and plant, living creatures, celestial and terrestrial bodies (I Cor. 15:35-50); triumphal procession, aroma or fragrance (II Cor. 2:14-16); letters of recommendation, the giving of the law at Mt. Sinai, the "new covenant" of Jeremiah (II Cor. 3:1-3); houses, garments, homeland (II Cor. 5:1-10); betrothal, Eve and the serpent (II Cor. 11:2 f.); a thorn in the flesh, a messenger (?) (II Cor. 12:7 f.); baptism, the death and resurrection of Christ, slavery (Rom. 6:1-14); slavery, harvest, military life (Rom. 6:15-23); firstfruit, lump of dough, root and branches, grafting branches (Rom. 11:16-24).

(7) In a large number of passages the nature of the material is such as to indicate the absence of any concern on the part of Paul for the careful or systematic application of a given analogy. This is particularly evident in the following passages: I Thess. 2:7; 5:1-11; Gal. 3:15-18; 3:23 to 4:7; 4:19; 4:21-31; I Cor. 3:5-17; 5:6-8; 9:4-14; 9:24-27; 12:12-30; II Cor. 2:14-16; 3:1-3; 5:1-10; 9:6; 11:2 f.; 12:7 f.; Rom. 5:7; 6:1-

14; 6:15-23; 7:1-6; 9:20-24; 11:16-24; Phil. 3:2; Philemon 10. In a very small number of cases, it is true, a picture is given a somewhat extended application, and this may suggest a conscious attempt at systematic usage. Such cases involve the pictures of a building (I Cor. 3:5-17), the human body (I Cor. 12:12-30), marriage (Rom. 7:1-6), and the grafting of branches (Rom. 11:16-24). In each of these instances, however, an analysis of the material shows that systematic application of a picture was not intended. It has been seen, furthermore, that the presence of elements or ideas *related* to a given picture appear as the result of a simple association of ideas, not as the result of conscious systematic development and application. See especially: a thief in the night, day and night, sleeping (I Thess. 5:1-11); the custodian, the minor heir, adoption, slavery, ransom (Gal. 3:23 to 4:7); leaven, lump of dough, the Passover observance, the paschal lamb, a festival (I Cor. 5:6-8); the soldier, the planter of a vineyard, the shepherd, the workmen on a farm (I Cor. 9:4-14); the footrace, the boxing match, the herald at the games (I Cor. 9:24-27); the triumphal procession, aroma or fragrance (perhaps, II Cor. 2:14-16); letters of recommendation, the giving of the law at Mt. Sinai, the "new covenant" of Jeremiah (II Cor. 3:1-3); houses, homeland (II Cor. 5:1-10); baptism, the death and resurrection of Christ, slavery (Rom. 6:1-14); the potter and the clay (Rom. 9:20-24); root and branches, grafting branches (Rom. 11:16-24).

(8) A few examples of so-called "reversals" should be noted. In Gal. 4:19 the picture of children with whom a woman is in travail suddenly becomes a picture in which the children themselves appear as pregnant mothers. In Gal. 4:21-31 Hagar is pictured as representing both the mother of the Jews, "bearing children for slavery," and also the children themselves (the Jews, "the present Jerusalem"). It is possible that reversals appear elsewhere also. If the correct reading in I Thess. 2:7 should include the noun "babes" rather than the adjective "gentle," then Paul likens himself and his companions both to babes and to their (mother)

nurse. If, in I Thess. 5:1-11, the plural form " thieves," should be read in v. 4, then the picture of a thief who surprises others suddenly becomes that of thieves who themselves are surprised. In Rom. 7:1-6 it appears that the woman who becomes free upon the death of her husband becomes the one (at least by implication) who has herself died (v. 4).

All these observations regarding Paul's analogical usage are based upon an analysis of his employment of pictures or of analogies generally. It is not enough, however, simply to catalog the characteristics of his analogical usage which thus have emerged. Of particular concern is the significance of these characteristics for the interpreter of Paul's thought, especially as his thought is expressed through the use of those analogies which may be designated as crucial in their bearing upon important theological questions. What, in other words, does the presence of these characteristics indicate with respect to principles of interpretation which the student of the Pauline literature must take into account as he attempts to determine the precise significance of any given analogy, primarily of those analogies involving central theological issues? Three major conclusions regarding such principles of interpretation can be drawn.

A. It must be recognized, first of all, that *Paul's analogies are intended to be applied to his thinking in a limited way only*. This becomes immediately apparent because of the fact — seen in (2) above — that in the case of a multitude of pictures there are elements within them which, if given application, would introduce ideas clearly inconsistent with his thought as that thought is expressed directly or indirectly either in the immediate contexts or elsewhere in his letters. The same conclusion is justified by the further fact — seen in (7) above — that the apostle persistently reveals an absence of concern for the kind of careful or systematic application that is involved when an attempt is made to find significance for his thought in all the various elements or ideas suggested by this or that picture. It is true that in a few passages — see (1) above — more than one element in a given picture may be intended to offer clarification or reinforcement for an idea that Paul wishes to convey. In every one of these passages, however, there are evidences of the absence of interest in full and extended application — compare (7) above. And although more than one element in these analogies does receive a measure of application, still further elements in some of these same analogies have been shown to be clearly inapplicable.[1] The presence of more than one element which is applied, therefore, does not show that still further application is intended. Yet another consideration is also relevant here. The fact that combinations of pictures are introduced in numerous passages — see (6) above — points to Paul's lack of concern for the full application of the various elements found in any one analogy. Since he can move with surprising rapidity from one picture to another, and since each group of pictures in a given combination is brought together for the sake of a common central idea, it is evident that Paul's interest is only in those elements in the pictures which serve to clarify or reinforce that central idea. There is created the clear impression that in Paul's mind the question of the appropriateness or inappropriateness of additional elements in the pictures has not even been raised. Upon occasion the application of such additional elements in the pictures of a given combination would lead to confusion within that combination.[2] Finally, the presence of the so-called reversals — as seen in (8) above — must be noted. The abrupt reversing of a picture, like the sudden joining of one picture to another, indicates the absence of concern for the systematic development and application of any one picture; and this, in turn, bespeaks the fact that Paul is interested only in that element — or in those elements — for the sake of which the picture is introduced in the first place.

In view of the evidence that Paul cannot have intended his analogies to be applied to his thought in full detail, it follows, of course, that it is wholly improper for the reader of the Pauline literature to interpret any detail or element within a given analogy as conveying an intended meaning or as having a particular significance unless there is some indication, either explicit or implied, that such an interpretation is warranted. It is as erroneous to attempt to apply to Paul's thought all the elements of his analogies as it is to give to the details of the parables in the Synoptic Gospels an allegorical significance that was never intended.

B. It is also to be recognized, more positively, that in a given analogy or picture *the only elements that can with certainty be taken as indicative of Paul's thinking — or as keys to his thought — are those elements which have relevance to the immediate context, to the issues that are under direct consideration.* This conclusion is implicit, of course, in what has just been said. It rests, however, on other considerations as well. It has been observed — see (3) above — that numerous pictures are applied by Paul in different ways in different contexts and even in different ways within the same general context. It is obvious that in all these cases the immediate setting must be taken as determinative for the meaning that the given analogy is intended to present. Or, to express it differently, a given analogy *in and of itself* offers no reliable clue for an understanding of Paul's thinking; rather, the analogy serves to clarify or reinforce an idea only as the context into which it is introduced provides an indication of the nature of the idea. The interpreter must begin with the idea that is being presented. Then, and only then, can he interpret the analogy. This is true even in those cases where the apostle has employed pictures that had already become associated with specific ideas. When Paul introduces a picture that had become a familiar analogy, it might be supposed that his thought is therefore to be understood in terms of the idea or ideas that that picture was commonly employed to suggest. It has been seen to be a Pauline characteristic, however — see (4) above — that although he sometimes uses an analogy in a more or less traditional manner, he deviates frequently from the traditional usage, sometimes in greater and sometimes in lesser degree. Since he does upon occasion thus use an analogy to express an idea somewhat different from that with which it had been associated, it is apparent that even a familiar analogy cannot be regarded as conveying necessarily a particular idea; it has relevance or significance only as the immediate context determines that relevance or significance.

C. It is to be recognized, finally, that in Paul's use of analogy *his pictures provide no reliable clue as to his thought or understanding with respect to the phenomena or life situations that those pictures represent or from which they are drawn.* Numerous pictures — as seen in (5) above — simply do not conform to reality. The apostle has adjusted them in order that they might serve his purpose, sketching into them, so to speak, certain elements that may illustrate or reinforce his thought or argument; but they do not correspond to what anyone could really believe with respect to the phenomena or life situations supposedly represented. One certainly cannot ascribe to Paul, for example, the ideas concerning building procedures or the ideas regarding horticultural practices that are incorporated in his pictures of a building (I Cor. 3:5-17) and of the grafting of branches (Rom. 11:16-24). This means that a picture *as he draws it* cannot be used by the interpreter to provide evidence as to what Paul really believed to be true in the area from which it was taken.[3] It can be used only as Paul himself used it — to clarify and reinforce the thought with which he is concerned in the given context.

Notes

Introduction

1. Adolf Deissmann, *St. Paul*, tr. by Lionel R. M. Strachan, p. 3.

2. A. E. Barnett, *Paul Becomes a Literary Influence* (The University of Chicago Press, 1941). Barnett shows that for a time the popularity of Paul's letters was greatly reduced, especially during the second quarter of the second century, "due to the espousal of Paul by heretical groups" (p. 186). The very fact that these heretical groups found it expedient to appeal to Paul, however, is indicative of the importance that was attached to him.

3. See, for example, the first chapter, "Paul or Paulinism," in James S. Stewart, *A Man in Christ*.

4. Joachim Jeremias, *The Parables of Jesus*, tr. by S. H. Hooke, p. 10.

5. These examples are discussed by Jeremias, *op. cit.*, pp. 52–70. Jeremias presents evidence that the process of allegorization began even before the writing of the Synoptic Gospels.

6. See, for example, C. H. Dodd, *The Parables of the Kingdom*, pp. 1 f.

7. Richard Chenevix Trench, *The Parables of Our Lord*, pp. 8 f.

8. *Ibid.*, p. 115.

9. *Ibid.*, p. 37, quoting Tholuck.

10. Adolf Jülicher, *Die Gleichnisreden Jesu*. Jülicher's work is, of course, of particular significance. It is often overlooked, however, that other men of his time were moving in the same direction. As early as 1886 W. M. Taylor wrote thus: "Just as, in the interpretation of the symbolism of the Jewish tabernacle, we run into trifling and conceit when we attempt to give a spiritual significance to every pillar, curtain, and coupling, and pin, so we miss the full force of a parable when we try to find a meaning in

every fold of its drapery " (*The Parables of Our Savior*, pp. 14 f.).

11. A. T. Cadoux, *The Parables of Jesus*.

12. B. T. D. Smith, *The Parables of the Synoptic Gospels*.

13. Dodd, *The Parables of the Kingdom*.

14. Jeremias, *op. cit.*

15. Rudolf Bultmann, *Der Stil der paulinischen Predigt und die kynisch-stoische Diatribe*, pp. 88–90.

16. Werner Straub, *Die Bildersprache des Apostels Paulus*.

17. *Bildwörter, bildhafte Redewendungen, Vergleiche, Metaphern, Bildsprüche*, and *Gleichnisse*.

18. Ernest De Witt Burton, *The Epistle to the Galatians* (International Critical Commentary), on Gal. 4:5, p. 221.

19. C. H. Dodd, *The Epistle of Paul to the Romans* (The Moffatt New Testament Commentary), on Rom. 7:1-6, p. 103.

20. Burton, *op. cit.*, on Gal. 4:1-2, p. 211.

21. There have been numerous treatments of the place of analogy in theological discourse. One of the more recent is that of E. L. Mascall, *Words and Images: A Study in Theological Discourse*. Although treatments of this kind deal with important questions that are relevant to a study of Pauline usages, they are concerned largely with the general rather than with the specific.

22. Hans Lietzmann has written a striking paragraph in which he suggests certain Pauline characteristics in this respect (*The Beginnings of the Christian Church*, tr. by Bertram Lee Woolf, pp. 148 f.), but he does not enter upon a discussion of the evidences that have led him to his observations.

23. See Rudolf Bultmann, *Theology of the New Testament*, tr. by Kendrick Grobel, Vol. I, pp. 205 f.

24. This expression is Bultmann's, in his *Theology of the New Testament*, Vol. I, p. 190. He includes among the " undoubtedly genuine " documents the same as those which are used here.

25. See, for example, Straub, *op. cit.*, pp. 20–97.

26. See the discussion of Rom. 7:1-6.

1.

The First Letter of Paul to the Thessalonians

I THESSALONIANS 2:7

1. Walter F. Adeney, *Thessalonians and Galatians* (New-Century Bible), p. 167.

2. Martin Dibelius, *An die Thessalonicher I, II* (Handbuch zum Neuen Testament), Zweite Auflage, p. 8.

3. George Milligan, *St. Paul's Epistles to the Thessalonians*, p. 21.

4. George G. Findlay, *The Epistles to the Thessalonians* (Cambridge Bible for Schools and Colleges), p. 67.

5. Rom. 2:20; I Cor. 3:1; 13:11; Gal. 4:1, 3. In addition, it appears as a verb form in I Cor. 14:20.

6. James Everett Frame, *The Epistles of St. Paul to the Thessalonians* (International Critical Commentary), p. 91. On p. 100, however, he suggests that a colon should be placed after the first clause.

7. Frame, *op. cit.*, p. 100. Frame also observes that as a contrast to " apostles " we should naturally expect a noun ("babes"), not an adjective ("gentle").

8. William Neil, *The Epistle of Paul to the Thessalonians* (The Moffatt New Testament Commentary), p. 40.

9. See Frame, *op. cit.*, p. 100.

10. The Greek word for " child "in Mark 10:15 is *paidion*, but "babes" are children too!

11. Willoughby C. Allen, *The Gospel According to S. Matthew* (International Critical Commentary), p. 194.

12. Alfred E. Garvie, *Romans* (New-Century Bible), on Rom. 2:20, p. 111. Lietzmann seems to agree when he suggests that Rom. 2:19 f. gives the impression of involving a quoting by Paul from some Jewish writing pertaining to proselytes (Hans Lietzmann, *An die Römer* [Handbuch zum Neuen Testament], Vierte Auflage), on Rom. 2:19 f., p. 43.

13. See James Moffatt, *The First Epistle of Paul to the Corinthians* (The Moffatt New Testament Commentary), on I Cor. 13:10, p. 201.

14. Note that here, as in I Cor. 3:1 f., milk is associated with "babes," and "solid food" with the "mature." Compare also I Peter 2:2.

15. Milligan, *op. cit.*, on I Thess. 2:7, p. 22.

I THESSALONIANS 5:1-11

1. The articles enclosed in parentheses are absent in Paul's Greek text.

2. See Joseph Henry Thayer, *A Greek-English Lexicon of the New Testament*, Corrected Edition, on *phulakē*, d.

3. Compare also Rev. 16:15. Some have regarded this verse as a gloss, however. See James Moffatt, *The Revelation of St. John the Divine* (Expositor's Greek Testament, Vol. V), p. 448.

4. Neil, *op. cit.*, p. 110.

5. For a brief discussion of this and other possibilities, see Frame, *op. cit.*, p. 181.

6. At other points, also, there are references to anguish, terror, and the like coming " suddenly " (Jer. 15:8; 18:22; 51:8).

7. The idea of suddenness is brought out with particular clarity in the picture of a woman in travail, to be discussed below.

8. See Thayer, *op. cit.*, on *kleptēs*.

9. This has been shown by Adolf Jülicher, in his discussion of the use of this analogy in Luke 12:39 f., as he comments upon the interpretation of Godet — namely, that the returning Messiah " is not only a beloved Lord, who replaces all that one has given up for him, but is also like a thief, who takes everything that one should not have retained" (translation mine). See *Die Gleichnisreden Jesu*, Vol. I, p. 84.

10. Compare Werner Straub, *Die Bildersprache des Apostels Paulus*, p. 51.

11. Paul's word, translated " surprise," is *katalabēi*, literally, " lay hold of," or " overtake," but " with a touch of surprise " (see Frame, *op. cit.*, pp. 183 f.).

12. Frame, *op. cit.*, p. 183.

13. Frame (*op. cit.*, p. 184) accepts this reading. Dibelius agrees that *kleptas* ("thieves") is not unsuitable here; he concludes, however, that this form must be considered as an emendation (*An die Thessalonicher*, p. 54).

14. Milligan, *op. cit.*, p. 66. Such inversion may also be found in I Thess. 2:7, if in that verse Paul indeed likens himself and his companions to " babes " and then to a " nurse " (who cares for the children).

15. See, for example, Isa. 13:8; 21:3; Jer. 22:23; 30:6; 49:24; 50:43; Micah 4:9-10.

16. R. H. Charles, *The Book of Enoch*, p. 123.

17. Frame, *op. cit.*, on II Thess. 1:9, p. 234. So also, essentially, Neil, *op. cit.*, p. 149.

18. See Archibald Robertson and Alfred Plummer, *The First Epistle of St. Paul to the Corinthians* (International Critical Commentary), on I Cor. 5:5, p. 99. See also Moffatt, *The First Epistle of Paul to the Corinthians*, pp. 56 f.

19. In essential agreement are Milligan, *op. cit.*, pp. 65 f.; Neil, *op. cit.*, p. 111; and Frame, *op. cit.*, p. 182. Findlay (*op. cit.*, p. 110), however, states that the image does signify the "intense pain" that will be found in the coming disaster.

20. Findlay, *op. cit.*, p. 110.

21. So Frame, *op. cit.*, p. 182.

22. So Neil, *op. cit.*, p. 112.

23. Neil, *op. cit.*, p. 112.

24. This picture is used more fully in Eph. 6:11-17, a passage that in several respects suggests the influence both of Isa. 59:17 and of the Wisd. of Sol. 5:17-20. Ephesians, however, lies outside the scope of the present study (see the Introduction).

25. So William Sanday and Arthur C. Headlam, *The Epistle to the Romans* (International Critical Commentary), on Rom. 13:11-14, p. 377. Also Dodd, *The Epistle of Paul to the Romans*, p. 209.

26. Thayer, *op. cit.*, on *oikodomeō*. See also I Cor. 6:19.

2.

The Letter of Paul to the Galatians

GALATIANS 3:15-18

1. For a careful treatment of the word and its usage, see Burton, *op. cit.*, pp. 496–505.

2. As Burton, *op. cit.*, p. 179; see also pp. 500–505; also George S. Duncan, *The Epistle of Paul to the Galatians* (The Moffatt New Testament Commentary), pp. 105 ff.; also E. H. Perowne, *The Epistle to the Galatians* (Cambridge Bible for Schools and Colleges), p. 36.

3. Burton, *op. cit.*, p. 180; Duncan, *op. cit.*, p. 106.

4. Duncan, *op. cit.*, p. 106.

5. Burton, *op. cit.*, p. 498.

6. *Ibid.*, p. 497.

7. For the same distinction, see Robertson and Plummer, *op. cit.*, on I Cor. 11:25, p. 247.

8. Paul's emphasis upon "the promises" in Gal. 3:15-18 seems to suggest the same thought.

9. Duncan, *op. cit.*, p. 106. See also R. H. Strachan, *The Second Epistle of Paul to the Corinthians* (The Moffatt New Testament Commentary), pp. 82 ff.

238 The Use of Analogy in the Letters of Paul

10. There is also strong manuscript evidence for the presence of "new" in Luke 22:20. The evidence is not strong for the presence of this adjective in the parallel verses of the other Synoptic Gospels (Matt. 26:28 and Mark 14:24).

11. "For Christ, our paschal lamb, has been sacrificed." (I Cor. 5:7.)

12. For a similar connection between "blood" and "covenant," see Zech. 9:11.

13. Compare Heb. 8:6-13 and 9:15-22.

14. See Strachan, op. cit., on II Cor. 3:4-11, pp. 84 f., and Hans Lietzmann, An die Korinther I, II (Handbuch zum Neuen Testament), Vierte Ergänzte Auflage, pp. 57 and 112 f.

15. Duncan, op. cit., p. 112.

16. This is probably the meaning intended in Gal. 3:19. Compare Rom. 3:20; 4:15; 5:13, 14, 20; 7:7-12. See Burton, op. cit., p. 188.

17. "It [the law] was added because of transgressions." (Gal. 3:19.)

18. Burton, op. cit., p. 188.

19. While Gal. 4:21-31 suggests that the giving of the law did involve the establishing of a covenant ("One is from Mount Sinai," ch. 4:24) — and for that reason is mentioned here — it provides no basis for the idea that one covenant comes after, or displaces, the other, unless there was consciously in Paul's mind the thought that in the book of Genesis, Hagar preceded Sarah as a bearer of Abraham's child; but this would be pressing that analogy beyond Paul's own application of it.

20. As Lietzmann, An die Galater (Handbuch zum Neuen Testament), Dritte Auflage, pp. 19 ff. Adeney (op. cit., p. 297) argues that in this instance Paul has in mind both "will" and "covenant": "The nature of the Greek 'will,' as public and unchangeable when once executed, would assimilate it to such a covenant as we meet with in the O. T., an agreement between two parties, but really determined in the first instance by one, since it is God's covenant offered to man."

21. Burton (op. cit., p. 502) refutes convincingly the claim that in Greek practice not even the maker of a will could revoke a will once made. It appears that a will was irrevocable only in a case involving adoption. Paul's language points to general, and not exceptional, practice.

22. "Das Gleichnis hinkt, denn Gott ist nicht als Erblasser gestorben." (Lietzmann, *An die Galater*, p. 20.)

GALATIANS 3:23 to 4:7

1. Thayer, *op. cit.*, on *paidagōgos*.

2. Burton, *op. cit.*, p. 200.

3. Literally, faith " of Jesus Christ," but see Adolf Deissmann, *Paulus*, Zweite Auflage, pp. 125 ff.

4. Duncan, *op. cit.*, p. 122. See also Lietzmann, *An die Galater*, p. 23.

5. Burton, *op. cit.*, p. 197.

6. So Lietzmann, *An die Galater*, p. 23.

7. See Burton, *op. cit.*, p. 200.

8. Lietzmann, *An die Korinther*, on I Cor. 4:15, p. 21.

9. Moffatt, *The First Epistle of Paul to the Corinthians*, on I Cor. 4:15, p. 51.

10. Adeney, *op. cit.*, on Gal. 3:24, p. 302.

11. So Duncan, *op. cit.*, p. 121.

12. *Ibid.*, p. 121.

13. See Burton, *op. cit.*, on Gal. 4:1-2, pp. 211–215; also Duncan, *op. cit.*, pp. 125 f.

14. For a discussion of this expression, see Burton, *op. cit.*, pp. 510–518.

15. *Ibid.*, p. 518.

16. Duncan, *op. cit.*, on Gal. 4:8-11, p. 135.

17. *Ibid.*, on Gal. 4:4, p. 129, and Burton, *op. cit.*, on Gal. 3:23, p. 198.

18. Lightfoot, *St. Paul's Epistle to the Galatians*, p. 267. It should also be noted that Paul's phrase, *genomenon hupo nomon*, may be translated " made subject to law " instead of " born under law." For a discussion of this point, see Burton, *op. cit.*, p. 218.

19. At least this would normally be true (see Thayer, *op. cit.*, on *epitropos*, 2), although Burton regards it as possible that " a guardianship may be created during the lifetime of the father " (*op. cit.*, p. 211).

20. So Adeney (*op. cit.*, on Gal. 4:2, p. 306), who observes, with respect to Paul, that this " would be the law of his own native province Cilicia, and that also of the churches to which he was writing."

21. Duncan, *op. cit.*, p. 127.

22. Burton (*op. cit.*, p. 214) mentions this account.

23. In Gal. 3:28 *doulos* ("slave") appears, but there it does not have analogical significance.

24. For a discussion of the unenviable position of a slave in the Greek and Jewish world, see the article on *doulos* in Gerhardt Kittel, ed., *Theologisches Wörterbuch zum Neuen Testament*, Vol. II, pp. 264 ff.

25. Although the RSV gives "servant" in most of these passages, Paul's word in each case is *doulos*.

26. Burton, *op. cit.*, on Gal. 3:13, p. 168.

27. Lightfoot, *St. Paul's Epistle to the Galatians*, on Gal. 3:13, p. 252. See Adolf Deissmann, *Light from the Ancient East*, tr. by Lionel R. Strachan, pp. 324 ff., for striking parallels in early inscriptions to Paul's picture of man's redemption in terms of a slave being ransomed through divine action.

28. It is thus designated in W. F. Moulton and A. S. Geden, *A Concordance of the Greek Testament*, on *huiothesia*, p. 966.

29. Sanday and Headlam, *op. cit.*, on Rom. 8:15, p. 203.

30. See Otto Michel, *Der Brief an die Römer* (Kritisch-exegetischer Kommentar über das Neue Testament), p. 168.

31. Lietzmann, *An die Galater*, on Gal. 4:5, p. 27.

32. That adoption among the Greeks and Romans involved a multitude of complications and ramifications has been shown in various treatments of the subject. See, for example, James Hastings, ed., *Encyclopaedia of Religion and Ethics*, under "Adoption," Vol. I, pp. 107–110 and 111–114.

33. James Hastings, ed., *A Dictionary of the Bible*, under "Adoption," Vol. I, p. 40.

34. Hastings, *Encyclopaedia of Religion and Ethics*, under "Adoption," Vol. I, p. 112.

35. Lightfoot, *St. Paul's Epistle to the Galatians*, p. 267. See also James Denney, *St. Paul's Epistle to the Romans* (Expositor's Greek Testament, edited by W. Robertson Nicoll), Vol. II, p. 648.

36. For reference to a very special kind of transaction which might be construed as the equivalent of a father adopting his own natural son, see Hastings, *Encyclopaedia of Religion and Ethics*, Vol. I, p. 112. It is unthinkable that Paul would presuppose on the part of his readers a knowledge of the complexities involved in this kind of situation.

37. Dodd comments, "We get the paradox that God is the 'Father' of all men, but not all men are His 'sons'" (*The Epistle of Paul to the Romans*, on Rom. 8:14-17, p. 131).

38. Duncan, *op. cit.*, on Gal. 4:5, p. 130.
39. Lietzmann, *An die Galater*, p. 26.
40. *Ibid.*
41. Deissmann, *St. Paul*, p. 153.
42. Barrett regards the reference in Rom. 8:15 as future also: "The 'Spirit of adoption' is . . . not 'the Spirit which actually effects adoption' but 'the Spirit which anticipates adoption,' which brings forward into the present what is properly an eschatological event" (C. K. Barrett, *A Commentary on the Epistle to the Romans*, p. 163).

GALATIANS 4:19

1. So Duncan, *op. cit.*, p. 141.
2. Burton, *op. cit.*, p. 248.

GALATIANS 4:21-31

1. Burton, *op. cit.*, p. 253.
2. For a survey of the various possibilities as to meaning, see Burton, *op. cit.*, pp. 254 ff.
3. It is assumed here that this section of the letter ends with v. 31, as in the KJV and the RSV (see Burton, *op. cit.*, pp. 270 ff.). Textual variations, however, do allow the possibility that Gal. 5:1 belongs with the preceding section, as in Moffatt's translation (so also Lightfoot, *St. Paul's Epistle to the Galatians*, pp. 282 f., and Duncan, *op. cit.*, pp. 151 f.). But if ch. 5:1 does belong with ch. 4:21-31, the section still closes with the same kind of contrast: slavery versus freedom.
4. Burton, *op. cit.*, p. 251.
5. W. M. Ramsay, *A Historical Commentary on St. Paul's Epistle to the Galatians*, pp. 431–433.
6. See Lietzmann, *An die Galater*, p. 30, and Burton, *op. cit.*, p. 252.
7. Lightfoot, *St. Paul's Epistle to the Galatians*, on Gal. 4:23, p. 278.
8. Burton, *op. cit.*, p. 259.
9. See Lightfoot, *St. Paul's Epistle to the Galatians*, pp. 361 ff., and Burton, *op. cit.*, pp. 259 ff.
10. For a discussion — and rejection — of this suggestion, see Lightfoot, on "The Meaning of Hagar in Gal. 4:25" (*St. Paul's Epistle to the Galatians*, pp. 363–368). Lietzmann (on Gal. 4:25, p. 31) regards the idea as *kaum denkbar*.

11. So Duncan, *op. cit.*, p. 146.

12. Compare Micah 4:8; Zeph. 3:14; S. of Sol. 1:5; 3:5; etc. In Gal. 4:25, " children" probably refers not so much to the actual inhabitants of the city as to " all the adherents of legalistic Judaism which has its center in Jerusalem" (Burton, *op. cit.*, p. 262).

13. For some discussion of this view ascribed to Zahn, see Lietzmann, *An die Galater*, p. 30.

14. Lightfoot, *St. Paul's Epistle to the Galatians*, on Gal. 3:29, p. 281.

15. The quotation from Isa. 54:1, in v. 27, shows that Paul is indeed relying on the LXX in this section, for the quotation reproduces exactly the form that is found in the LXX, omitting, with the LXX, the reference to " singing" found in the Hebrew text.

16. See the examples given in Hermann L. Strack and Paul Billerbeck, *Kommentar zum Neuen Testament*, Vol. III, pp. 575 f.

17. So Duncan, *op. cit.*, p. 149; see Lightfoot, *St. Paul's Epistle to the Galatians*, p. 281.

18. Burton, *op. cit.*, on Gal. 4:21, p. 252; also p. 459.

19. *Ibid.*, on Gal. 3:29, p. 266.

20. The question as to whether or not Philo attached historical as well as allegorical significance to the Torah is one that need not be treated here.

21. Lightfoot, *St. Paul's Epistle to the Galatians*, p. 370.

3.

The First Letter of Paul to the Corinthians

I CORINTHIANS 2:11

1. See Robertson and Plummer, *op. cit.*, pp. 43 f.

2. Rudolf Bultmann, *Theology of the New Testament*, Vol. I, p. 206. Bultmann recognizes that in a passage like I Thess. 5:23 Paul's language suggests a trichotomous " scheme of anthropology." He insists, however, that this is a matter of form only, and that " the formulation is to be explained as coming from liturgical-rhetorical (perhaps traditional) diction" (pp. 205 f.).

3. Still a different meaning is involved in I Cor. 2:12a (" the spirit of the world"), but this need not be considered here. See Robertson and Plummer, *op. cit.*, on I Cor. 2:12, p. 45, and Thayer, *op. cit.*, on *pneuma*, 5.

4. Bultmann, *Theology of the New Testament*, Vol. I, p. 205.

5. Lietzmann observes that "die Parallele ist nicht völlig durchführbar" (*An die Korinther*, p. 13).

6. Dodd, *The Epistle of Paul to the Romans*, on Rom. 8:26, p. 135.

7. C. K. Barrett, *A Commentary on the Epistle to the Romans*, p. 168. However, Barrett also suggests the possibility of Gnostic influence here, although he adds that "Paul does not mean what the Gnostics meant."

8. Sanday and Headlam, *op. cit.*, on Rom. 7:15, p. 182.

9. Barrett, *op. cit.*, p. 147.

10. So Lightfoot, *St. Paul's Epistle to the Galatians*, on Gal. 4:9, p. 269.

11. To accept this distinction would bring the picture of man in I Cor. 2:11 into closer agreement with the thought of Rom. 7:15, since in the latter the verb is *ginōskō:* a man may "know" (*oida*) his own thoughts and yet may not understand *thoroughly* (*ginōskō*) some aspects of his experience. This would not account for the contrast found between the picture of I Cor. 2:11 and the thought of Rom. 8:26, however, for in both of these passages the *same* verb (*oida*) is employed.

12. See Thayer, *op. cit.*, on *ginōskō*.

13. Robertson and Plummer, *op. cit.*, p. 44.

14. The words are absent in G and in the Latin fathers. See Lietzmann, *An die Korinther*, p. 13.

I CORINTHIANS 3:5-17

1. See Robertson and Plummer, *op. cit.*, p. 57.

2. Lietzmann translates "eins (in ihrer Arbeit)" (*An die Korinther*, p. 14).

3. Compare Paul's reference to his "blamelessness" before men (Phil. 3:6) as over against his sense of guilt before God (Rom. 7:15-25).

4. The rendering of I Cor. 3:9a in the KJV is "For we are laborers together with God." The translation (RSV) given here, however, is preferable, for it preserves the idea of the subordination of the human leaders under God as seen in the larger context (ch. 3:5 ff.). See Moffatt, *The First Epistle of Paul to the Corinthians*, p. 39.

5. See Moffatt, *ibid.*, p. 39; Robertson and Plummer, *op. cit.*, p. 58.

6. See J. Albani, "Die Parabel bei Paulus," *Zeitschrift für wissenschaftliche Theologie,* Zweites Heft, 1903, p. 164.

7. Weiss is quoted by Straub, *op. cit.,* p. 73.

8. Moffatt, *The First Epistle of Paul to the Corinthians,* p. 39.

9. Dobschütz refers to the fact that "die Verbindung der Gleichnisse vom Ackerbau und Hausbau . . . seit Plato weit verbreitet ist" (Ernst von Dobschütz, *Der Apostel Paulus,* Vol. I, p. 56, Anm. 22).

10. In Rom. 11:17 ff. Paul moves similarly to a second picture, combined with a first picture in v. 16, just as here (I Cor. 3:10 ff.) he takes up the second analogy, which is combined with the first in v. 9.

11. See the Introduction.

12. See below, however.

13. The Greek words, *lithous timious,* are rendered "precious stones" not only in the RSV but also in the KJV and by Moffatt. The American Translation has "costly stones." The latter, together with the view of Deissmann, will be considered below.

14. Moffatt, *The First Epistle of Paul to the Corinthians,* p. 40.

15. Lietzmann, *An die Korinther,* p. 17.

16. *Ibid.,* p. 16.

17. Straub, *op. cit.,* p. 87.

18. "Innerhalb seiner Allegorie fühlt er sich nicht daran gebunden, wirklichkeitsgetreu zu schildern." *Ibid.,* p. 86.

19. Strack and Billerbeck (*op. cit.,* p. 333) prefer also, as the meaning, valuable building material, such as marble and alabaster.

20. Deissmann, *Paulus,* p. 244. He directs particular attention to Tobit 13:16 and Rev., ch. 21.

21. Compare Rev. 21:19-21.

22. Deissmann, *Paulus,* footnote on p. 244. Robertson and Plummer, interpreting *lithous timious* as "precious stones," regard all the first three items in I Cor. 3:12 as included because they are suitable for ornamentation (*op. cit.,* pp. 62 f.).

23. Compare I Thess. 5:4.

24. See especially Dan. 7:9 f.; Mal. 4:1; Isa. 10:16 f.; 47:14 f.; 66:15; Ezek. 22:20-22; II Thess. 1:5-8; II Peter 3:7.

25. See Robertson and Plummer, *op. cit.,* p. 63.

26. The term "reward," of course, carries certain implications that Paul does not accept. On its use in I Cor. 3:14, Moffatt writes: "Firmly as Paul held to the grace of God, to whom all credit

went . . . , he never abandoned his pharisaic conviction that those who were bound to serve the Lord as best they could received a recompense at the end (9:14; II Cor. 5:10) " (*The First Epistle of Paul to the Corinthians*, p. 41).

27. See, for example, Ps. 66:10; Prov. 17:3; Wisd. of Sol. 3:5 f.

28. Jer. 9:7 (LXX, 9:6); compare Mal. 3:3.

29. Zech. 13:9. Paul specifically mentions " the Day " in I Cor. 3:13.

30. Compare Zech. 14:14.

31. Thayer, *op. cit.*, on *archi*.

32. In the Septuagint version of Isa. 3:3 the word is included in a list of offices or positions where at least a certain measure of preeminence is involved. This is less clear in the use of the term in Ecclus. 38:27.

33. Robertson and Plummer, *op. cit.*, p. 61.

34. Moffatt, *The First Epistle of Paul to the Corinthians*, p. 41.

35. Paul uses the word in this sense in I Cor. 15:33; II Cor. 7:2; 11:3.

36. Footnote to I Cor. 3:17, p. 67.

37. *Ibid.*, p. 66.

38. Similar evidence of the influence of previously used terminology is seen in I Cor. 4:3, although the English versions generally conceal this fact. When Paul is made to say there, " It is a very small thing that I should be judged by you or by any human court," the Greek for the last phrase says literally, " by a human day." The expression is undoubtedly suggested by " the Day " (the Day of Judgment) of ch. 3:13. A " day " of human judgment means little as over against the " Day " of God's Judgment. As in the case discussed above, a picture may *suggest* the terminological usage that follows, without, however, involving further development or application of the *original* picture.

39. The connection between I Cor. 3:16 f. and the previous section is so limited that Lietzmann prefers to speak of vs. 16-17 as introducing " a new picture " (" ein neues Bild ") (*An die Korinther*, p. 17).

I CORINTHIANS 4:9; 15:30-32

1. The Greek word (*epithanatious*) translated as " sentenced to death " appears in Bel and the Dragon (32) with reference to that which was given to the lions.

2. Robertson and Plummer, *op. cit.*, p. 85. The word has a

similar connotation in Acts 2:22 and in II Thess. 2:4.

3. So Moffatt, *The First Epistle of Paul to the Corinthians,* p. 254. The same phrase seems to have a similar meaning in Rom. 3:5 (Sanday and Headlam, *op. cit.,* p. 73) and in Gal. 3:15. Compare Rom. 6:19 (*anthrōpinon*). In other contexts, however, *kata anthrōpon* does not suggest metaphorical usage (see Gal. 1:11; I Cor. 3:3; 9:8). For other suggestions as to the meaning in I Cor. 15:32, see Lietzmann, *An die Korinther,* p. 83, and Robertson and Plummer, *op. cit.,* pp. 361 f.

4. Thayer, *op. cit.,* on *thēriomacheō.* So also Robertson and Plummer, *op. cit.,* p. 362, and Lietzmann, *An die Korinther,* p. 83.

5. J. J. Lias, *The First Epistle to the Corinthians* (Cambridge Bible for Schools and Colleges), p. 152. Moffatt, it is true, cites the case of Acilius Glabrio, who, though a Roman citizen, was compelled to engage in such combat. Moffatt agrees, however, that Paul is speaking metaphorically (*The First Epistle of Paul to the Corinthians,* p. 254).

6. Bultmann has claimed, it should be noted, that Paul never draws upon the theater for his analogical material. He insists that no comparison is intended, for example, in I Cor. 4:9. (In this passage " liegt kein Vergleich vor.") See Bultmann, *Der Stil der paulinischen Predigt,* p. 91. It is true that Paul does not present a clear picture of the gladiatorial arena, but the combination of words found here (" spectacle " and " exhibited ") suggests strongly that the arena was indeed in his mind as he wrote.

I CORINTHIANS 5:6-8

1. In spite of this the RSV renders the Greek of I Cor. 5:6, " a little leaven ferments the whole lump of dough." The verb in D is *doloi* (" corrupt," " spoil ") rather than *zumoi* (" leaven "), but in that manuscript this is true for both Gal. 5:9 and I Cor. 5:6, so that identity of wording is also found there. For similar variations in Latin texts, see Lietzmann, *An die Korinther,* pp. 23 f.

2. Matt. 16:6-12; Mark 8:15; Luke 12:1. For non-Biblical references, see James Hastings, ed., *A Dictionary of the Bible,* Vol. III, p. 90. A notable exception occurs in Matt. 13:33 and Luke 13:20 f., where leaven is likened to the Kingdom of God. Even in these parables leaven has sometimes been interpreted as representing something evil. Trench refers to such interpretations in his *Parables of Our Lord,* pp. 113 f., though he himself firmly rejects them.

3. So Burton, *op. cit.*, p. 283; so also Thayer, *op. cit.*, on *zumē*, and Perowne, *op. cit.*, p. 62.

4. So Lightfoot, *St. Paul's Epistle to the Galatians,* p. 286, and Adeney, *op. cit.*, p. 323.

5. However one may interpret " deliver this man to Satan for the destruction of the flesh," etc., at least the idea of expulsion from the church must be involved (Moffatt, *The First Epistle of Paul to the Corinthians,* p. 56; also Robertson and Plummer, *op. cit.*, p. 99).

6. Moffatt, *The First Epistle of Paul to the Corinthians,* on I Cor. 5:8, p. 58.

7. Robertson and Plummer, *op. cit.*, p. 101.

8. Although the RSV has " lump " of dough in I Cor. 5:6 and " dough " in v. 7, the Greek has the same noun, *phurama,* in both places. Since the noun represents the Corinthian Christians in v. 7, it presumably does so also in the preceding verse.

9. For numerous statements of regulations regarding this observance, see Strack and Billerbeck, *op. cit.*, Vol. III, pp. 359 f.

10. See, for example, Ex., ch. 12, and Deut. 16:4-6.

11. Robertson and Plummer, *op. cit.*, pp. 102 f.

12. So, for example, Lietzmann, who renders the clause, " So wollen wir denn (das Passah) feiern . . ." (*An die Korinther,* p. 24).

13. Moffatt, *The First Epistle of Paul to the Corinthians,* pp. 58 f., quoting Thucydides, i. 70.

I CORINTHIANS 9:4-14

1. The position of Barnabas in this section is not entirely clear. The name must have been included by Paul himself, since there is no textual evidence to the contrary. The inclusion appears to be an " afterthought " (Robertson and Plummer, *op. cit.*, p. 182), however, since in the Greek (literally, " alone I and Barnabas ") the " alone " is in the singular.

2. For numerous references to rabbinical rulings on such matters, see Strack and Billerbeck, *op. cit.*, Vol. III, pp. 379–382.

3. The reference cannot be to the farmer-owner, who does his own work, for in that case he would certainly both plow and thresh; in v. 10 the sentence construction suggests that the one who plows and the one who threshes may be different persons. Also, the farmer-owner would hardly be said " to have a share " in the crop, since the entire crop would be his.

4. Moffatt, *The First Epistle of Paul to the Corinthians*, p. 117. "Gott redet nur scheinbar von den Ochsen, in Wahrheit von etwas ganz anderem" (Johannes Weiss, *Der erste Korintherbrief* [Kritisch-exegetischer Kommentar über das Neue Testament], p. 236).

5. *Op. cit.*, pp. 183 f.

6. See Strack and Billerbeck, *op. cit.*, Vol. III, pp. 385–399, for an extended treatment of allegorical interpretation.

7. "Gott meint also an jener Stelle, dass der Pflügende und der Dreschende . . . Anteil am Ertrag erhalten soll" (Straub, *op. cit.*, p. 82). J. Weiss, however, understands v. 10b to mean: It was written for our sake *that* the plowman should plow. . . . That which was "written" is regarded by him as referring, not to Deut. 25:4 at all but to the following words, quoted from some now-unknown source (*op. cit.*, p. 237).

8. See Deut. 18:1-4; Num. 18:8-20.

9. See Matt. 10:10; Luke 10:7.

10. Robertson and Plummer, *op. cit.*, p. 182.

11. Lietzmann, *An die Korinther*, on II Cor. 10:4, p. 141.

12. Strachan, *op. cit.*, on II Cor. 10:4-6, p. 10. See also Thayer, *op. cit.*, on *ochurōma*.

13. See his use of *hopla* and *hoplōn* ("weapons") in Rom. 6:13; 13:12; II Cor. 10:4; 6:7. See also *perikephalaian* ("helmet") and *thōraka* ("breastplate") in I Thess. 5:8, where, as in Rom. 13:12, the emphasis is upon right conduct in life rather than upon warfare against evil. Paul uses *machaira(n)* ("sword") twice (Rom. 8:35; 13:4), but never metaphorically (compare Eph. 6:17).

14. Note again that Paul quotes Deut. 25:4 in I Cor. 9:9 and refers to Deut. 18:1 in I Cor. 9:13.

15. Compare Hos. 10:13 and Job 4:8. See especially Gal. 6:7.

16. Judg. 14:18; Job 4:8; Ps. 129:3; Isa. 28:24; Jer. 26:18; Hos. 10:12, 13; Amos 6:12; Luke 9:62.

17. Robertson and Plummer, *op. cit.*, on I Cor. 5:10, p. 185.

I CORINTHIANS 9:24-27

1. See especially Phil. 3:12-14. For a discussion of games of this sort and for further references to Pauline language drawn from this field, see Moffatt, *The First Epistle of Paul to the Corinthians*, pp. 126 f., and Hastings, *A Dictionary of the Bible*, Vol. II, pp. 107 f.

2. See the previous section.

3. " For the sake of the gospel " can hardly mean " to help the preaching of the gospel " (J. Massie, *Corinthians* [New-Century Bible], p. 198), but rather, " for the sake of what the gospel means to me," as the following words suggest: " that I may share in its blessings," or, more literally, " that I might be a joint partaker of it." Lietzmann's translation brings out this meaning effectively: " Alles (das) aber tue ich um des Evangeliums willen, um an ihm Anteil zu bekommen." Compare Rom. 11:17.

4. See Robertson and Plummer, *op. cit.*, p. 194, in their reference to the thought of Origen.

5. Lietzmann, *An die Korinther*, p. 44.

6. Compare Phil. 2:3 f.

7. " In the sports, one gains at the expense of others, but not so in the Christian effort, where there is nothing competitive." (Moffatt, *The First Epistle of Paul to the Corinthians*, p. 128.)

8. The award was often a pine wreath. In the classic period it was a wreath of parsley. See Massie, *op. cit.*, p. 198.

9. Compare Wisd. of Sol. 4:1 f.:

" Better than this is childlessness with virtue,
   for in the memory of virtue is immortality,
   because it is known both by God and by men.
   When it is present, men imitate it,
   and they long for it when it has gone;
   and throughout all time it marches crowned in triumph,
   victor in the contest for prizes that are undefiled."

10. So, fundamentally, J. Weiss (*op. cit.*, p. 248), Lietzmann (*An die Korinther*, p. 44), Robertson and Plummer (*op. cit.*, p. 176), Massie (*op. cit.*, p. 198), Moffatt (*The First Epistle of Paul to the Corinthians*, p. 126).

11. J. J. Lias, *The First Epistle to the Corinthians* (Cambridge Greek Testament for Schools and Colleges), p. 109.

12. The Greek word here rendered " pommel " (*hupōpiazō*) generally meant " to beat black and blue " — sometimes, " to strike under the eye."

13. Robertson and Plummer, *op. cit.*, p. 196.

14. American Translation.

15. The word *hupōpiazō* (" pommel ") has not only the meaning " to beat black and blue," but also (metaphorically), " to mortify," " to afflict."

16. Thayer, *op. cit.*, on *doulagōgeō,* which is Paul's word here. The term means literally to "bring into slavery."

17. Bultmann, *Theology of the New Testament,* Vol. I, p. 195. See the entire treatment of "Body" by Bultmann, pp. 192–203.

18. Moffatt comes close to this interpretation when he says that Paul "is referring . . . to discipline voluntarily inflicted upon himself" (p. 127), but he fails to relate this adequately to the context.

19. See Thayer, *op. cit.*, on *adokimos,* which is Paul's word here.

20. So Robertson and Plummer, *op. cit.*, p. 197.

21. So Moffatt, *The First Epistle of Paul to the Corinthians,* p. 128.

22. Straub (*op. cit.*, p. 90) states that "die . . . Schilderung aus dem Lebens des Apostels vorbildlich zu verstehen ist."

I CORINTHIANS 12:12-30

1. It "beherrscht den ganzen Abschnitt" (J. Weiss, *op. cit.*, p. 302). The analogy does not "dominate," however, in the sense that it is determinative for the ideas that Paul expresses. As will be shown, the apostle uses the picture extensively here, but only as a vehicle for saying what is inspired by the Corinthian situation, not by the picture itself.

2. Chapter 14 of I Corinthians, especially, gives this impression. For a discussion of "speaking with tongues," see especially Moffatt, *The First Epistle of Paul to the Corinthians,* pp. 206–217.

3. Or "members." The Greek word here is exactly the same as that which is generally rendered "members."

4. See Lietzmann, *An die Korinther,* p. 63.

5. Moffatt, *The First Epistle of Paul to the Corinthians,* p. 184.

6. Lietzmann, *An die Korinther,* on I Cor. 12:12, p. 62. The translation is that of the present writer.

7. The use of "body" as representing "a society" is not exclusively Pauline. (For further evidence of this, see below.) His designation of the Christian society *as the body of Christ,* does, however, introduce an original kind of concept. See Moffatt, pp. 185–190. See also Dodd, *The Epistle of Paul to the Romans,* on Rom. 12:4-5, pp. 194 f.

8. Robertson and Plummer, *op. cit.*, on Rom. 12:15, p. 273.

9. This is true unless declining value is attached to seeing

("eye"), then hearing, then smelling. It is hardly likely, however, that such declining value is intended. Certainly the four parts of the body mentioned in a similar series in I Cor. 12:21 do not fall into any recognizable pattern either of declining or of increasing value.

10. The aorist tense of the verbs indicates the kind of past action (on the part of God) to which the act of Creation, best of all, belongs.

11. See Thayer, *op. cit.*, on *kai*, I, 3.

12. We do this because it is in agreement with the plan of God himself (I Cor. 12:24b). Paul seems to mean that "it is in reality God who blends and balances the whole by endowing men with this instinctive sense of propriety" (Robertson and Plummer, *op. cit.*, p. 276). In I Cor. 11:14 he suggests even more clearly that certain practices of men in regard to their bodies are due to more than merely human invention.

13. See above. See also J. Weiss, *op. cit.*, on I Cor. 12:15, 16, p. 304; Lietzmann, *An die Korinther*, p. 63.

14. Shakespeare uses this in *Coriolanus* (Act I, Scene I). See Moffatt, *The First Epistle of Paul to the Corinthians*, pp. 183 f.

15. See Robertson and Plummer, *op. cit.*, p. 273, for references to further early writings in which the analogy of the body is used to illustrate harmony or cooperation as over against disharmony or discord.

16. Strack and Billerbeck, *op. cit.*, on I Cor. 12:12 ff., Vol. III, pp. 446-448.

17. J. Weiss emphasizes this point (*op. cit.*, p. 306).

18. Moffatt, *The First Epistle of Paul to the Corinthians*, p. 187; see also Robertson and Plummer, *op. cit.*, p. 277.

19. J. Weiss refers to it as present in the Diatribe (*op. cit.*, p. 305).

20. Straub, *op. cit.*, p. 77.

21. II Kings 14:9; Isa. 14:8; 29:16.

22. In Rom. 9:20 Paul suggests speech on the part of the object molded by the potter.

23. For a comment upon this use of "head," see Thayer, *op. cit.*, on *anthrax*.

24. Rom. 3:15 corresponds closely to the Septuagint version of Isa. 59:7 (see also Prov. 1:15 f.). Romans 10:15 is based on Isa. 52:7 (compare Nahum 1:15). Romans 3:18 reproduces almost exactly the Septuagint version of Ps. 36:1 (LXX, 35:2). Romans

12:20 includes the same language as that found in the Septuagint form of Prov. 25:22.

25. There are at least seventeen examples of such usage in the New Testament. See Moulton and Geden, *A Concordance of the Greek Testament,* on *kephalē.*

26. Eph. 1:22 f.; 4:15 f.; 5:23; Col. 1:18; 2:19.

27. See the Introduction.

I CORINTHIANS 13:12

1. See Hastings, *A Dictionary of the Bible,* Vol. III, pp. 396 f. See also Hans Lamer, *Römische Kultur im Bilde,* p. 71 and p. 43. There is nothing in the text that indicates that Paul had in mind a "mirror on the wall" (H. Weinel, *St. Paul, the Man and His Work,* tr. by G. A. Bienemann, p. 19). The Greek word *esoptron* does not mean a "window-pane" (see Robertson and Plummer, *op. cit.,* pp. 298 f.).

2. For present purposes it is unnecessary to discuss the question whether or not the lyric "may have been already composed in whole or in part by Paul" (Moffatt, *The First Epistle of Paul to the Corinthians,* p. 191).

3. See Moffatt, *The First Epistle of Paul to the Corinthians,* p. 201.

4. So William Smith, *A Dictionary of the Bible,* under "Mirror."

5. Robertson and Plummer, *op. cit.,* p. 98. See also Lietzmann, *An die Korinther,* p. 66. The reference to the use of a mirror in James 1:23 may possibly suggest *accuracy* or *clarity* of reproduction (Straub, *op. cit.,* p. 45), though this is not necessarily so. See W. H. Bennett, *The General Epistles* (New-Century Bible), on James 1:23, p. 154. In any case this need not affect the interpretation of the Pauline passage.

6. See Straub, *op. cit.,* p. 45.

7. See Moffatt, *The First Epistle of Paul to the Corinthians,* p. 201.

I CORINTHIANS 14:6-12

1. So Moffatt, *The First Epistle of Paul to the Corinthians,* p. 218. Lietzmann, on the other hand, believes that the thought is of differences in rhythm primarily (*An die Korinther,* p. 71). See also Straub, *op. cit.,* p. 84. Robertson and Plummer center attention upon the *mood* created by the sounds: "The music

must be different, if it is to guide people to be joyous, or sorrowful, or devout" (*op. cit.*, p. 308).

2. See Thayer, *op. cit.*, on *dēlos*.

3. So Massie, *op. cit.*, p. 235, and also Robertson and Plummer, *op. cit.*, p. 309.

4. There are eighteen such cases in these chapters (I Cor., chs. 12 to 14).

5. J. Weiss, *op. cit.*, p. 335, emphasizes this point.

6. *Ibid.*, pp. 335 f.

7. See J. Weiss, *op. cit.*, p. 325.

8. See Thayer, *op. cit.*, on *glōssa*.

I CORINTHIANS 15:35-50

1. J. Weiss, *op. cit.*, p. 367.

2. On I Cor. 15:35-58, p. 366. Compare the American Translation, " How can the dead rise? "

3. See Massie, *op. cit.*, p. 249.

4. So J. Weiss, *op. cit.*, p. 371; Robertson and Plummer, *op. cit.*, p. 372; Massie, *op. cit.*, p. 250; also Thayer, *op. cit.*, under *phthora* and *atimia* and *speirō*.

5. See Thayer, *op. cit.*, as indicated in the previous note.

6. See especially I Cor. 9:11, where the reference is to the sowing of " spiritual things "; in this case the idea of the seed being " buried " in the soil is particularly out of place. See also the other metaphorical usages of *speirō* in II Cor. 9:6, 10 and Gal. 6:7, 8.

7. See Thayer, *op. cit.*, on *phthora*.

8. See Rom. 1:26; I Cor. 11:14; II Cor. 6:8; 11:21.

9. See I Cor. 2:3; II Cor. 11:30; 12:5, 9, 10; Gal. 4:13.

10. Robertson and Plummer, *op. cit.*, p. 369.

11. J. Weiss, *op. cit.*, p. 370, quoting Sanhedrin f. 91a. Lietzmann (*An die Korinther,* on I Cor. 15:37-38, p. 83) quotes the same passage.

12. So also Robertson and Plummer, *op. cit.*, pp. 369 f.

13. Thayer, *op. cit.*, on *gumnos*.

14. Moffatt, *The First Epistle of Paul to the Corinthians*, p. 259.

15. This particular antithesis appears also in II Cor. 6:8.

16. Compare I Cor. 2:3 f.; II Cor. 12:9; 13:4.

17. There are eleven Pauline usages of the noun. The KJV renders six of these as " soul " (plus an additional marginal reading). Three are rendered as " life," and one as " mind." The RSV

uses "life," "person," "self," "soul," etc.

18. Bultmann, *Theology of the New Testament,* Vol. I, p. 205.

19. For discussions of Paul's thought here in relation to Hebraic, Greek, and Gnostic concepts, see Bultmann, *Theology of the New Testament,* Vol. I, p. 174 and pp. 203–210.

20. Compare the implications of Mark 12:25.

21. See R. H. Charles, *The Apocalypse of Baruch,* pp. xii f.

22. See Moffatt, *The First Epistle of Paul to the Corinthians,* p. 260.

23. See Bultmann, *Theology of the New Testament,* Vol. I, pp. 192–203.

24. J. Weiss, *op. cit.,* p. 368; Lietzmann, *An die Korinther,* p. 83. Commentators generally compare this verse to John 12:24.

25. Robertson and Plummer use this phrase (*op. cit.,* p. 369).

26. Moffatt, *The First Epistle of Paul to the Corinthians,* p. 259.

27. J. Weiss, *op. cit.,* pp. 368 f.; Lietzmann, *An die Korinther,* pp. 83 f.; Moffatt, *The First Epistle of Paul to the Corinthians,* p. 258; Robertson and Plummer, *op. cit.,* p. 370.

28. The tense (aorist) of the verb *ēthelēsen* ("has chosen," or "chose") places the decision at a point in past history. This naturally suggests the time of Creation.

29. J. Weiss, *op. cit.,* p. 369.

30. Moffatt, *The First Epistle of Paul to the Corinthians,* p. 258. It was claimed, for example, that "if we are to have clear knowledge of anything, we must get rid of the body." This is possible after death; "for then, and only then, will our souls be by themselves, apart from our bodies" (Plato's *Phaedo,* 66, translated with Introduction and Commentary by R. Hackforth, The University Press, Cambridge, 1955).

31. Flavius Josephus, *The Jewish War (The Works of Flavius Josephus,* Whiston's Translation), II, viii, 11.

32. Massie, *op. cit.,* p. 250.

33. Moffatt suggests, in a different connection, that Paul may have believed in "the varying nature of recompense for the shining spirits of the faithful," noting I Cor. 3:8b: "Each shall receive his wages according to his labor" (*The First Epistle of Paul to the Corinthians,* on I Cor. 15:41, pp. 258 f.). But even if the resurrection life should involve variation in terms of recompense, this would not bespeak differences as to kinds of resurrection bodies. After all, corresponding variations among men in the present earthly life do not bespeak differences as to their "physi-

cal bodies." Their bodies are all of the same *kind*.

34. Compare John 12:24.

35. In the Greek the word *sarx* ("flesh") appears four times in this sentence.

36. Robertson and Plummer, *op. cit.*, p. 370.

37. J. Weiss overstates the case, however, when he speaks of "glory" as utterly foreign, in Paul's thinking, to everything earthly (*op. cit.*, p. 370). It is true that the apostle generally associates *doxa* ("glory") either with God himself or with the future state of man, but see Rom. 9:4; I Cor. 2:7; 11:7, 15; II Cor. 6:8; Phil. 3:19; I Thess. 2:20.

38. See, for example, Deut. 4:19; II Kings 23:5; Ezek. 8:16. See also Hastings, *A Dictionary of the Bible,* under "Sun," Vol. IV, pp. 627 ff.; "Moon," Vol. III, pp. 433 ff.; and "Star," Vol. IV, p. 613.

39. This seems to be the case in *The Apocalypse of Baruch,* ch. 51:10 and in Enoch 18:13-16; 21:3-6.

40. Lietzmann believes that he did (*An die Korinther,* p. 84). J. Weiss also seems to believe that Paul did thus regard them, for he speaks of the context here as concerned with "animate bodies" (*op. cit.*, p. 370).

41. See Moffatt, *The First Epistle of Paul to the Corinthians,* pp. 258 f.

42. Robertson and Plummer, *op. cit.*, p. 371.

43. *Ibid.*, pp. 371 f.

4.

The Second Letter of Paul to the Corinthians

II CORINTHIANS 2:14-16

1. There are some who regard Paul as having in mind here, not two pictures, but rather, two aspects of a single picture. This view will be considered below.

2. See Moffatt's translation of the New Testament.

3. See especially II Cor. 2:1-4 and 7:2-16.

4. Lietzmann, *An die Korinther,* p. 108; Massie, *op. cit.*, p. 271; Alfred Plummer, *The Second Epistle of St. Paul to the Corinthians* (International Critical Commentary), p. 68; Allan Menzies, *The Second Epistle of the Apostle Paul to the Corinthians,* p. 17; James Denney, *The Second Epistle to the Corinthians* (Exposi-

tor's Bible), pp. 86 ff. Lias, however, prefers the causative sense "by the analogy of other verbs used causatively" (J. J. Lias, *The Second Epistle to the Corinthians* [Cambridge Bible for Schools and Colleges], p. 43).

5. Compare Col. 2:15, where the author of that document uses the same expression.

6. Denney, *The Second Epistle to the Corinthians*, p. 88.

7. Menzies, *op. cit.*, p. 17.

8. Massie, *op. cit.*, p. 271.

9. See Strachan, *op. cit.*, p. 74.

10. So Denney, *The Second Epistle to the Corinthians*, p. 90; Menzies, *op. cit.*, pp. 17 f.; and Lias, *The Second Epistle to the Corinthians*, p. 43.

11. So Strachan, *op. cit.*, p. 74.

12. So Lietzmann, *An die Korinther*, p. 108, and Strachan, *op. cit.*, p. 74.

13. In Paul's expression, "fragrance of the knowledge" (*osmēn tēs gnōseōs*), the fragrance is to be understood *as* the knowledge, since the latter term is in the "genitive of apposition" (see Denney, *The Second Epistle to the Corinthians*, p. 91).

14. The antecedent of the pronoun *autou* ("of him") may be either God (Lietzmann, *An die Korinther*, p. 108) or Christ (Plummer, *op. cit.*, p. 70). In this case the distinction is not important since it is Christ who manifests the knowledge of God (II Cor. 4:6).

15. Lietzmann, *An die Korinther*, p. 108.

16. For parallels in rabbinical literature, see Strack and Billerbeck, *op. cit.*, Vol. III, pp. 498 f., and Lietzmann, *An die Korinther*, p. 109.

17. Straub compares the contrast to the difference between "poison gas" and "a beneficial, invigorating draught of air" (*op. cit.*, p. 41).

18. Strachan, *op. cit.*, pp. 74 f.; Lias, *The Second Epistle to the Corinthians*, p. 44.

19. See Gen. 8:21; Ex. 29:18, 25; Lev. 1:9, 13, 17; Ezek. 6:13; 20:41; etc.

20. See the previous note. Plummer contends that the absence of this phrase "makes any allusion to sacrifice doubtful" (*op. cit.*, p. 71).

II CORINTHIANS 3:1-3

1. See Strachan, *op. cit.*, p. 79.

2. II Cor. 10:12, 17 f.; 11:5 f., 12-15, 18, 21-29; 12:11. It is assumed here that chs. 10 to 13 of this letter were originally part of the previous letter mentioned in ch. 2:3 f.

3. II Cor. 3:1; 4:2; 5:12; 6:4; 10:12, 18. See also chs. 7:11; 12:11. Lietzmann observes that Paul has made a "catchword" ("*Schlagwort*") of the idea of self-commendation (*An die Korinther*, p. 109).

4. Deissmann, *Light from the Ancient East*, pp. 157 f. and pp. 182 ff.

5. The Codex Sinaiticus has *humōn* ("your"). Certain scholars would retain as original only the first clause of v. 2 (see Plummer, *op. cit.*, p. 80).

6. Straub suggests that these words were not intended to have any connection with the picture (*op. cit.*, p. 83).

7. See Plummer, *op. cit.*, p. 81.

8. See Thayer, *op. cit.*, under *diakoneō*, 4. There is little evidence that the Greek word, meaning literally "to minister," was intended to convey the idea that Paul was the "bearer of the letter" as he tells the story of the Corinthians to others (as Massie, *op. cit.*, p. 273, and Lietzmann, *An die Korinther*, p. 110).

9. In the Greek the parallels are closer than the RSV indicates. Paul's word (*sarkinais*), here translated "human," is the same as that which, in the Septuagint version of Ezekiel, is rendered "of flesh."

10. See Ex. 24:12; 31:18; 34:1, 4; Deut. 4:13; 9:9-11.

11. Jer. 31:31-33 (Septuagint, ch. 38:31-33).

12. See Lietzmann, *An die Korinther*, pp. 110 f.

II CORINTHIANS 5:1-10

1. See the treatment of I Cor. 15:35-50.

2. "Tent" is in the genitive case, but it is the genitive of apposition.

3. So Plummer, *op. cit.*, p. 141, and especially Deissmann, *St. Paul*, p. 51 and p. 62.

4. Menzies prefers "frame" (p. 35), contending that the word itself does not mean "tent" (*op. cit.*, p. 34).

5. See Plummer, *op. cit.*, p. 142. See also Lietzmann, *An die Korinther*, p. 117. Compare II Peter 1:13 f. For examples of the

use of "house" as a metaphor for the body, see Plummer, *op. cit.*, pp. 142 f. Strack and Billerbeck, however, note the fact that "house" was not a common picture for "body" in rabbinical literature (*op. cit.*, p. 517).

6. The more common adjective *arestos* ("pleasing"), is also used in Wisd. of Sol. 9:9 and 9:18.

7. See Plummer, *op. cit.*, p. 155.

8. Rom. 3:19; 7:14; 8:22, 28; I Cor. 8:1, 4; 13:9; II Cor. 5:16.

9. See Bultmann, on "'Soma' (Body)," *Theology of the New Testament*, Vol. I, pp. 192–203.

10. *Ibid.*, p. 201.

11. Deissmann stresses particularly the fact of the impermanence of the "tent-house" (*St. Paul*, p. 62).

12. It is somewhat surprising that commentators generally make no connection between II Cor. 5:1 and Dan. 2:34, 45.

13. Plummer, *op. cit.*, p. 142.

14. See Heb. 11:13-16 and I Peter 1:17; 2:11. Compare I Peter 1:1, 4. For non-Biblical references, see Plummer, pp. 142 f.

15. Plummer, *op. cit.*, p. 142.

16. Compare I Cor. 15:51b f. and I Thess. 4:17.

17. So Lietzmann, *An die Korinther*, p. 117.

18. Plummer, *op. cit.*, p. 144.

19. Bultmann regards v. 3 as also having reference to the occurrence of death before the giving of the new body. Accepting the text of the Codex Bezae (D), he reads, "For we will not be found naked when we have divested ourselves (of our present physical body)" (*Theology of the New Testament*, Vol. I, p. 202).

20. See Bultmann, *Theology of the New Testament*, Vol. I, p. 202.

21. See especially I Cor. 4:5, and compare I Cor. 1:8; 5:5; II Cor. 1:14. Compare also the association of judgment with the appearance of the "Son of Man" or the "Elect One" in Enoch 45:3; 49:4; 55:4; 61:8 f.; 62:3, 11. For a discussion of this subject see Lietzmann, *An die Korinther*, pp. 122 f.

22. Bultmann, *Theology of the New Testament*, Vol. I, p. 192.

23. *Ibid.*, p. 202.

II CORINTHIANS 9:6

1. The Greek expression translated "bountifully" (*ep' eulogiais*) has to do literally with "blessings." To sow and reap "with blessings," as opposed to doing so "sparingly," must be intended

to suggest the idea of abundance.

2. Compare Mark 4:3-8; Matt. 13:3-8; Luke 8:5-8.

3. See note 1, above.

II CORINTHIANS 10:3-6

1. It is possible that the words translated as "every proud obstacle" (*pan hupsōma epairomenon*) in v. 5 are intended to suggest towers or walls set up to withstand attacks (so Plummer, *op. cit.*, p. 277); if this is the case, the language is analogical. On the other hand, the words follow the reference to "arguments" (or "theories," *logismous*), and seem to be parallel to the following "every thought" (*pan noēma*); in view of this, "every proud obstacle" may refer directly to the arguments or reasoning of Paul's opponents.

2. Compare II Cor. 13:10.

3. See the discussion of I Thess. 5:1-11. Compare Eph. 4:8; 6:11-17; I Tim. 1:18; II Tim. 2:3 f.; 3:6.

II CORINTHIANS 11:2 f.

1. Hos., chs. 1; 2; Isa. 50:1; 54:1-6; Jer. 2:2; 3:1; Ezek. 16:8; etc.

2. See especially Eph. 5:23-30; Rev. 19:7; 21:3, 9.

3. Compare II Cor. 12:14. See Hastings, *A Dictionary of the Bible,* on "Marriage," Vol. III, p. 270.

4. See Strachan, *op. cit.*, p. 17; also Lietzmann, *An die Korinther,* p. 145.

5. See the American Translation of II Cor. 11:3. Compare Moffatt's translation.

6. Plummer, *op. cit.*, p. 293.

7. Menzies, *op. cit.*, p. 77.

8. See note 1, above.

9. For different interpretations, see Lias, *The Second Epistle to the Corinthians,* p. 109.

10. Strachan, *op. cit.*, p. 17.

11. Plummer, *op. cit.*, p. 294. See v. 4.

12. Lias, *The Second Epistle to the Corinthians,* p. 110. Bousset and Windisch also regard v. 3 as an extension of the analogy of v. 2; see Straub, *op. cit.*, p. 79.

13. See Plummer, *op. cit.*, p. 296; also Lietzmann, *An die Korinther,* p. 145; also Strachan, *op. cit.*, p. 18.

14. See Lietzmann, *An die Korinther,* p. 145.

15. Menzies, *op. cit.*, p. 77.

16. Plummer, *op. cit.*, on II Cor. 11:3, p. 295.

II CORINTHIANS 11:8

1. See I Cor., ch. 9.

2. See Thayer, *op. cit.*, on *sulaō*, and Plummer, *op. cit.*, p. 303.

3. See the treatment of I Cor. 9:4-14.

4. Lias, *The Second Epistle to the Corinthians*, p. 112.

5. See Phil. 4:17.

6. In the compound form (*hierosuleis*) in Rom. 2:22 the term has reference to evil action ("rob temples"). Compare *sulagōgōn* ("make a prey of") in Col. 2:8.

II CORINTHIANS 12:7 f.

1. Revised Standard Version, King James Version, Moffatt.

2. The latter is possible in view of the contexts, although both the King James Version and the Revised Standard Version give "thorns" in Hos. 2:6 (8).

3. See below, however.

4. For summaries of the various views, see Lias, *The Second Epistle to the Corinthians*, pp. 13–18; Plummer, *op. cit.*, on II Cor. 11:7, pp. 348–351; Lietzmann, *An die Korinther*, pp. 156 f.; Lightfoot, *St. Paul's Epistle to the Galatians*, pp. 354–361. In a rather recent article, "Paul's Thorn in the Flesh" (*Journal of Biblical Literature*, December, 1957, Vol. LXXVI, Part IV, pp. 299–303), Terence Y. Mullins argues strongly that Paul is "referring to a person, an enemy."

5. See Thayer, *op. cit.*, on *exorussō*.

6. Although the verb *aphistēmi* ("leave") is used by Paul only in this passage, it is always used in the New Testament (in thirteen other places) with reference to *persons*.

II CORINTHIANS 12:14

1. Compare II Cor. 11:7-11 and I Cor. 9:4-18.

2. See especially I Cor. 4:14-17; compare Gal. 4:19. See the discussion of Philemon 10.

3. Jesus is represented as emphasizing such responsibility (Mark 7:9-13; Matt. 15:3-6).

4. Plummer (*op. cit.*, p. 362), noting Mark 2:17; 6:4; 9:37; Luke 10:20; 14:12; 23:28; John 12:44.

5. Straub, *op. cit.*, p. 66.

6. Plummer, *op. cit.*, p. 362.

5.

The Letter of Paul to the Romans

ROMANS 4:4

1. Compare his reference to Abraham also in Gal. 3:6-9, 15-18.

2. Bultmann, *Theology of the New Testament*, Vol. I, p. 323. Bultmann adds: "Paul makes this unmistakably clear by never using *pisteuein* in the simple sense of 'trust' and hence never construing it with the dative, . . . except in the Old Testament quotations about the 'trust' of Abraham, Gal. 3:6; Rom. 4:3."

3. Lietzmann, *An die Römer*, p. 53.

4. See Dodd, *The Epistle of Paul to the Romans*, pp. 64 f., and Duncan, *op. cit.*, on Gal. 3:6, p. 84.

ROMANS 5:7

1. Compare Rom. 3:9 and 3:24, especially.

2. Garvie, *op. cit.*, p. 150; H. C. G. Moule, *The Epistle of Paul the Apostle to the Romans* (Cambridge Bible for Schools and Colleges), p. 102.

3. Denney, *St. Paul's Epistle to the Romans*, Vol. II, p. 625.

4. So Moule, *The Epistle of Paul the Apostle to the Romans*, p. 102. In Rom. 7:12 Paul applies the same Greek words to the same thing. Compare also Luke 23:50.

5. See Thayer, *op. cit.*, on *molis*.

6. Lietzmann, *An die Römer*, p. 59.

7. Sanday and Headlam, *op. cit.*, p. 128.

8. Denney, *St. Paul's Epistle to the Romans*, p. 625. This kind of distinction is sometimes compared to the Gnostic idea of a contrast between the Old and the New Testament portrayals of deity; in the former God appears as "just"; in the latter he is shown to be "good" (Garvie, *op. cit.*, p. 149; Sanday and Headlam, *op. cit.*, p. 128).

9. Dodd, *The Epistle of Paul to the Romans*, p. 75.

ROMANS 6:1-14

1. That such a conclusion was sometimes expressed is suggested in Rom. 3:7 f.

2. Dodd, *The Epistle of Paul to the Romans*, pp. 92 f. Compare Phil. 3:12.

3. Michel, *op. cit.*, pp. 128 f.

4. Lietzmann, *An die Römer*, p. 66.

5. Dodd, *The Epistle of Paul to the Romans*, p. 87.

6. Lietzmann, *An die Römer*, p. 65.

7. Bultmann, *Theology of the New Testament*, Vol. I, p. 312. For a consideration of the influence of the mystery religions upon the Pauline language and thought concerning baptism, see Bultmann, pp. 140 f. and pp. 311 ff. See also Martin Dibelius and Werner Georg Kümmel, *Paul*, tr. by Frank Clarke, pp. 93 f.

8. Lietzmann suggests that the idea of death through drowning is involved (*An die Römer*, p. 65).

9. In the parallel passage in Col. (ch. 2:12) the picture of baptism is much more clearly related to being "raised" (as well as to being "buried"). At least this is true if the relative pronoun there (in the prepositional phrase *en hōi*) refers to "baptism" rather than to "Christ." See J. B. Lightfoot, *Saint Paul's Epistles to the Colossians and to Philemon*, p. 183.

10. Denney, *St. Paul's Epistle to the Romans*, p. 633.

11. Michel speaks of the resurrection of Christ, thus mentioned here, as the "archetype" ("*Urbild*") of *baptism*. Just as the *procedure* involved in baptism provides a picture of "newness of life" for the Christian, so also the resurrection of Christ provides a picture of that which *actually occurs* in baptism (see above). See Michel, *op. cit.*, p. 130.

12. While he lived among men sin did have this claim upon him, not in the sense that he sinned, since he "knew no sin" (II Cor. 5:21), but rather, in the sense that man's sin "hung about him and wreaked its effects upon him" (Sanday and Headlam, *op. cit.*, on Rom. 6:10, p. 160). See also Dodd, *The Epistle of Paul to the Romans*, pp. 89 f.

ROMANS 6:15-23

1. In a sense the position expressed here is the same as that in the preceding verses: "Through faith in Christ a man passes from the sinful order into a new order of life in which sin has no place" (Dodd, *The Epistle of Paul to the Romans*, p. 96).

2. The picture of slavery is touched upon in the previous section (Rom. 6:6 f.), but there it is not developed.

3. See Sanday and Headlam, *op. cit.*, p. 166.

4. Dodd, *The Epistle of Paul to the Romans*, p. 97.

5. Sanday and Headlam, *op. cit.*, p. 168.

6. Lietzmann, *An die Römer*, p. 70.

7. Compare Luke 16:13; John 8:34; II Peter 2:19.

8. See Sanday and Headlam, *op. cit.*, p. 168.

9. Dodd observes that "it is certainly not felicitous to suggest that the master who is obeyed is Obedience!" (*The Epistle of Paul to the Romans*, p. 97).

10. See especially Gal. 4:1-7 and Rom. 8:14 f.

11. See Rom. 8:21. Compare Gal. 2:4; 4:21-31; 5:1, 13a.

12. Compare Rom. 3:5; I Cor. 3:1; Gal. 3:15.

13. Dodd, *The Epistle of Paul to the Romans*, p. 98.

14. Moule, *The Epistle of Paul the Apostle to the Romans*, p. 120.

15. Compare Rom. 8:15; II Cor. 3:17; Gal. 5:1, 13a. See Lietzmann, *An die Römer*, p. 71.

16. Denney observes that in the use of the picture of the slave "nothing else than obedience to his master alone is contemplated" (*St. Paul's Epistle to the Romans*, p. 635).

17. The special problem raised by the use of this term has been noted above.

18. Dodd, *The Epistle of Paul to the Romans*, p. 98. Denney, similarly, speaks of teachings regarding "ethical requirements" (*St. Paul's Epistle to the Romans*, p. 636).

19. Garvie, *op. cit.*, p. 169.

20. Lietzmann, *An die Römer*, p. 70. Lietzmann's treatment suggests that specific teachings (which would presumably include those of an ethical nature) can hardly be meant, for if the Roman Christians had indeed "become obedient" to them, then it would have been unnecessary for Paul to write this chapter. This judgment fails to take into account, however, the fact that Paul can upon occasion offer such commendation when it is not wholly deserved and when further improvement in conduct must yet be urged (compare I Cor. 1:5-7; 11:2; II Cor. 8:7).

21. Dodd, *The Epistle of Paul to the Romans*, p. 99.

22. It is true that in the Greek there are found *phrases* rather than *clauses:* "sin *unto death,*" "obedience *unto righteousness.*" But the point that has just been made is not affected by this fact.

23. Moule, *The Epistle of Paul the Apostle to the Romans*, p. 119.

24. See the treatments of I Cor. 9:4-14 and II Cor. 10:3-6.

25. Compare I Cor. 7:22.

26. Dodd, *The Epistle of Paul to the Romans*, p. 98.

27. "Paul thanks God that his readers have already made their choice, and made it for obedience" (Denney, *St. Paul's Epistle to the Romans*, p. 635).

28. Michel proposes that in v. 18 Paul is thinking of the Christians as "having been set free from sin" at *baptism* (*op. cit.*, pp. 136 f.). If this is correct, a choice on the part of the Christian is certainly involved, since the decision to be baptized would obviously have been made.

29. See Lietzmann, *An die Römer*, p. 70.

30. Michel, *op. cit.*, p. 135, note 1.

ROMANS 7:1-6

1. In these verses other pictures are combined with that of baptism, but they play a lesser role insofar as the language is concerned.

2. See especially Rom. 7:5, 7-11, 13.

3. Compare also Gal. 5:23b, where it is suggested that no law is needed where the Spirit — rather than sin — prevails. Lightfoot comments on this passage, "Law exists for the purpose of restraint, but in the works of the Spirit there is nothing to restrain" (*St. Paul's Epistle to the Galatians*, p. 294). It is worth noting that Paul similarly regards the law of the Roman state as existing primarily for the purpose of restraining wrongdoing (Rom. 13:4c). (See my article, "Paul's View of the State," *Interpretation*, Vol. 6, 1952, pp. 409–414.)

4. Compare Dodd, *The Epistle of Paul to the Romans*, p. 102.

5. That Rom. 7:1-6 is intended to stand in close relationship to ch. 6 is suggested further by the large number of parallel expressions that appear. See Michel, *op. cit.*, p. 141.

6. This seems to be the intended meaning of "the law concerning the husband" (literally, "the law of the husband"). See Garvie, *op. cit.*, pp. 171 f., and Sanday and Headlam, *op. cit.*, p. 173. The expression "law of the husband" came to be used in preference to "law of marriage" (or something similar) probably because in antiquity the rights of the husband over the wife were dominant (Michel, *op. cit.*, p. 141, note 3). Compare "the law of the leper" (Lev. 14:2) and "the law for [literally, "of"] the Nazirite" (Num. 6:13).

7. This implication, as already noted, becomes more explicit in Rom. 7:4 ff.

8. Dodd suggests that the relevance of the analogy to v. 1 is found only in " the bare fact that, in one way or another, death puts an end to obligations " (*The Epistle of Paul to the Romans*, p. 101).

9. Compare Sanday and Headlam, *op. cit.*, p. 173, and Garvie, *op. cit.*, p. 171.

10. Sanday and Headlam, *op. cit.*, p. 172.

11. " Thus ' law ' plays a double part. The whole story is an example of the working of a law, and at the same time, ' Law ' is a character in the story! " (Dodd, *The Epistle of Paul to the Romans*, p. 101).

12. Denney, *St. Paul's Epistle to the Romans*, p. 638.

13. *Ibid.*

14. Lietzmann, *An die Römer*, pp. 71 f.

15. Moule, *The Epistle of Paul the Apostle to the Romans*, p. 124.

16. Dodd, *The Epistle of Paul to the Romans*, p. 102. See v. 6c, and compare the " fruit of the Spirit " (Gal. 5:22 f.).

17. Garvie so contends (*op. cit.*, p. 172).

18. Of the approximately sixty-five usages of the noun in the New Testament only two refer to offspring (Luke 1:42 and Acts 2:30).

19. Denney contends that it is " both needless and grotesque " to interpret the verb " to bear fruit " as referring to the offspring of a marriage (Denney, *St. Paul's Epistle to the Romans*, p. 638).

20. See the discussion of Rom. 6:15-23.

21. Dodd, *The Epistle of Paul to the Romans*, p. 100.

22. *Ibid.*, p. 101.

ROMANS 9:20-24

1. It is of course beyond the scope of the present study to enter upon a discussion of the theological and ethical problems that are raised here. These will be considered only as they are relevant to the analogical usage of the apostle.

2. So Moffatt translates.

3. So Michel, *op. cit.*, p. 211.

4. Dodd, *The Epistle of Paul to the Romans*, on Rom. 9:20 f., p. 159.

5. Michel, *op. cit.*, p. 212.

6. Sanday and Headlam observe that "the image of the previous verse is continued" (*op. cit.*, p. 261).

7. Thayer suggests "for a low use (as, a urinal)" (*op. cit.*, on *skeuos*).

8. Compare I Cor. 12:22 ff., where it is emphasized that certain parts of the body are not to be regarded as useless because they serve a less "honorable" function.

9. See especially Isa. 29:16; 45:9; 64:8; Jer. 18:1-12; Ecclus. 33:12 f.; Wisd. of Sol. 15:7.

10. See Strack and Billerbeck, *op. cit.*, Vol. III, pp. 271 f.

11. This verb, *plassō*, is found in Gen. 2:7, 8, and 19.

12. See J. Skinner, *Isaiah* (Cambridge Bible for Schools and Colleges) (The University Press, Cambridge), on Isa. 45:9-13, p. 61; also Owen C. Whitehouse, *Isaiah* (New-Century Bible) (Oxford University Press, n.d.), p. 123.

13. The word for "vessel" (*angeion*) in Jer. 18:4 (LXX) is not the same as the one (*skeuos*) used by Paul.

14. Jeremiah 18:1-12 is being treated here as a unity. Though certain interpreters have regarded some of the verses in the application as a later editorial insertion, there is no reason to think that Paul would thus have regarded them. For purposes of comparison with the Pauline material, therefore, the passage must be considered as the apostle himself undoubtedly considered it.

ROMANS 11:16-24

1. Garvie, *op. cit.*, p. 238.

2. See especially Michel, *op. cit.*, p. 243.

3. So Sanday and Headlam, *op. cit.*, p. 326; Dodd, *The Epistle of Paul to the Romans*, pp. 178 f.; and others.

4. Lietzmann, *An die Römer*, p. 104. Lietzmann adds, however, that this assertion stands "on weak feet" logically.

5. So Strack and Billerbeck, *op. cit.*, Vol. III, p. 290; see also Moule, *The Epistle of Paul the Apostle to the Romans*, p. 193.

6. So Sanday and Headlam, *op. cit.*, p. 326; Dodd, *The Epistle of Paul to the Romans*, pp. 178 f.; Denney, *St. Paul's Epistle to the Romans*, pp. 679 f.; and others.

7. See Strack and Billerbeck, *op. cit.*, Vol. III, p. 290; also Michel, *op. cit.*, p. 243.

8. Lietzmann very properly asks, "Where are the proofs for this view?" (*An die Römer*, p. 104, my translation).

9. Dodd, *The Epistle of Paul to the Romans*, p. 178.

10. In this Paul seems to agree with the position that is presented in Ezek. 14:12-20. There it is flatly denied that the status or destiny of a whole people may be affected by the status or destiny of the few. See also Ezek., ch. 18, and Jer. 31:29 f.

11. Dodd, *The Epistle of Paul to the Romans*, p. 179.

12. *Ibid.*, pp. 182 f.

13. Garvie, *op. cit.*, p. 246; Moule, *The Epistle of Paul the Apostle to the Romans*, p. 194.

14. See Michel, *op. cit.*, p. 243.

15. Strack and Billerbeck, *op. cit.*, Vol. III, p. 290.

16. So Lietzmann, *An die Römer*, p. 104.

17. Dodd, *The Epistle of Paul to the Romans*, p. 179.

18. Compare — and contrast — Matt. 7:17 f. and Luke 6:43 f. See also Matt. 12:33 and James 3:12.

19. Compare Matt. 7:17 f.; 12:33; and Luke 6:43 f.

20. Dodd, on the other hand, proposes that the root of a tree *might* be thought of as holy if it is presupposed that the picture concerns a tree dedicated to deity — " sacred trees being common in most ancient religions" (*The Epistle of Paul to the Romans*, p. 178). The whole discussion about grafting, however, seems to indicate that Paul is thinking, not of a tree dedicated to deity, but rather, of a tree that is being cultivated for the production of fruit.

21. See above, point (4).

22. Dodd speaks of the "elaborate allegory" here (*The Epistle of Paul to the Romans*, p. 179). Straub suggests, however, that the mingling of picture and idea does not provide an allegory in the strict sense of the term (*op. cit.*, p. 75).

23. It is true that in v. 20 the thought is centered upon the issue under discussion rather than upon the picture. Paul's use of the verb "broken off" (*exeklasthēsan*), however, shows that the picture is still sufficiently in his mind to provide a part of the vocabulary.

24. Since the overwhelming majority of the Jews seem to fall in this category, Paul's use of "some" (*tines*) is regarded by Lietzmann as indicative of the fact that the apostle was a "warm-hearted patriot" (*An die Römer*, p. 105).

25. Garvie, *op. cit.*, p. 246.

26. Both Lietzmann (*An die Römer*, p. 105) and Michel (*op. cit.*, p. 244) refer to this claim, made especially by W. M. Ramsay

(*The Expositor* [1905], pp. 16 ff. and 152 ff.).

27. Lietzmann, *An die Römer*, p. 105. Numerous scholars doubt that Paul was even well informed regarding the more normal practice. See especially Dodd, *The Epistle of Paul to the Romans*, p. 180.

28. Albani, "Die Parabel bei Paulus," *Zeitschrift für wissenschaftliche Theologie*, p. 163.

29. Michel comments, especially in regard to vs. 23 f., that one is surprised how strongly the allegory is determined by the meaning that Paul wishes to convey (*op. cit.*, p. 247).

30. Sanday and Headlam, *op. cit.*, p. 330.

31. *Ibid.*, p. 327.

32. Garvie, *op. cit.*, p. 246. And Deissmann writes that Paul is "bent on demonstrating something that is really against nature" (*Light from the Ancient East*, p. 273).

33. Lietzmann's translation of v. 24 suggests this: "Wenn nämlich du aus dem *deiner* Natur entsprechenden wilden Ölbaum ausgeschnitten und wider *deine* Natur in den edlen Ölbaum eingepfropft wurdest . . ." (Italics mine.)

34. This is a possibility suggested by Weinel, *op. cit.*, p. 18.

35. Dodd, *The Epistle of Paul to the Romans*, p. 180.

6.

The Letter of Paul to the Philippians

PHILIPPIANS 3:2

1. The KJV renders Paul's verb as " Beware." Vincent notes that in the Greek the force of the expression is somewhat less than this. " A caution, however, is implied." See Marvin R. Vincent, *The Epistles to the Philippians and to Philemon* (International Critical Commentary), on Phil. 3:2, p. 92.

2. Strack and Billerbeck, *op. cit.*, on Matt. 15:26, Vol. I, p. 722. (My translation.)

3. *Ibid.*, Vol. I, pp. 722 ff.

4. J. B. Lightfoot, *Saint Paul's Epistle to the Philippians*, p. 144.

5. Ernst Lohmeyer, *Die Briefe an die Philipper, an die Kolosser und an Philemon* (Kritisch-exegetischer Kommentar über das Neue Testament), p. 125.

6. When it is stated in Luke 16:21 that " the dogs came and

licked his [Lazarus'] sores," the point is not that the dogs showed kindness, but rather, that the man's misery was thus increased. Among the Egyptians a more favorable view of dogs is said to have been found. See Straub, *op. cit.*, p. 125.

7. Thayer, *op. cit.*, on *kuōn*.

8. Kittel, *op. cit.*, on *kuōn*, Vol. III, p. 1100.

9. For numerous examples of such application, see Strack and Billerbeck, *op. cit.*, on Matt. 15:26, Vol. I, pp. 724 f.

10. Vincent, *op. cit.*, on Phil. 3:2, p. 92. Lightfoot presents fundamentally the same position (*Saint Paul's Epistle to the Philippians*, pp. 143 f.).

11. For a discussion of these possibilities, see Lohmeyer, *op. cit.*, pp. 124 ff.

12. Thayer, *op. cit.*, on *katatomē*. The two words differ only in the prefix.

13. For references to other views, see Vincent, *op. cit.*, p. 93.

14. In Paul's Greek there is found no word corresponding to the adjective " true." Its use in the translation seems to be justified, however, in order to bring out the force of the intended contrast between " mutilation " and " circumcision."

15. Lohmeyer, *op. cit.*, p. 125. (My translation.)

16. Lightfoot, *Saint Paul's Epistle to the Philippians*, p. 144.

17. See Vincent, *op. cit.*, on Phil. 3:8, p. 101.

18. Thayer, *op. cit.*, on *skubalon*. See also Lohmeyer, *op. cit.*, p. 135.

19. Vincent, *op. cit.*, p. 92. So also, essentially, Lohmeyer, *op. cit.*, p. 125. Paul's use of " bite " and " devour " in Gal. 5:15 suggests the picture of wild animals in general if not of dogs in particular. These words were so commonly employed in a metaphorical sense, however, that their use need not indicate the presence of the picture in the apostle's mind.

7.

The Letter of Paul to Philemon

PHILEMON 10

1. Whether the owner was Philemon, as has commonly been held, or Archippus, as has more recently been urged, need not be debated here.

2. The word for " my " is absent in some of the early manuscripts.

3. Lohmeyer, *op. cit.*, p. 186.

4. *Ibid.* (My translation.)

5. Moffatt, *The First Epistle of Paul to the Corinthians*, on I Cor. 4:15, p. 51.

6. Thayer, *op. cit.*, on *gennaō*, quoting Sanhedrin fol. 19, 2.

7. See E. F. Scott, *The Epistles of Paul to the Colossians, to Philemon and to the Ephesians* (The Moffatt New Testament Commentary), on Philemon 11, p. 108.

8. See Vincent, *op. cit.*, on Philemon 20, p. 191.

9. H. C. G. Moule, *The Epistles to the Colossians and to Philemon* (Cambridge Bible for Schools and Colleges), on Philemon 11, p. 173.

8.

Conclusions

1. This is especially true in the case of the pictures of the minor heir and of adoption (Gal. 3:23 to 4:7), marriage (Rom. 7:1-6), and the potter and the clay (Rom. 9:20-24).

2. See especially the discussion of Gal. 3:23 to 4:7.

3. It means, for example, that the picture of Adam which Paul draws in Rom. 5:12-20 cannot be used as a basis for a reliable judgment as to what the apostle actually believed with respect to Adam, since in that passage an analogical usage is involved (see the Introduction). What is said in an analogical usage must be interpreted in terms of the emphasis that is being made; it does not necessarily constitute a true picture of Paul's thought in the area out of which the picture arises.

Bibliography

Adeney, Walter F., *Thessalonians and Galatians* (New-Century Bible). Henry Frowde, n.d.

Albani, J., "Die Parabel bei Paulus," *Zeitschrift für wissenschaftliche Theologie*, Zweites Heft, pp. 161–171. O. R. Reisland, Leipzig, 1903.

Allen, Willoughby C., *The Gospel According to S. Matthew* (International Critical Commentary). Charles Scribner's Sons, 1925.

Barrett, C. K., *A Commentary on the Epistle to the Romans.* Harper & Brothers, 1957.

Bennett, W. H., *The General Epistles* (New-Century Bible). Henry Frowde, n.d.

Bultmann, Rudolf, *Der Stil der paulinischen Predigt und die kynisch-stoische Diatribe.* Vandenhoeck & Ruprecht, Göttingen, 1910.

—— *Theology of the New Testament,* tr. by Kendrick Grobel. Charles Scribner's Sons, 1951.

Burton, Ernest De Witt, *The Epistle to the Galatians* (International Critical Commentary). Charles Scribner's Sons, 1920.

Cadoux, A. T., *The Parables of Jesus.* The Macmillan Company, 1931.

Charles, R. H., *The Apocalypse of Baruch.* The Macmillan Company, 1918.

—— *The Book of Enoch.* The Clarendon Press, Oxford, 1912.

Deissmann, Adolf, *Light from the Ancient East,* tr. by Lionel R. M. Strachan. Hodder & Stoughton, Ltd., London, 1910.

—— *Paulus,* Zweite Auflage. J. C. B. Mohr (Paul Siebeck), Tübingen, 1925.

—— *St. Paul,* tr. by Lionel R. M. Strachan. Hodder & Stoughton, Ltd., London, 1912.

271

Denney, James, *The Second Epistle to the Corinthians* (Expositor's Bible). Hodder & Stoughton, Ltd., London, 1894.

—— *St. Paul's Epistle to the Romans* (Expositor's Greek Testament). Dodd, Mead and Company, 1900.

Dibelius, Martin, *An die Thessalonicher I, II* (Handbuch zum Neuen Testament), Zweite Auflage. J. C. B. Mohr (Paul Siebeck), Tübingen, 1923.

—— *Paul,* edited and completed by Werner Georg Kümmel, tr. by Frank Clarke. The Westminster Press, 1953.

Dobschütz, Ernst von, *Der Apostel Paulus.* Buchhandlung des Waisenhauses, Halle (Saale), 1926 (Vol. I), 1928 (Vol. II).

Dodd, C. H., *The Epistle of Paul to the Romans* (The Moffatt New Testament Commentary). Ray Long and Richard R. Smith, Inc., 1932.

—— *The Parables of the Kingdom.* Charles Scribner's Sons, 1961.

Duncan, George S., *The Epistle of Paul to the Galatians* (The Moffatt New Testament Commentary). Harper & Brothers, 1934.

Findlay, George G., *The Epistles to the Thessalonians* (Cambridge Bible for Schools and Colleges). The University Press, Cambridge, 1891.

Frame, James Everett, *The Epistles of St. Paul to the Thessalonians* (International Critical Commentary). Charles Scribner's Sons, 1912.

Gale, Herbert Morrison, "Paul's View of the State," *Interpretation,* Vol. 6, 1952.

Garvie, Alfred E., *Romans* (New-Century Bible). Henry Frowde, n.d.

Hastings, James, editor, *A Dictionary of the Bible.* Charles Scribner's Sons, 1901.

—— editor, *Encyclopaedia of Religion and Ethics.* Charles Scribner's Sons, 1928.

Jeremias, Joachim, *The Parables of Jesus,* tr. by S. H. Hooke. SCM Press, Ltd., London, 1954.

Josephus, Flavius, *The Jewish War* (*The Works of Flavius Josephus,* Whiston's Translation). George Bell and Sons, London, 1890.

Jülicher, Adolf, *Die Gleichnisreden Jesu.* J. C. B. Mohr (Paul Siebeck), Freiburg, 1899.

Kittel, Gerhardt, editor, *Theologisches Wörterbuch zum Neuen Testament,* Vols. II and III. W. Kohlhammer, Stuttgart, 1950.

Lamer, Hans, *Römische Kultur im Bilde*. Quelle & Meyer, Leipzig, 1910.

Lias, J. J., *The First Epistle to the Corinthians* (Cambridge Greek Testament for Schools and Colleges). The University Press, Cambridge, 1886.

—— *The First Epistle to the Corinthians* (Cambridge Bible for Schools and Colleges). The University Press, Cambridge, 1892.

—— *The Second Epistle to the Corinthians* (Cambridge Bible for Schools and Colleges). The University Press, Cambridge, 1893.

Lietzmann, Hans, *An die Galater* (Handbuch zum Neuen Testament), Dritte Auflage. J. C. B. Mohr (Paul Siebeck), Tübingen, 1932.

—— *An die Korinther I, II* (Handbuch zum Neuen Testament), Vierte von Werner Georg Kümmel Ergänzte Auflage. J. C. B. Mohr (Paul Siebeck), Tübingen, 1949.

—— *An die Römer* (Handbuch zum Neuen Testament), Vierte Auflage. J. C. B. Mohr (Paul Siebeck), Tübingen, 1933.

—— *The Beginnings of the Christian Church*, tr. by Bertram Lee Woolf. Charles Scribner's Sons, 1937.

Lightfoot, J. B., *Saint Paul's Epistles to the Colossians and to Philemon*. The Macmillan Company, 1897.

—— *Saint Paul's Epistle to the Philippians*. The Macmillan Company, 1890.

—— *St. Paul's Epistle to the Galatians*. Warren F. Draper, 1870.

Lohmeyer, Ernst, *Die Briefe an die Philipper, an die Kolosser und an Philemon* (Kritisch-exegetischer Kommentar über das Neue Testament), Neunte Abteilung, 11. Auflage. Vandenhoeck & Ruprecht, Göttingen, 1956.

Mascall, E. L., *Words and Images: A Study in Theological Discourse*. The Ronald Press Co., 1957.

Massie, J., *Corinthians* (New-Century Bible). T. C. and E. C. Jack, Ltd., Edinburgh, n.d.

Menzies, Allan, *The Second Epistle of the Apostle Paul to the Corinthians*, Macmillan & Co., Ltd., London, 1912.

Michel, Otto, *Der Brief an die Römer* (Kritisch-exegetischer Kommentar über das Neue Testament). Vandenhoeck & Ruprecht, Göttingen, 1957.

Milligan, George, *St. Paul's Epistles to the Thessalonians*. Macmillan & Co., Ltd., London, 1908.

Moffatt, James, *The First Epistle of Paul to the Corinthians* (The

Moffatt New Testament Commentary). Harper & Brothers, n.d.

—— *The Revelation of St. John the Divine* (Expositor's Greek Testament, Vol. V). Hodder & Stoughton, Ltd., London, n.d.

Moule, H. C. G., *The Epistle of Paul the Apostle to the Romans* (Cambridge Bible for Schools and Colleges). The University Press, Cambridge, 1896.

—— *The Epistles to the Colossians and to Philemon* (Cambridge Bible for Schools and Colleges). The University Press, Cambridge, 1894.

Moulton, W. F., and Geden, A. S., *A Concordance of the Greek Testament*. T. & T. Clark, Edinburgh, 1957.

Mullins, Terence Y., "Paul's Thorn in the Flesh," *Journal of Biblical Literature*, Vol. LXXVI, December, 1957.

Neil, William, *The Epistle of Paul to the Thessalonians* (The Moffatt New Testament Commentary). Harper & Brothers, 1950.

Perowne, E. H., *The Epistle to the Galatians* (Cambridge Bible for Schools and Colleges). The University Press, Cambridge, 1896.

Plummer, Alfred, *The Second Epistle of St. Paul to the Corinthians* (International Critical Commentary). Charles Scribner's Sons, 1915.

Ramsay, W. M., *A Historical Commentary on St. Paul's Epistle to the Galatians*. G. P. Putnam's Sons, 1900.

Robertson, Archibald, and Plummer, Alfred, *The First Epistle of St. Paul to the Corinthians* (International Critical Commentary). Charles Scribner's Sons, 1925.

Sanday, William, and Headlam, Arthur C., *The Epistle to the Romans* (International Critical Commentary). Charles Scribner's Sons, 1896.

Scott, E. F., *The Epistles of Paul to the Colossians, to Philemon and to the Ephesians* (The Moffatt New Testament Commentary). Hodder & Stoughton, Ltd., London, 1930.

Smith, B. T. D., *The Parables of the Synoptic Gospels*. The University Press, Cambridge, 1937.

Smith, William, *A Dictionary of the Bible*. Fleming H. Revell Company, n.d.

Stewart, James S., *A Man in Christ*. Hodder & Stoughton, Ltd., London, 1947.

Strachan, R. H., *The Second Epistle of Paul to the Corinthians*

(The Moffatt New Testament Commentary). Harper & Brothers, 1935.

Strack, Hermann L., and Billerbeck, Paul, *Kommentar zum Neuen Testament*. C. H. Beck'sche Verlagsbuchhandlung, München, 1926.

Straub, Werner, *Die Bildersprache des Apostels Paulus*. J. C. B. Mohr (Paul Siebeck), Tübingen, 1937.

Taylor, William M., *The Parables of Our Savior*. A. C. Armstrong and Son, 1886.

Thayer, Joseph Henry, *A Greek-English Lexicon of the New Testament*. Corrected Edition. American Book Company, 1889.

Trench, Richard Chenevix, *The Parables of Our Lord*. D. Appleton and Company, 1884.

Vincent, Marvin R., *The Epistles to the Philippians and to Philemon* (International Critical Commentary). Charles Scribner's Sons, 1897.

Weinel, H., *St. Paul, the Man and His Work*, tr. by G. A. Bienemann. G. P. Putnam's Sons, 1906.

Weiss, Johannes, *Der erste Korintherbrief* (Kritisch-exegetischer Kommentar über das Neue Testament). Vandenhoeck & Ruprecht, Göttingen, 1910.

Index

Subjects

Abraham, 11, 41 f., 44 f., 64 ff., 73, 173 ff., 199, 206 ff., 223 f., 238, 261

Adam, 14, 16, 138, 166, 206, 270

Adoption, 7, 46, 53, 57 ff., 223 f., 226 f., 238, 240 f., 270

Agriculture, 19, 79 ff., 106, 143, 163, 188, 197 f.

Allegory, 12 ff., 18, 44, 64 f., 67, 72 ff., 84, 102, 125, 211, 230, 233, 242, 244, 248, 267 f.

Apollos, 80 ff., 93

Architecture, 38 f., 83, 85, 88 ff.

See also Building(s). *See also* House(s)

Arena. *See* Gladiatorial arena

Armor, 38

Aroma, 148 ff., 224 ff., 256

Awake, to be, 29, 34 ff., 224 ff.

Babes, 21 ff., 64, 223 f., 227, 235 f.

Baptism, 82, 122, 178 ff., 190, 194, 226 f., 262, 264

Barnabas, 101, 108, 247

Beasts, 94 f.

Betrothal, 164 ff., 223, 225 f.

Body: celestial and terrestrial, 146 f., 224, 226; head of, 126; human, 7, 11, 113 f., 116 ff., 135 ff., 155 ff., 179, 223 ff., 227, 250 f., 254 f., 258, 266; of Christ (the church), 7, 117 ff., 122, 124, 126 f., 208, 250; resurrection, 134 ff., 155, 157 ff., 254, 258

Boxing match, 109, 111 ff., 224 ff.

Branches. *See* Root and branches. *See also* Grafting branches

Breastplate, 37 f., 248

Building(s), 38 f., 81, 83 ff., 157 f., 161, 225 ff., 231

See also House(s)

Child. *See* Parent-child obligations

Church (the body of Christ). *See* Body

Circumcision, 96, 218, 269

Clay. *See* Potter and clay

Clothing, 158 f., 161 f.

277

Scripture References
(*Passages discussed briefly*)